SPREADSHEET MARKETING

To IDV, without which this would not have been possible.

Spreadsheet Marketing

Alan West

Gower

Published by
Gower Publishing Company Limited,
Gower House,
Croft Road,
Aldershot,
Hants GU11 3HR,
England

British Library Cataloguing in Publication Data
West, Alan
  Spreadsheet marketing.
  1. Marketing—Data processing
  2. Electronic spreadsheets
  I. Title
  658.8′0028′553   HF5415.125

ISBN 0–566–02663–5

Printed and bound in Great Britain
by Billing & Sons Limited, Worcester.

Contents

Illustrations

Figures

Each chapter contains at least one Listing, Proforma and Example illustrating the model discussed.

When the illustration of a spreadsheet occupies more than one page, the book uses the cartographic convention of indicating the position of a detail relative to the whole by showing a small-scale map with the relevant detail highlighted. This has been done here using open and closed squares arranged in the shape of the whole spreadsheet.

Preface

'What can I do with a spreadsheet apart from cash flow forecasting?' As the personal computer becomes a more and more familiar part of the business process, this is a question heard increasingly from managers.

The present book is designed to show, with worked examples, how spreadsheets can help the marketing function in any business. The examples range from simple exercises for the manager or student new to the spreadsheet approach to sophisticated material dealing with quite complex issues.

The sequence of chapters does not follow any particular pattern, and readers will inevitably find some more relevant than others to the task in which they are involved, be it management information, product development or pricing. All the topics described are, however, relevant to the marketing function in one or more specific areas, and the emphasis throughout is on the application of computing to the 'real' business world.

I hope that my book will stimulate interest in the whole field of quantification in marketing even where subjective assessment is all that is available. At the very least it will show that the spreadsheet is a powerful and versatile tool. The ideal outcome would be for readers to use the examples given to develop control systems for themselves and thereby integrate the spreadsheet and the personal computer into their own decision-making process.

Alan West

Introduction

The introduction of the personal computer into the business world has provided the manager with steadily increasing sophistication in the level of control that can be developed through the evaluation of the data available both inside and outside the company.

Classically, the use of the computer within companies has been linked with the needs of accountants and there exists a multitude of systems which track invoices, maintain the company cash flow, and other aspects of the company's financial well-being. The considerable amount of information that the control of these problems involves has meant that the computer is now central to business activity in these areas.

Any quick reading of the computer journals will show that the majority of computer software is still directed at this market. More detailed analysis of the packages available underlines the lack of systems for the business planner or marketeer. Indeed in the British journal *Micro Decision*, of the more than a thousand programs listed only one was specifically designated under a 'Marketing' heading (1). This supports the view that the development of approaches to a wide range of problems within the marketing or business strategy environment has been limited.

One reason often put forward for the restricted use of computer technology in the business strategy/marketing sphere is that the lack of standardisation is a major obstacle. Thus the nature of the sales ledger will be similar for both the manufacturer of gas turbines and ice-cream with standard accounts for all major clients. The marketing dilemmas will be considered different by the respective marketing departments.

Why this should be so, against the wisdom of business school teaching which strongly supports the common ground approach to tackling the challenges ahead, is perhaps a reflection that marketing personnel tend to be educated 'on the job' in contrast to the accounting profession, with its emphasis on precedent and laid-down procedure. The marketeer is expected to function with 'flair' and 'feel' as the marketing mix is considered too difficult to quantify. In other words, this

1

means that the gap between the information available and the information necessary to reach the most sensible decision should be filled by experience and creativity.

The main objective of this book is to question this belief by demonstrating that it is possible to standardise marketing decision-making using models structured around the spreadsheet designed for the business computer. It will show that a number of problems faced by our hypothetical gas turbine and ice-cream manufacturers are, in reality, common to each firm. For example, the problems that both meet in respect of product development are very similar. They both have to ensure that the product fits into the current company philosophy and distribution systems, has long-term potential, and so on. It is not merely the sales ledger that is similar for both types of company, as is too often assumed. The genesis of standardisation in a number of key areas of marketing is made possible by the spreadsheet which can be regarded, as far as the exercise undertaken in this book is concerned, as the marketing equivalent of the sales ledger.

Why a model

The classical definition of a marketing information system is:

> A structured interacting complex of persons, machines and procedures designed to generate an orderly flow of pertinent information collected from both intra-and extra-firm sources for use as a basis for decision-making (2).

In all such systems a loop is being established (see Figure Intro.1) whereby the

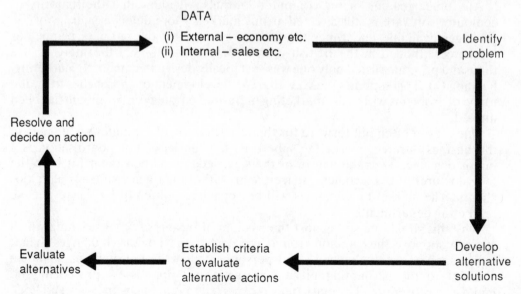

DATA
(i) External – economy etc.
(ii) Internal – sales etc.

Identify problem

Resolve and decide on action

Evaluate alternatives

Establish criteria to evaluate alternative actions

Develop alternative solutions

Figure Intro.1   Management information control loop

data is being evaluated against a set of criteria to produce alternative paths to action. The decision taken will affect the data and therefore close the loop.

The marketing manager has to aim at achieving the best possible results for his company while resolving a series of complex problems involving both objective facts as well as subjective assessments. The amount of data required to reach a decision is often large and needs to be correctly structured if only to make sure that key areas are separated from less-important considerations. Models are simply a system of ordering data known to be crucial within a particular context, piecing together seemingly unrelated facts which experience has shown to have a possible impact, and identifying areas where subjective assessment is necessary.

In marketing where, as mentioned earlier, there has been a tendency to stress subjectivity by emphasising 'flair' and 'feel', the systematisation of all factors through the use of a model when trying to resolve a particular problem will also help the manager to be clear about what is involved. Muddle about fact and fantasy, about whether a decision is based on hard data, or personal judgement, or a mixture of both tends to be a notorious feature of organisations where marketing is regarded as 'instinctive' behaviour.

Imagine you are the ice-cream manufacturer. You should know from sales information your selling price and those of your competitors. You have some information concerning the interaction of price and demand in the market. There are a number of historical lessons that you know from earlier price changes which indicate that the relationship between price and demand is not necessarily a simple one. How do you come to the most effective assessment of your pricing policy?

A model can combine the historical data you have available to give a number of possible options based on your subjective assessment of the market. It both narrows the area of uncertainty and also highlights the data one would require to further minimise the problem. Thus, the framework of a model which could provide this sort of information for the ice-cream manufacturer would be one that combines an analysis of straightforward price effects – demands changing smoothly with increases in price – with an overlay of non-standard price responses.

From such a system one would gain the information:

1 What the price effects would be if the response was a straightforward relationship between price and demand
2 How this would be affected by non-quantifiable problems in the market

A concrete example which would be relevant in the ice-cream market follows. The manufacturer considers his production costs, his advertising investment and the volume of production that best suits his operation. These are then assessed by the use of a straightforward price/volume relationship equation. However, the manufacturer is aware that other problems exists in the market place. The price suggested by the straightforward analysis might be $1.02, but the manufacturer knows full well that a phenomenon of price points exists in that particular market. Thus, a product will sell for 99 cents but not for $1.02. The use of a model in this particular instance would enable an assessment of the risks or benefits following upon a change in price. In other words, it enables the manager to forecast the future behaviour of his product in the market with greater accuracy than would be the case if he did not use a formally structured approach.

Readers may understandably be sympathetic towards the predicament of the marketing manager. Like Little Jack Horner he is expected to pull out a golden plum for his employer when he may be totally in the dark about the pudding's ingredients and their effects on each other. The circumstances described so far highlight the intricacy of the mix. How can they be separated?

The spreadsheet

The simplicity of the spreadsheet makes it exceptionally well suited to disentangling a multiplicity of data. There is nothing mysterious about it. A spreadsheet is simply a blank table divided by verticals and horizontals into boxes which are described in the jargon as 'cells'. Harnessed to the skills of the computer it is able to manipulate the information supplied to those cells with the help of simple mathematical functions. In addition, the size of the spreadsheet table means that it is possible to compare and contrast an enormous amount of data on any one topic. The models developed in this book depend heavily upon the ability of the spreadsheet to manipulate information using simple calculations to draw attention to special relationships between data. The models could be handled manually, but the task would be much more cumbersome than on a spreadsheet.

Spreadsheets such as the *Lotus 1-2-3*, *Visicalc* and *Supercalc* are available for practically all computer systems and they share a variety of standard features which has made it possible to write this book. The models described in the following chapters can be used with any spreadsheet system and will adapt to new systems such as *Framework* and *Symphony*. All have a Value Option and a Label Option. The functions used for calculation are given their common form in the book: $* = $ multiply; $/ = $ divide; $+ = $ add; $- = $ subtract. The models also use the Log 10 and square root functions accompanying most spreadsheets.

An important function that appears frequently in the models is the "IF" command. This is always followed by a mathematical statement. For example, "IF(BI$>=$9) true (X), false (Y)". This varies in the exact form it takes in the various spreadsheets. It is presented in this book in the standard form "IF(B$>=$9)THEN (VALUE) ELSE (VALUE)" as this format is more understandable for the model builder.

The building of each model is explained on a cell by cell basis. As you gain experience with the spreadsheet system a number of cells can be replicated to other cells using commands which vary with the spreadsheet system. Learning these techniques will considerably reduce the labour involved in the construction of the models. With this in mind the early chapters of the book contain more basic models than the later ones. The author suggests that readers totally unused to spreadsheet systems should start at the beginning.

Each chapter of the book is structured more or less similarly: the opening sections explain the theory behind the model. Next, the use of the model is explained and each step given in the Listing. The Proforma accompanying each Listing illustrates the formula for each cell as viewed on screen. One or more Examples are given for each model, each of which illustrates the actual answers calculated. These are discussed in the closing paragraphs of the chapter.

The best way of understanding the relationship between the models and the spreadsheet is to take an example from scratch. This we shall do in the next section.

An introductory model: competitive bidding

Within the business environment the organisation faces a large number of constraints on distribution, production and the like. In a free market it can normally set its prices and its costs at whatever level it wants (providing of course that this is a coherent decision, enabling continuing profitability to be maintained).

There are two exceptions to this general statement both relating to one-off events, the wage bargaining process and the sealed bidding system in operation for major capital projects. Both of these activities operate in an environment which is largely isolated from both the market and the underlying cost constraints. In other words the process at work is very similar to betting, each particular bet (price point) having associated odds (probability of occurrence) and possible winnings (consequent profitability/cost effect).

Thus for both wage negotiation and sealed bidding the organisation needs to evaluate the *value* of each level of bid and the *profit* or cost of each level of decision. From this the most cost effective approach can be developed, which should maximise the firm's position over the long term. Naturally, other constraints may be more important. For example the firm may choose to pay their employees more than the suggested level of wage settlement because of changes in the working environment, or it may choose to complete a contract at marginal cost to gain access to new markets, as a form of introductory pricing.

The factors involved

The spreadsheet model will provide a convenient and rapid framework in which to evaluate alternative strategies. Price is the proposed range of bid values, ranging from the lowest possible, to the highest price that could be feasibly attained. Cost is the underlying costs associated with the bid, similar in each case, and is an ideal opportunity to develop a marginal costing system (see Chapter 5). The organisation would also need to consider the implications of opportunity costing, especially important in one-off bids. For the wage negotiation, the cost will obviously be the same as the bid price. Lastly, the probability that each bid can be successful should be assigned for each event occurring. The range of probability with 100 comprising certainty that the bid will be successful, should be individually considered by each of the responsible managers, so that the best group consensus can be arrived at. The higher the price the lower the probability of success will be. The model will compare the level of probability with the expected profitability at differing pricing levels, allowing the most cost effective mix of price and probability to be developed. Obviously the probability of success will be a subjective assessment involving experience of the market conditions, competitors' likely pricing levels, and any special factor that may exist (foreign exchange problems for example).

Using the competitive bidding model

Using a step by step approach, let us apply the model based on the principles discussed above to a spreadsheet system. This will teach you the practicalities of using the system and will help you to assess the arguments for and against a particular course of action.

Before you begin you will have loaded your spreadsheet system into the computer, or it will be displayed on the screen in front of you. All the spreadsheet actions are placed between inverted commas to help you to pick them out at a glance, but as the inverted commas are not part of the data input they should not be typed on the keyboard! Beware that some spreadsheets, the *Lotus 1-2-3* for example, format the Label Option by using the inverted-comma key.

1   Load the spreadsheet and have it before you on the screen. In Listing Intro.1 the *Go To* column tells you the cell number and the cursor position. The next column specifies the spreadsheet option (LO = Label Option; VO = Value Option). The *Type In* column gives you instructions within the inverted commas which you must type in or asks you to supply the necessary data. R in the *Return* column instructs you to commit the information to memory by pressing the Return key.

2   Move the cursor to cell B2 and choose the Label Option. Type "Competit" on the status line and enter into memory by pressing the Return key. "Competit" will appear in cell B2 in the body of the spreadsheet. This last, described here in order to familiarise you with what to expect when you are using a spreadsheet, will take place automatically on pressing the Return key and will be taken as read for the subsequent instructions. Note that you will have to type the remainder of the word "Competitive" in cell C2.

3   When you choose the Value Option (VO) the information entered will be used for calculation purposes. The Value Option also includes the whole range of equations provided for the model. When you select the Value Option and type in the values or equation in the model the spreadsheet follows the procedure you have decided upon. For example, if you have located the cursor at say cell E83 and you type in C10*A15 the spreadsheet will multiply the values in those two cells together and the answer will appear in cell E83 on the screen. Thus if the value of C10 was 5 and the value of A15 was 3 the result in E83 would be 15.

Note: * = multiply; / = divide

Listing Intro.1   Competitive bidding model

Go To		Type In	Return
B2/	LO	"COMPETITIVE	R
C2/		BIDDING	R
D2/		MODEL"	R
E2			R
A6	LO	"PRICE"	R
C6	LO	"COST"	R
D6	LO	"% PROBAB" for Probability	R
E6	LO	"VALUE"	R
F6	LO	"EXP RET" for Expected Return	R
A10	VO	Insert possible bidding price $	R
A12	VO	Insert second possible bidding price	R
A14	VO	Insert third possible bidding price	R
A16	VO	Insert fourth possible bidding price	R
A18	VO	Insert fifth possible bidding price	R
C10	VO	Insert cost of bid in A10	R
C12	VO	Insert cost of bid in A12	R
C14	VO	Insert cost of bid in A14	R
C16	VO	Insert cost of bid in A16	R
C18	VO	Insert cost of bid in A18	R

Note the estimated cost of C10–C18 will be similar in each case because the production cost will be identical in each case.

Go To		Type In	Return
D10	VO	Insert probability of achieving respective target price for A10	R

When price goes up probability of success goes down.

Go To		Type In	Return
D12	VO	Insert probability of achieving target price for A12	R
D14	VO	Insert probability of achieving target price for A14	R
D16	VO	Insert probability of achieving target price for A16	R
A18	VO	Insert probability of achieving target price for A18	R
E10	VO	"A10–C10"	R
E12	VO	"A12–C12"	R
E14	VO	"A14–C14"	R
E16	VO	"A16–C16"	R
E18	VO	"A18–C18"	R
F10	VO	"E10*D10/100"	R
F12	VO	"E12*D12/100"	R
F14	VO	"E14*D14/100"	R
F16	VO	"E16*D16/100"	R
F18	VO	"E18*D18/100"	R

Remember: Save your model.

Competitive bidding commentary

Let us consider two examples (Example Intro.1.1 and Example Intro.1.2) which show how the model can often produce unexpected and therefore thought provoking results. In Example Intro.1.1 the cost associated with the bid is $900 000, similar for all levels of bid pricing (entered in column C). The price at which the bid can be made is entered in column A, varying from $1 million to $1.2 million. At each price the sales management enter a probability of the bid being accepted, in column D. For the bid priced at $1 million it is considered that the firm is practically certain to win the contract, with a 95 per cent chance of success. At the other end of the scale, the bid priced at $1.2 million is much less likely to succeed and is given a 45 per cent chance of success. The model then calculates the total value to the company of achieving the bid (column E) and the overall likely return (column F).

Proforma Intro.1 Competitive bidding model

	A	B	C	D	E	F
		A	B	C	D	E	F
2		COMPETITIVE	BIDDING	MODEL		
6	PRICE		COST	% PROBAB	VALUE	EXP RET
10	1000000		900000	95	A10-C10	E10*D10/100
12	1050000		900000	85	A12-C12	E12*D12/100
14	1100000		900000	75	A14-C14	E14*D14/100
16	1150000		900000	60	A16-C16	E16*D16/100
18	1200000		900000	45	A18-C18	E18*D18/100

At the lowest level of pricing, $1 million, the expected return to the company would only be $95 000. The rate of return rises considerably as the price increases to $1.1 million, with a return of $150 000. At this point rises in price (and profit) begin to be offset by the decline in the probability of achieving the bid and so whereas the overall level of profitability of the bid at $1.2 million would obviously be the highest, the expected return would be very similar to a bid priced at $1.05 million.

Example Intro.1.2 shows considerably more variation in both bid price and probabilities. The model would provide the conclusion that the most satisfactory level of expected return would be a bid priced at $1.75 million. However examination of the model would lead one to question the assumptions behind some of the probabilities assigned to certain bidding prices. Does, for instance, the difference of $80 000 between the bids of $1.83 million and $1.75 million *really mean* a decline of a full ten percentage points in the probability of achieving the bid? Experience might suggest that this was not likely to be the

Example Intro.1.1   Competitive bidding model

	A	B	C	D	E	F
2		COMPETITIVE	BIDDING	MODEL		
6	PRICE		COST	% PROBAB	VALUE	EXP RET
10	1000000		900000	95	100000	95000
12	1050000		900000	85	150000	127500
14	1100000		900000	75	200000	150000
16	1150000		900000	60	250000	150000
18	1200000		900000	45	300000	135000

case, and the probability level would need to be reconsidered by the sales management team.

The model can also be used not only to highlight such discrepancies in judgement, but to allow rapid and easy evaluation of the sensitivity of the figures to changes in price, probability, and expected rate of return.

This approach can also be used, as initially stated, to consider various levels of pay settlement in industrial relations exercises, enabling management to finely tune any wage proposal that may be considered. The aim in such a case would obviously be the reverse of the examples stated above – management attempting to find the minimal cost solution rather than the maximum profit.

Other considerations

The competitive bidding model is a simple one, but it should by now be perfectly plain that even in this case the factors tied into the model are really quite complicated. Furthermore as the commentary on Example Intro.1.2 of the

Example Intro.1.2   Competitive bidding model

	A	B	C	D	E	F
2		COMPETITIVE	BIDDING	MODEL		
6	PRICE		COST	% PROBAB	VALUE	EXP RET
10	1830000		1000000	70	830000	581000
12	2490000		1000000	40	1490000	596000
14	1750000		1000000	80	750000	600000
16	2800000		1000000	30	180000	540000
18	1500000		1000000	90	500000	450000

model demonstrates, careful judgements are required. This means that the systems described in this book will also make demands on you. No great knowledge of computers is assumed, but you will inevitably be required to become more familiar with them, especially in the use of the computer keyboard. You will have to spend time in a number of instances finding the information demanded by the model and then you will have to order it. Concentration and patience will be required especially when following the instructions for building the model on the spreadsheet. Because the exercise is presented in a simple fashion, this does not mean that the task will be an easy one. On the other hand, there is a great deal of satisfaction to be gained from building a working tool from scratch.

Different problems require different solutions. The structure of the model for the assessment of pricing problems will differ from others developed to deal with other matters, for example, to analyse the structure of marketing investment. The data involved will obviously vary considerably as will the area of subjective assessment. The analysis of sales force productivity will be very much a matter of straightforward calculation, whereas packaging will demand a totally different approach. There are a number of instances where the decision-making will be entirely based on the intelligent use of judgement in which there will be no external data which can be used. Examples of this type of model include product diversification, packaging, product viability and personnel appraisal.

Others will demand a mixture of external data and evaluation of likely changes in the business environment. Among these are the models in this book on pricing, direct mail, marketing investment, and test markets.

Lastly there are instances where the spreadsheet is used to manipulate data and evaluate alternative possible actions. These include the models presented later on export pricing, forecasting, marginal profitability, sales productivity and promotions.

Models are always criticised on the basis that the design of the system does not reflect adequately the real world and that the information put in is inaccurate, producing suspect conclusions: the classic 'garbage in, garbage out' syndrome.

These criticisms miss the main object of any model. Its aim is to provide a logical framework into which the best available information can be manipulated to provide an insight into the workings of any particular problem. What it then initially should prompt is the questioning of the assumptions on which the decisions are taken. Does one believe, for example, that demand changes smoothly with price or are there breaks in the line indicating other factors at work?

It is hoped that using models will encourage all organisations to structure the information available internally or externally in a coherent fashion. Thus a multinational organisation with whom the author worked did not have available details of how consumer prices were built up in export countries, even in wholly owned distribution companies. This information could have been regarded as crucial to the organisation to enable it to maximise overall profitability and strategic development of what at the time was a weak operation. The development of a model in this particular instance would have supplied valuable management information. This is how models should be applied.

The way ahead

The purpose of this book is to define areas in which modelling can be valuable and to examine the theory underlying the model.

In each case the models are structured with the examples discussed in the book providing the basis on which company examples can be developed. The formulas that produce the model have been copied across the spreadsheet (presented as 'Proformas') so that the data entered in columns D.E.F.G.H.I. will produce the standard model response.

Each chapter is divided into three parts. The first covers the conceptual aspects of the problem – the 'logical framework' on which the system is built. This is always where models are most suspect and any user of the system should consider whether the approach suggested is the correct one. The author would never claim to have received any topic carved on tablets of stone and, in an area as contentious as marketing, opinions will always differ. The second part of the chapter describes the structure of the model and the variables that are being considered. The final part contains a brief description of the uses to which the model can be put with a worked example (or two) followed by a commentary.

Each chapter also contains a listing, cell by cell, of the formulas that need to be entered to produce the models described. The early chapters have the simpler models so that the reader without experience can become familiar with the spreadsheet approach.

The topics covered in this book are those that lend themselves to a structured approach; concepts such as creativity are impossible to quantify and readers searching for such a philosopher's stone will be disappointed. The reduction of any area of endeavour to the interaction of data cells will perhaps appear over-scientific, but it does at least allow the problems to be examined in a systematic way on which can be built the particular skills of the individual.

References

1   *Micro Decisions*, No. 2, 1984.

2   S.V. Smith, R.H. Brien, J.C. Stafford, *Readings in Marketing Information Systems*, Houghton Mifflin Company, Boston, 1968.

1 Product viability

Classic marketing theory postulates that the majority of products and services will follow a standard sales pattern over time: a period of growth, a period of stability (the maturity phase) and then decline. This process is known as the product life cycle, and is used to explain the high levels of product failure in, for example, the fast moving consumer goods area in the United States.

Closer examination of any particular product sector will begin to raise doubts on the universal applicability of such a hypothesis. In soaps for example the brands long ago developed remain the dominant factors in the market, with toothpaste, detergents, scourers, fabric conditioners, hairspray, French perfumes and petfood showing continuing domination by long-established brands. Even in the highly competitive confectionery market Mars and Hersey bars still remain on every shelf.

The test of a hypothesis in the scientific sense is whether it has any predictive value. For example, one would know beforehand that an experiment involving the addition of sulphuric acid to water would produce large quantities of heat. The reality would follow the theory, and in actuality large amounts of heat would be generated. Knowledge of the amount of sulphuric acid involved will enable the experimenter to accurately calculate the quantity of heat that the experiment would precipitate.

When one contrasts the product life cycle hypothesis with this situation it can be seen to have little predictive value, particularly when so many brands appear to manage to overcome the restraints that it would theoretically impose. The counter argument claims that differing products have differing maturity phases, and that even these will eventually decline. Similar conclusions are put forward about trade cycles. Historical graphing can show that these exist but the variation in the amplitude and frequency of the peaks are still largely unexplained. Currency movements also remain an area where after the event analysis is a rich field. The movement of the dollar against European currencies will doubtless be explained to the satisfaction of everyone in the future, but at present no economic forecaster can effectively predict short-term (or long-term) currency movements. The conclusion that can be drawn from all these hypotheses is that though they provide a framework to which the product, service, or economy *may* comply, they have no predictive value for the actual performance of the specific item over a period of time.

Product successes and failures can however be analysed to yield some guidelines as to the long-term viability of any particular product, subject to one important qualifying statement. The nature of the firm and how, historically, it has approached the market place can be the most important factor in determining the future of a product. Procter and Gamble and Mars follow closely a management philosophy of continued support for major brands often in highly adverse market conditions. The brand becomes a 'property' with continuing site value, and the companies have little intention of selling up and moving to new locations with all the consequent dislocation this causes. Should the property be on the wrong site as it is argued that Ariel Automatic in the UK is (see Chapter 9 on product diversification) the high level of commitment will be enormously expensive, but even so may eventually win through.

The contrast is provided by companies such as Black and Decker with high levels of product innovation. Here the emphasis is heavily on supporting the new items with the remainder of the existing range being expected to find their own level, receiving, compared with the business philosophy at Procter and Gamble, little continuing support.

The risks of product innovation are considerable with increasingly high investment levels required. The suitable mix between the maintenance of existing products, their re-development and the introduction of new concepts requires careful planning and understanding of the current market position of the company's products. An assessment of the product viability can help to develop the requirements for product change by identifying the problem areas for solution.

General criteria

1 Economic conditions

The first general criterion must be the underlying economic conditions and whether it will affect the product in the present or near future. Within the Nigerian market no one would claim that imported beer is ending its product life cycle. The reality in the sales figures for Carlsberg and Heineken is however very similar to that theoretical effect. The market has disappeared practically overnight due to the dearth of foreign exchange. In contrast cement has still been imported – its product life cycle has continued because construction projects have still been funded by a Nigerian government reluctant to allocate foreign exchange for imported beer. Reduced economic activity will inevitably lower demand for a wide range of goods with the reverse being equally true.

Unilever for example takes the view that there is an underlying correlation between bar soap, powder detergents, and per capita income. As per capita income increases, bar soap consumption declines, while powder detergents increase in sales (see Figure 1.1). Readers will doubtlessly be able to think of many

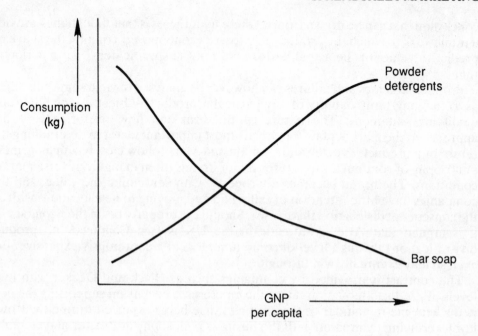

Figure 1.1 GNP and detergent consumption patterns

more illustrations. The fact that sales are booming or slumping due to economic factors, while relevant to the viability of the product, does not necessarily affect the notion of the product life cycle. Bar soap is available on the shelves of most Western industrialised countries, and should some of these economies continue in their decline, consumption will tend to increase.

2 Population structure

In conjunction with the economic trends, the changes in population structure will independently affect the product. Babies' rattles will be more in demand in a predominantly youthful population, whereas in the 'sunset' towns of the United States they will have little use except for those individuals entering their second childhood!

3 Consumer living styles

The living style of a community can mean that a product has to be specially adapted in order to become acceptable. In the world of model railways the standard European gauge has for many years been HO or OO (roughly 1/72 scale). Changes favouring more compact living accommodation for a majority of families, particularly in the Far East, led to the introduction of a smaller, far more compact system N-gauge (roughly 1/144 scale). In this, the basic product has remained the same, but the way in which it is presented has changed. The manufacturer clinging to the continuation of HO gauge would by now be complaining that his product was in the final stages of its product life cycle. In reality the emphasis of the product has slightly shifted, and though demand overall may have also declined due to other circumstances – economic strength or whatever – the product remains a viable one, even though at a lower level of production in a slightly different form.

Specific criteria

As well as the general criteria there are other identifiable product trends that make long-term viability more questionable.

4   Management capabilities

One of the themes running through this book is that the management resources of any company need far greater attention than they are normally accorded. This is no less true for the continuing viability of existing products than for the development of new ones. The issues fall into two broad categories: management faith and management abilities. An example from the author's experience illustrates the role of management faith, or the Pandora principle, whereby continual denigration or praise becomes a self-fulfilling prophecy. Unilever sold large quantities of a germicidal soap, Asepso, mainly in West Africa, at very high profit margins, and without promotional support. Due to changes in health legislation it was decided to change the active ingredient from mercuric iodide to a standard germicidal mix. This alteration led to the export management totally discounting the new product and drastically cutting production. Fortuitously, the gap in availability while the new formulation was being introduced had led to a backlog in demand producing $2 million net profit in the first six months. Continuing management indifference to the product did however ensure a rapid tail-off in sales, regardless of any objective assessment of underlying benefits or defects. Part of this problem seems to have been the status of the brand within the company – individuals prefer working on high-status projects which attract the more competitive management because their seniors on the company ladder give these areas their greatest attention.

Similarly, the abilities of management may play a role in the success or failure of products within very diverse companies. Managers always have favourite products or areas of business which will receive most of their attention even if this may be less profitable for their organisation as a whole. An ardent nationalist happened to be managing director of a combined wine, port, and sherry multinational company. He inevitably favoured the expansion of his own country's side of the business ensuring that it received the maximum of investment – perhaps to the detriment of other areas of the business in other countries.

Such examples suggest that management are extremely important in determining product viability, a reflection of that tedious statement 'Where there is a will there is a way'.

5   Distribution

One of the key tests of product viability is the history of distribution gains and losses that the brand has made. The concentration of retailing in fewer and fewer groups has meant that the number of alternatives within each product sector is increasingly under the microscope, with the retailer more and more conscious of the need to maximise return per square foot or metre. In the early stages of a product's development, gaining distribution is a vital measure of increasing the success of the product, and when no further distribution gains can be attained, the maturity phase of the product has been reached. Loss of distribution at this plateau can have serious escalating effects with the delisting of one store group often being followed by others, producing a downward distribution spiral.

6   Profit margins

In common with distribution levels, the analysis of profit margins can yield valuable insights into the continuing viability of the product. Classically, the life cycle theory holds that during the initial growth phase profit margins will be small for various reasons. First the firm may be using a form of introductory pricing to ensure that a high level of trial is achieved (commented on in Chapter 12, on test markets). Second, a high level of promotional activity may be involved as well as the attractive, low price. Third, the costs of investment in new plant, components and man-power is being amortised over only a small volume, producing high unit costs. Naturally if the product can be manufactured using old technology at a high price – such as the IBM Personal Computer – most of these comments are invalidated. Once the product is established, advertising costs diminish, greater volumes are achieved, and introductory pricing strategies can be abandoned. This period should generate greater per unit profit and obviously considerably greater overall return.

Adverse market conditions can unwind this spiral of increased profitability. Promotional expenditure may have to be increased; pricing reduced to maintain sales; and overall market share may drop. Future profitability will remain a key element in the analysis of product viability, but never in isolation, for many of the other factors outlined in this chapter can have a contributing influence on profitability.

7   Trial

The early stages of a product's life are characterised by a high level of trial when compared with repeat purchases. As the product acquires customers, the balance will change as repeat purchase becomes more important. The decline of the product may be presaged by a further drop in the level of trial followed by a decline in repeat purchase levels. Whether this is so – and there does not appear to be research on the subject – the level of trial remains a useful criterion for inclusion in the assessment of any brand's long-term position.

8   Competitors

The arrival of other companies' products within a market sector may either expand the market, or in the case of the majority of sectors where demand is relatively inelastic, reduce market share of the existing product ranges.

Competition may also lead to the introduction of a large number of variants, with a resulting rise in overall costs (higher inventories, lower unit production runs) of the product. Growth in competition will therefore tend to have a deleterious effect on brand performance and viability in the long term.

9 Packaging

The role of packaging in maintaining the viability of the product can either be over-estimated or drastically under-estimated. Minimal attention to the packaging demands of the market place will pose problems for the product in the medium term, as visibility in the increasingly competitive market becomes more and more important. Continual changes in the packaging may also affect both the brand identity and consistency of pack design – both important elements in packaging decisions (see Chapter 8 on packaging dilemmas).

10 Technical superiority

The degree of technical advantage one particular product field may have over another is crucial to many industries. It is most apparent in areas such as electronics but is no less important in product areas such as toys, cars, ships, generators, pumps and aeroplanes. The issues raised by improved technology can be clearly seen in the case of Volkswagen and the development of the Golf. In the late 1960s certain radical changes in motor car manufacture were appearing. Car bodies and chassis were lighter due to improvements in metallurgy and design; car engines became more powerful although smaller; soundproofing techniques were considerably improved as cars became more comfortable with the use of improved shock absorbers and the like. In consequence, the Beetle which had been upgraded with a series of minor modifications on a basically unchanged design over a fifteen-year period suddenly faced many technical problems. The concept that had provided one of the most successful post-war cars became outmoded in a very short period causing major financial problems for the parent company. Volkswagen have however managed to change direction as the technology demanded, introducing the highly successful Golf and Polo family cars.

The time horizon that each industry faces for technological change will vary. Within the canning industry for example, the introduction of ring-pull cans occurred relatively slowly in Europe over a five- to six-year period. In computers, both hardware and software are changing much more rapidly. From 1980 to 1984 the home computer industry in the United Kingdom managed to move from the 1 kilobyte storage standard to 48k; and similar changes have taken place within software over the same time. So the knowledge of where a particular product in the range is with respect to changing technology is essential to an understanding of its viability.

Other factors

Many commentators on the product life cycle also see the level of media support, and the percentage of the firm's total profit that an individual line makes up, as important factors in overall viability. In general terms the promotional expenditure per unit is considered high in the growth phase, medium in the maturity phase and low in the declining phase. But tactical changes in promotional expenditure – say to prevent a competitor becoming established in the market – may well disturb this standard pattern. Similarly, the importance to the organisation of a particular product should be regarded in terms of a return on investment rather than percentage of total profitability. Provided all the additional costs of small product production runs are properly accounted for (see Chapter 5 on marginal profitability), and the item is still producing an effective rate of return on capital employed it should still be regarded as a viable proposition.

The product viability model

The model provides a simple decision framework for evaluating the various criteria over a number of time spans, which link up with the majority of firms' planning horizons. The short-term option is generally the length of time that the annual plan still has to run, which by the time it has been completed, with modifications, is normally of the order of a maximum of nine months. Medium-term planning can be considered as the period of time beyond the detailed annual plans where information is still regarded as accurate, a period of an additional eighteen months or two years. Beyond that the bulk of organisations will tend to rely on pencilled-in general statements of policy, unless a particular manager is attempting to justify some speculative long-term investment leading to detailed ten- or fifteen-year flights of fantasy. Within these time horizons the viability of the particular product can be assessed.

The criteria evaluated are those described in the sections on general and specific criteria:

1 Economic conditions
2 Population structure
3 Social conditions
4 Management capabilities
5 Distribution
6 Profit margin
7 Trial
8 Competitors
9 Packaging
10 Technical superiority

For the three different time horizons the risk that these criteria will deteriorate can be assessed. Should the event be imminent, and highly deleterious it is obviously of far greater risk to the product viability than a long-term, low-level change as it can only with difficulty be offset. It is much easier to develop alternative plans to cope with long-term changes.

The model will simply calculate on the user's own assumptions the viability of the product, over the varying time horizons. The higher the score achieved, the greater the problems that the brand faces. The model also serves as an interesting planning aid to ensure that the strategic thinking underlying the prospects for the company's products are considered on a line-by-line basis and not in an amorphous general sense. Particular problems can then be identified earlier, enabling the management to take corrective action to ensure that their product, at least, will not be explained away in future years as a casualty of the product life cycle.

Using the product viability model

In Listing 1.1 the *Go To* column tells you the cell number and the cursor position. The next column specifies the spreadsheet option (LO = Label Option; VO = Value Option). The *Type In* column gives you instructions within the inverted commas which you must type in or asks you to supply the necessary data. These inverted commas are not part of the instructions supplied here and should not be typed in. Beware however that some spreadsheets, the *Lotus 1-2-3*, for example, enter the Label Option by using the inverted-comma key. Under the *Type In* column the symbols * = multiply and / = divide. R in the *Return* column instructs you to commit the information to memory by pressing the Return key.
Remember: When you have finished, save your model.

Listing 1.1 Product viability model

Go To		Type In	Return	Go To		Type In	Return
C2/	LO	"PRODUCT	R	A16/	LO	"Distribution"	R
D2/		VIABILITY"	R	B16			R
E2			R	A18/	LO	"Profit	R
A4	LO	"FACTOR"	R	B18		margin"	R
C4/	LO	"Planning	R	A20	LO	"Trial"	R
D4		horizon"	R	A22/	LO	"Competitors"	R
C6	LO	"Short"	R	B22			R
D6	LO	"Medium"	R	A24/	LO	"Packaging"	R
E6	LO	"Long"	R	B24			R
A8	LO	"Economic"	R	A26/	LO	"Tech.	R
A10/	LO	"Population"	R	B26		superior" for tech-	
B10			R			nical superiority	R
A12/	LO	"Social	R	C8	VO	Insert values for level	
B12		conditions"	R	to		of risk that worsening	
A14/	LO	"Management"	R	E8		of economic condi-	
B14			R			tions will occur during	
						the three stages of the	
						planning horizon	R

Listing 1.1 *(continued)*

Go To		Type In	Return	Go To		Type In	Return
				F12	VO	"SUM(C12:E12)"	R
				G12	VO	"IFF12<=30THENF12 ELSE0"	R

If you don't think anything dramatic will happen leave column blank, if you think that there are some prospects that things will change allocate 5; if you think things will alter dramatically allocate 10. At the extremes of dramatic changes in the short, medium and long term this line would add up to 30; the model will not accept a higher value.

Go To		Type In	Return	Go To		Type In	Return
				C13	VO	"C12*12"	R
				D13	VO	"D12*6"	R
F8	VO	"SUM(C8:E8)"	R	E13	VO	"E12*4"	R
G8	VO	"IFF8 <=30THENF8ELSE0"	R	F13	VO	"SUM(C13:E13)"	R
				G13	VO	"IFG12>0THENF13 ELSE0"	R
C9	VO	"C8*12"	R	C14 to E14	VO	Enter values of levels of risk pertaining to management as per C8 to E8	R
D9	VO	"D8*6"	R				
E9	VO	"E8*4"	R				
F9	VO	"SUM (C9:E9)"	R	F14	VO	"SUM(C14:E14)"	R
G9	VO	"IFG8>0THENF9 ELSE0"	R	G14	VO	"IFF14<=30THENF14 ELSE0"	R
C10 to E10	VO	Enter values for levels of risk pertaining to population factors as per C8 to E8	R	C15	VO	"C14*12"	R
				D15	VO	"D14*6"	R
				E15	VO	"E14*4"	R
F10	VO	"SUM(C10:E10)"	R	F15	VO	"SUM(C15:E15)"	R
G10	VO	"IFF10<=30THENF10 ELSE0"	R	G15	VO	"IFG14>0THENF15 ELSE0"	R
C11	VO	"C10*12"	R	C16 to E16	VO	Enter values of levels of risk pertaining to distribution as per C8 to E8	R
D11	VO	"D10*6"	R				
E11	VO	"E10*4"	R				
F11	VO	"SUM (C11:E11)"	R	F16	VO	"SUM(C16:E16)"	R
G11	VO	"IFG10>0THENF11 ELSE0"	R	G16	VO	"IFF16<=30THENF16 ELSE0"	R
C12 to E12	VO	Enter values of levels of risk pertaining to social conditions as per C8 to E8	R	C17	VO	"C16*12"	R
				D17	VO	"D16*6"	R
				E17	VO	"E16*4"	R
				F17	VO	"SUM(C17:E17)"	R
				G17	VO	"IFG16>0THENF17 ELSE0"	R

Listing 1.1 *(concluded)*

Go To		Type In	Return	Go To		Type In	Return
C18 to E18	VO	Enter values of levels of risk pertaining to profit margin as per C8 to E8	R	F23	VO	"SUM(C23:E23)"	R
				G23	VO	"IFG22>0THENF23 ELSE0"	R
F18	VO	"SUM(C18:E18)"	R	C24 to E24	VO	Enter values of levels of risk pertaining to packaging as per C8 to E8	R
G18	VO	"IFF18<=30THENF18 ELSE0"	R				
C19	VO	"C18*12"	R	F24	VO	"SUM(C24:E24)"	R
D19	VO	"D18*6"	R	G24	VO	"IFF24<=30THENF24 ELSE0"	R
E19	VO	"E18*4"	R	C25	VO	"C24*12"	R
F19	VO	"SUM(C19:E19)"	R	D25	VO	"D24*6"	R
G19	VO	"IFG18>0THENF19 ELSE0"	R	E25	VO	"E24*4"	R
C20 to E20	VO	Enter values of levels of risk pertaining to trial as per C8 to E8	R	F25	VO	"SUM(C25:E25)"	R
				G25	VO	"IFG24>0THENF25 ELSE0"	R
F20	VO	"SUM(C20:E20)"	R	C26 to E26	VO	Enter values of levels of risk pertaining to technical superiority as per C8 to E8	R
G20	VO	"IFF20<=30THENF20 ELSE0"	R				
C21	VO	"C20*12"	R	F26	VO	"SUM(C26:E26)"	R
D21	VO	"D20*6"	R	G26	VO	"IFF26<=30THENF26 ELSE0"	R
E21	VO	"E20*4"	R	C27	VO	"C26*12"	R
F21	VO	"SUM(C21:E21)"	R	D27	VO	"D26*6"	R
G21	VO	"IFG20>0THENF21 ELSE0"	R	E27	VO	"E26*4"	R
C22 to E22	VO	Enter values of levels of risk pertaining to competitors as per C8 to E8	R	F27	VO	"SUM(C27:E27)"	R
				G27	VO	"IFG26>0THENF27 ELSE0"	R
F22	VO	"SUM(C22:E22)"	R	A29/	LO	"VIABILITY	R
G22	VO	"IFF22<=30THENF22 ELSE0"	R	B29		INDEX"	R
C23	VO	"C22*12"	R	B31	VO	"G9 + G11 + G13 + G15 + G17 + G19 + G21 + G23 + G25 + G27"	R
D23	VO	"D22*6"	R				
E23	VO	"E22*4"	R				

Proforma 1.1   Product viability model

	A	B	C	D	E	F	G
2			PRODUCT VIABILITY				
4	FACTOR		Planning Horizon				
6			Short	Medium	Long		
8	Economic		10	10	0	SUM(C8:E8)	IFF8<=30THENF8ELSE0
9			C8*12	D8*6	E8*4	SUM(C9:E9)	IFG8>0THENF9ELSE0
10	Population		0	1	1	SUM(C10:E10)	IFF10<=30THENF10ELSE0
11			C10*12	D10*6	E10*4	SUM(C11:E11)	IFG10>0THENF11ELSE0
12	Social condition		5	5	5	SUM(C12:E12)	IFF12<=30THENF12ELSE0
13			C12*12	D12*6	E12*4	SUM(C13:E13)	IFG12>0THENF13ELSE0
14	Management		10	5	5	SUM(C14:E14)	IFF14<=30THENG14ELSE0
15			C14*12	D14*6	E14*4	SUM(C15:E15)	IFG14>0THENF15ELSE0
16	Distribution		5	5	5	SUM(C16:E16)	IFF16<=30THENF16ELSE0
17			C16*12	D16*6	E16*4	SUM(C17:E17)	IFG16>0THENF17ELSE0
18	Profit margin		2	8	10	SUM(C18:E18)	IFF18<=30THENF18ELSE0
19			C18*12	D18*6	E18*4	SUM(C19:E19)	IFG18>0THENF19ELSE0
20	Trial		10	10	10	SUM(C20:E20)	IFF20<=30THENF20ELSE0
21			C20*12	D20*6	E20*4	SUM(C21:E21)	IFG20>0THENF21ELSE0
22	Competitors		0	5	10	SUM(C22:E22)	IFF22<=30THENF22ELSE0
23			C22*12	D22*6	E22*4	SUM(C23:E23)	IFG22>0THENF23ELSE0
24	Packaging		5	5	8	SUM(C24:E24)	IFF24<=30THENF24ELSE0
25			C24*12	D24*6	E24*4	SUM(C25:E25)	IFG24>0THENF25ELSE0
26	Tech. superior		8	7	7	SUM(C26:E26)	IFF26<=30THENF26ELSE)
27			C26*12	D26*6	E26*4	SUM(C27:E27)	IFG26>0THENF27ELSE0
29	VIABILITY INDEX						
B31	G9+G11+G13+G15+G17+G19+G21+G23+G25+G27						

The explanatory notes for this chart are given in the line by line listings.

Product viability commentary

The model (Example 1.1.1) indicates that the particular product under study faces some significant problems in several areas. Economic factors, management, the level of trial, and technical superiority are all major short-term handicaps. The economic constraints on the product's future are likely to improve in the long-term, and management shortcomings will be solved to an extent over this period either by training or recruitment. In contrast, profit margins will face greater difficulties over time, as competitive activity grows significantly. The level of trial will remain low over the entire period suggesting that the product is well

Example 1.1.1   Product viability model

	A	B	C	D	E	F	G
2			PRODUCT VIABILITY				
4	FACTOR		Planning Horizon				
6			Short	Medium	Long		
8	Economic		10	10	0	20	20
9			120	60	0	180	180
10	Population		0	1	1	2	2
11			0	6	4	10	10
12	Social condition		5	5	5	15	15
13			60	30	20	110	110
14	Management		10	5	5	20	20
15			120	30	20	170	170
16	Distribution		5	5	5	15	15
17			60	30	20	110	110
18	Profit margin		2	8	10	20	20
19			24	48	40	112	112
20	Trial		10	10	10	30	30
21			120	60	40	220	220
22	Competitors		0	5	10	15	15
23			0	30	40	70	70
24	Packaging		5	5	8	18	18
25			60	30	32	122	122
26	Tech. superior		8	7	7	22	22
27			96	42	28	166	166
29	VIABILITY INDEX						
31		1270					

established in the market place. Packaging is another area which is judged likely to experience future problems.

From this analysis the firm could examine the costs of improvement in various areas, such as packaging, and technical features. Distribution could also be improved and action taken on the overall profitability by cutting product variants, production lines and so on. Should these remedial steps be carried out, the product's long-term viability might significantly improve and in consequence it might remain a valuable company product over a greater number of years than might otherwise be the case. The model is providing, in this instance, a framework within which the organisation can identify problem areas and take action to minimise them.

Example 1.1.2 shows a different pattern, one that might be associated with a product newly introduced into a growing market sector. Trial is not judged to be an immediate problem, and economic, population and social conditions are also much more favourable. In addition the management is seen as far more able to deal with the problems that the product may or may not encounter. With the low level of competitive activity; the technical edge that the product is seen to have in the short to medium term; and the up-to-date nature of the packaging, this particular product is much more viable than Example 1.1.1. Nevertheless there are trends apparent in the long term – declining technical superiority and the increase in competitive activity – that could repay further investigation to ensure that the product maintains its competitive superiority.

Example 1.1.2   Product viability model

	A	B	C	D	E	F	G
2			PRODUCT VIABILITY				
4	FACTOR		Planning Horizon				
6			Short	Medium	Long		
8	Economic		0	2	5	7	7
9			0	12	20	32	32
10	Population		0	1	1	2	2
11			0	6	4	10	10
12	Social condition		0	2	3	5	5
13			0	12	12	24	24
14	Management		2	3	2	7	7
15			24	18	8	50	50
16	Distribution		5	1	1	7	7
17			60	6	4	70	70
18	Profit margin		2	8	10	20	20
19			24	48	40	112	112
20	Trial		0	2	5	7	7
21			0	12	20	32	32
22	Competitors		0	3	7	10	10
23			0	18	28	46	46
24	Packaging		1	3	3	7	7
25			12	18	12	42	42
26	Tech. superior		2	5	7	14	14
27			24	30	28	82	82
29	VIABILITY INDEX						
31		512					

2 Direct marketing

Any firm faces a dilemma when communicating with the market: how to achieve the maximum of effective contact at the minimum cost. The problem is especially acute for those firms or parts of companies whose customers are not the general public and for whom mass media advertising may be both costly and impotent since it will not adequately convey the highly specialised information essential to the selling of their products. In this chapter we shall be concerned with the highly specialised needs catered for through direct marketing which covers such areas as industrial detergents, vending machines, the components industry, computers, luncheon vouchers, insurance and other forms of service industry.

The difficulties of examining the issues involved in direct marketing are evident from the diversity of the examples cited. Within any one operation there are many interlocking factors comprising the nature of the market, the form of the product and type of customer.

The markets can be small or large; distribution may be evenly spread or concentrated; and there may be extremes of fluctuation and continuous stability.

The products may range from the highly technical equipment to the most simple; shape and weight will be multifarious thereby influencing distribution methods. Of course pricing too will differ considerably.

In number and usage patterns, customers will also be a mixed bag and will vary in geographical concentration and location as well. They will also show heterogeneity of response to the products ranging from nearly universal to highly specialised interest.

Direct marketing and cost effectiveness

We are mainly concerned with such communication methods as direct mail, advertising in specialised or localised journals, exhibitions, or other media with a sufficiently specific target. In a market where there is a profusion of radio and television channels, cable networks for instance, the media may be used.

25

For the small organisation the method of communication will tend to be the salesman who may easily be the owner or managing director of the firm. The use of the salesman to promote the sales message is a very high-cost route. The amount of time concerned with travelling between customers must be taken into account as well as the magnitude of the effort that is required once the customer is in front of the seller. Thus the door-to-door trader in dustpans and brushes only faces the problem of outright rejection – the housewife either likes the product or not, and does not require an explanation of the uses to which a carpet brush can be put. The vendor of a complicated steam carpet cleaner would require an initial period of explanation before being able to gauge whether the sale would be successful. In consequence the costs of attempting to sell this sort of equipment by this method will greatly outweigh profit unless margins are very high. It is interesting to note that even companies in the highly profitable home improvements markets, which heavily employ 'cold' calling techniques, are increasingly developing filter systems to weed out the obvious unlikely candidates using canvassers or 'market researchers'.

Using the mass media – television, press or radio – to communicate with the customer again confronts the issue of whether or not this is a cost effective way of reaching those with buying power. The broader the spread of the user the more cost effective mass media will be within certain constraints. The most obvious of these is the level of technical information that needs to be imparted about the product which tends to mitigate against its use, though certain car manufacturers, notably BMW, have successfully mobilised the press in particular to dominate the market.

Guidelines for direct marketing

It is possible to identify guidelines for where it is most appropriate to develop direct marketing systems for communicating with specific individuals or groups interested in a highly specialised market.

1 Direct marketing will become more appropriate if the potential number of customers is small.
2 Highly technical products requiring a high level of explanation are ideally suited to the development of specialist literature which can overcome some of the initial hurdles faced by the salesman.
3 Targeted activity is also more effective when the purchase frequency is low, as otherwise the costs of maintaining exposure would be too high.
4 It is inappropriate in countries with poorly developed specialised media or where the postal service is limited. Thus in many developing countries the use of such direct methods would not prove particularly effective.

Once the decision is taken that the direct method offers a cost effective way of reaching the consumer the development of the programme can be carried forward and then evaluated.

As in all marketing exercises, the first stage will involve the definition of the market. This includes all possible information about buyers, the level of competition, pricing information and so on. From this the ways of overcoming the marketing problem can be defined and the means identified for converting the buyer from the state of no, limited, or extensive knowledge concerning your product into making a purchase.

During the second stage moves will be made towards the creation of the list of possible purchasers. This will often require a major investment and continual refining by the company to ensure that the information is constantly updated otherwise it will rapidly become valueless over time. It will eventually enable the company to segment the market geographically and by other criteria, for example by former user/non-user; or major/minor consumers.

The combination of the list marketing objectives and background information will determine the selling strategy for the particular item being considered. To illustrate the point, the buying criteria of the engineering departments within target organisations will undoubtedly be different from those of the marketing directors. The nature of the planned response will also be an important factor. In some contexts with highly technical information the initial result required may only be to persuade the end-user to send for some more information on the product or product range. In others the aim is the immediate placing of orders or a request for a follow up sales call.

Assessing the response will therefore vary according to how that particular item was being considered. Within the public relations area a straightforward comparison between two activities could yield information on cost effectiveness. Thus two items each requiring response of a demand for a company brochure can be compared on a cost per brochure basis. This is only relevant when comparing like with like: brochures distributed at exhibitions will tend to fall into a different category.

For the majority of operations the comparison will tend to be made on the response rate as a measure of the success or effectiveness of the activity carried out. This is not always totally valid as the value of the particular sales lead needs to be evaluated. To take an extreme example one can consider the case of the vending machine manufacturer carrying out a series of mailings to differing market sectors, one to hospitals and the others to snack-bars. Based on initial criteria of cost per sales lead, the mailing to the snack-bars would be considered far more cost effective to the company than that to the hospital. However when the order size is considered together with the level of repeat business which is generated, a single hospital conversion may be worth several hundred snack bars.

Any evaluation that is carried out must therefore consider the same level of sales – in other words comparing the effectiveness of the activity in rates of return to the company.

The direct marketing analysis model

The model considers the interactions of direct marketing costs in relation to overall return to the company. By comparing and contrasting the achievements of a sales force supported by advertising with one that is not, the model provides a framework for assessing the relative cost-effectiveness of each. Advertising expenditure is measured against the sales force base activity, that is the cost of achieving a level of sales using only the sales force working mainly through 'cold' call techniques. The following information is necessary for the model to function effectively:

1   Total costs

This includes the total expenditure on the direct marketing effort including the research expenditure necessary to develop the list, though this will obviously be amortised over a period of time. Costs will include material origination, printing and postage if direct mail is being used; the costs of media space if specialised magazines are chosen; and stand costs, display costs and so on when exhibitions are used as the ideal direct response method.

2   Total sales force costs

This covers all administrative costs such as personnel involved with the sales force as well as the expenditure specifically related to the representatives such as salary and travelling expenses.

3   Average days in market

Within the sales force there will be an average number of days spent in the market. A normal figure allowing for holidays, weekends, and conferences will be in the region of 220 days per year (see Chapter 7 on sales productivity).

4   Total number of new accounts visited

This can be obtained from analysis of the sales force daily sales records (DSRs) over the time period under consideration.

5   Total number of accounts opened

The account listings will be available in the accounts department together with the date of their commencement. It is common practice in sales forces' record keeping to indicate whether a new client is obtained from personal contact; the 'cold call' approach; or as a follow up to a trade enquiry generated by one of the direct marketing items.

6   Total value of orders placed during year

For the evaluation of any investment in direct marketing it is necessary to gain an accurate idea of the rate of return on the investment involved. One of the common pitfalls in significant areas of sales force management is the lack of monitoring of the existing client base. This is particularly true in a young company with sales representatives targeted on the acquisition of new clients – the clients gained tend to have very little long-term value to the organisation producing an initial order and then no further business.

7 Profit margin percentage on business gained

This will be very important to companies selling a variety of merchandise with differing profit margins, the return on investment of the marketing effort again being a crucial factor.

What the model does not consider is the long-term return from the accounts opened with or without advertising. Should the accounts be substantially different in their long-term potential, the comparison between the two using the first year sales as a measure of success may not be totally accurate. In many product areas however the initial order from the newly opened account is a very effective measure of long-term return for that particular account.

Similarly, the model does not take into account the amount of time the salesmen are taking to open differing types of new account which may also affect the profitability comparisons between the two systems. Should they be spending a substantial amount of time canvassing for and then obtaining new accounts, the level of repeat business will inevitably suffer, and as repeat business is not considered in the model the manager must still bear it in mind.

In the interests of simplicity these items have been omitted, but can be included by readers both searching for greater control over the question and wishing to increase their knowledge of the use of spreadsheets.

Using the direct marketing analysis model

The *Go To* column in Listing 2.1 tells you the cell number and the cursor position. The next column specifies the spreadsheet option (LO = Label Option; VO = Value Option). The *Type In* column gives you instructions within the inverted commas which you must type in, or asks you to supply the necessary data. These commas are not part of the instructions supplied here but beware that some spreadsheets, the *Lotus 1-2-3* for example, enter the Label Option by using the inverted-comma key. Under the *Type In* column the symbols * = multiply and / = divide. R in the *Return* column instructs you to commit the information to memory by pressing the Return key.

Remember: When you have finished, save your model.

Listing 2.1 Direct marketing analysis model

Go To		Type In	Return	Go To	Type In	Return
C2/	LO	"Direct	R	E5	"Base act"	R
D2/		Marketing	R			
E2/		Analysis"	R			
F2			R			
C5/	LO	"Investment"	R			
D5/		for advertising invest-ment		A7/	LO "Total	R

Note that in columns C and E you will be inserting data to compare a situation where advertising supports the sales force against a base (column E) where there is none.

Listing 2.1 *(continued)*

Go To		Type In	Return
B7		adv costs$" for total advertising costs	R
C7	VO	Insert figures for total advertising costs in $	R
A9/	LO	"Sales	R
B9/		Force	R
C9		Cost$"	R
E7	VO	Insert figure for base activity	R

Note: As we are comparing the effects of investing money in direct marketing with a situation where there is none there will be no figure in this cell.

C9	VO	Insert figure for sales force costs in $ when there is advertising support for sales force	R
E9	VO	Insert figure for sales force costs in $ when there is no advertising	R
A11/	LO	"Total	R
B11		Costs$"	R
C11	VO	"C7+C9"	R
E11	VO	"E7+E9"	R
A13/	LO	"Total days	R
B13		worked"	R

Note: this consists of the number of salesmen multiplied by the number of days at work.

C13	VO	Insert figure for total days worked by sales force with advertising support	R

Go To		Type In	Return
E13	VO	Insert figure for total days worked by sales force without advertising	R
A15/	LO	"Total	R
B15		leads" for total prospective customers visited	R
C15	VO	Insert figure for total sales leads acquired by advertising	R
E15	VO	Insert figure for total leads without advertising	R
A17/	LO	"Total new	R
B17		accounts"	R

Note: This refers to the actual number of accounts that are opened in the accounting period.

C17	VO	Insert figure for total number of accounts opened with advertising	R
E17	VO	Insert figure for total number of accounts opened through sales force efforts without advertising	R
A19/	LO	"Total	
B19		order val$" for total order value in accounting period	R
C19	VO	Insert figure for total order value from new accounts generated by advertising in the accounting period	R

Listing 2.1 *(concluded)*

Go To		Type In	Return	Go To		Type In	Return
E19	VO	Insert figure for total order value of new accounts achieved by sales force unaided by advertising	R	A31/	LO	"Acc sales$"	R
				B31		for average value of each new customer	R
A21	LO	"Profit %"	R	C31	VO	"C19/C17"	R
C21	VO	Insert value for profit % achieved through advertising	R	E31	VO	"E19/E17"	R
E21	VO	Insert value for profit % achieved by sales force without advertising support	R				

Note that the formula for both C31 and E31 calculates the business generation cost. This is the pure cost of generating new business treating the sales force as an advertising force.

Go To		Type In	Return	Go To		Type In	Return
A23/	LO	"Total		A33/	LO	"Net bus.	R
B23		profit$"	R	B33		gen$" for net business generated	R
C23	VO	"C19*C21/100"	R	C33	VO	"C23−E23−C7"	R
E23	VO	"E19*E21/100"	R				

Note: If this figure is negative the direct marketing investment has created a loss; if positive a gain to the business.

Go To		Type In	Return	Go To		Type In	Return
A25/	LO	"Improved	R	A35/	LO	"New acc/	R
B25		profit$"	R	B35		man day" for the number of new accounts opened per sales force effective day	R
C25	VO	"C23−E23"	R				
A27/	LO	"Return	R				
B27		on invest." for return on investment	R				
C27	VO	"(C25−C7)/C7*100"	R				
A29/	LO	"Cost of	R				
B29		new acc.$"	R	C35	VO	"C17/C13"	R
C29	VO	"C11/C17"	R	E35	VO	"E17/E13"	R
E29	VO	"E11/E17"	R				

Direct marketing analysis commentary

The model compares the return on investment in two contexts: (1) the combined costs of advertising and the sales force, with (2) sales force costs alone. In Example 2.1.1, the amount of money spent on advertising is $180 000, with the sales force costing an additional $500 000. Each organisation should keep a record of accounts

Proforma 2.1   Direct marketing analysis model

	A	B	C	D	E	F
2			Direct Marketing	Analysis		
5			Investment		Base act.	
7	Tot. adv. costs		180000		0	
9	Sales force cost		500000		500000	
11	Total costs		C7+C9		E7+E9	
13	Total days work		3500		3500	
15	Total leads		1500		1770	
17	Total new accs		750		450	
19	Total order value		860000		570000	
21	Profit %		35		30	
23	Total profits$		C19*C21/100		E19*E21/100	
25	Improved profit		C23-E23			
27	Return on invest		(C25-C7)/C7*100			
29	Cost of new acc $		C11/C17		E11/E17	
31	Acc sales$		C19/C17		E19/E17	
33	Net bus gen$		C23-E23-C7			
35	New acc/man day		C17/C13		E17/E13	

that the sales force open on their own initiative compared with accounts that are generated by advertising. This can be an instance where as stated in the Introduction the model is demanding information that is not currently available. Obviously an organisation should have such data; for otherwise sensible decisions concerning the level of sales force expenditure versus advertising cannot be quantified.

Details of new accounts visited (leads) with and without advertising are entered in cells C15 and D15. The numbers of new accounts actually opened are entered in C17 and D17, and in this example it can be seen that the total number of accounts visited when advertising is used is considerably lower than when the sales force are 'cold-calling'. The conversion of accounts visited to actual business is however higher in the case of the advertising programme indicating that higher quality accounts are being generated. This is as would be expected; the response to advertising indicates a level of initial interest not generally present when the salesman calls on his own. The profit levels achieved from accounts gained from advertising is also higher, yielding a substantially greater profit figure than that gained by the use of the sales force alone. This is provided by the improved profit figure in cell C25.

Example 2.1.1   Direct marketing analysis model

	A	B	C	D	E	F
2			Direct Marketing		Analysis	
5			Investment		Base act.	
7	Tot. adv. costs		180000		0	
9	Sales force cost		500000		500000	
11	Total costs		680000		500000	
13	Total days work		3500		3500	
15	Total leads		1500		1770	
17	Total new accs		750		450	
19	Total order value		860000		570000	
21	Profit %		35		30	
23	Total profits$		301000		171000	
25	Improved profit		130000			
27	Return on invest		-27.778			
29	Cost of new acc $		906.667		1111.11	
31	Acc sales$		1146.67		1266.67	
33	Net bus gen$		-50000			
35	New acc/man day		0.21429		0.12857	

However, the model shows that the extra investment in advertising in this example is not paying for itself (producing a negative rate of return on the investment even though overall profitability is higher – cell C27), compared with the column where the sales force is generating new business without the help of advertising support. Though the number of accounts visited has declined, and the conversion rate had increased, the total return on the investment is negative in the first year.

The model also analyses the cost of each new account opened and the business that each account has provided in the first year or accounting period. This particular example shows that while the conversion rate of leads to new accounts is considerably higher with advertising, the actual business generated is lower compared with those accounts opened by the sales force – a fact that would require further investigation.

In Example 2.1.2 the model is being used to consider reductions in sales force numbers and the replacement by advertising of the account generation function. The manager in this instance considers that the value of sales in these new accounts will be significantly higher than the normal level of account generation (cells C19

Example 2.1.2   Direct marketing analysis model

	A	B	C	D	E	F
2			Direct Marketing	Analysis		
5			Investment		Base act.	
7	Tot. adv. costs		250000		0	
9	Sales force cost		300000		500000	
11	Total costs		550000		500000	
13	Total days work		2100		3500	
15	Total leads		1670		1770	
17	Total new accs		950		450	
19	Total order value		1500000		450000	
21	Profit %		30		30	
23	Total profits$		450000		135000	
25	Improved profit		315000			
27	Return on invest		26			
29	Cost of new acc $		578.947		1111.11	
31	Acc sales$		1578.95		1000	
33	Net bus gen$		65000			
35	New acc/man day		0.45238		0.12857	

and E19). In consequence, at the reduced level of sales force and higher advertising expenditure the exercise will be more profitable for the company. Thus an improved profit of $315 000 is considerably more than is needed to break even on advertising costs. But should the lead generation target not be reached and the conversion rate be lower than that postulated, the expenditure of money on advertising would need to be considered.

The model can therefore be useful in the planning of direct mail campaigns to control the level of return that companies are making in this particular area of business activity, isolating important areas where further information may be necessary. Many companies concentrate on the cost of lead generation alone – a campaign producing a high level of leads will be more successful than a lower level of achievement. What should be considered is the dollar value of these accounts to the company and from that the return to the organisation. This may produce a very different picture.

3 Personnel analysis

You may be surprised to see a chapter on personnel matters in a book on marketing, particularly since it is a subject which is absent from most books on the subject. One aim of this book is to provoke thought about traditional attitudes to marketing and directions for the future. The managers themselves are the hub of the exercise: however useful the models presented in this book are, they will be little more than seeds scattered in the wind in the absence of the right people to use them and put them into effect. Taking a fresh look at marketing within the context of the company's best interests must therefore also involve the discusssion of staffing matters.

Typically, the hiring and firing of staff is regarded as an unwelcome task, with managers preferring to distance themselves from the complexities of making decisions about the careers of members of staff for whom they are responsible. Yet however hard managers may pretend that these are matters for their companies' personnel departments, the fact remains that they are the ones who will undertake job appraisals to assess the abilities and achievements of the staff working under them, making recommendations for action to the personnel departments. For this task they will have had little or no training and because the subject is sensitive and the risks tend to outweigh the benefits for the individual staff manager – competence as a manager of people having a low or no job status rating – personnel management issues fail to become integrated as a cornerstone of achieving company objectives. Only one of the companies for whom the author worked had a policy of systematically directing its most able managers into personnel work.

In any organisation progress will be determined by the interaction of people, machines, and resources. The majority of the literature on marketing management tends to ignore the impact of people on a company's development, a fact that is doubly strange when practical experience within organisations suggests that rational solution of a specific problem will often be impossible because the people needed to implement the project within the organisation are either opposed to it or incapable of producing the desired result.

Studies of large organisations reveal the importance of internal politics in hampering or promoting a project – however sensible it may be (1). Thus the position of the individual in the firm can often become more important to him or her than the tasks of the department in which he or she is involved. The effects of such management can be seen clearly in areas such as packaging, product development and the control of media expenditure – topics discussed in other chapters.

A clear view of the human resources within the firm is as vital to its long-term health as audits of its present and future strategy and physical resources. It will ensure that the correct managerial team is available to cope with the future problems the firm will face. The efficient organisation needs to be aware of the essential human skills present and required, and to develop its thinking on manpower planning. One study of 75 companies using regression techniques has shown that approximately 65 per cent of the changes in financial performance and productivity could be explained by analyses of the company's personnel policy within areas of decision making, the amount of information in the organisation, and the level of trust between management levels (2).

The case for standardisation

Any planning procedure demands a degree of formalisation with standard reporting structures so that a measure of common ground can be developed. Thus for capital investment projects a common approach will be the return on capital employed, with some assessment of the risk factor of achieving the planned level of profit. Because resources are scarce, the two or more competing projects will be compared to decide which is the most profitable. The allocation of resources within the personnel sector can also be viewed in the same light.

First, there will be limited opportunities available for promotion, and where promotion occurs it should be to those people who are most valuable to the organisation as a whole, rather than a particular sectional interest. Second, the amount of money that the organisation has available for salaries will also be limited and it is to its advantage to achieve the maximum rate of return on the investment made in this area. This should imply that personal merit will be recognised within the organisation if promotion is not possible by a degree of financial reward. This may take the form of such management perks as company cars, subsidised health insurance and the like, rather than increased salary. It could also include foreign travel and training courses which are not normally regarded as classic 'fringe' benefits – except perhaps by the employee.

Indeed the development of non-financial rewards should be seen as a very important aspect of personnel planning. A well-known saying holds that 'if you pay peanuts you get monkeys'. An article in the *Harvard Business Review* considered senior executive pay in relation to overall company performance, finding that there was if anything a negative correlation – the most highly paid executives being found in the least successful firms. The conclusion was that 'paying golden peanuts produces golden monkeys' (3).

The standardisation of an appraisal system will benefit an organisation by creating awareness of the short- and medium-term requirements of people and other resources. It may well reduce management and employee turnover levels. Though the research on this is fragmented there are indications that where formalised appraisal systems are in operation the level of employee turnover is diminished. On a practical level it is possible to see why this should be so. Individuals who are interviewed in depth at least once a year will have an opportunity to reveal at least part of their problems as well as their ambitions for the future. It departs from the mushroom principle often used by some firms as their main personnel tactic. This, for the uninitiated, is to keep everyone as much in the dark as possible, occasionally opening the door to throw something unpleasant in.

The effective use of an efficient appraisal system which is continually searching for ways of improving the value of the personnel pool should also prevent the development of a stagnant pool of manpower which can often have serious consequences on the long-term viability of the organisation. Many of the problems of low performance in bureaucracies are often laid at the door of an unchanging personnel pool.

Properly applied, personnel analysis can determine job prospects (promotion or increasingly more relevant, redundancy) and the salary/benefit level of the employee. It should also increase the awareness about the employees' problems throughout the organisation. For example, it should encourage supervisors to take a more active interest in their subordinates: in how they can be encouraged and in how their performance can be improved by the sensible use of training schemes.

Some of its problems

As within other areas of management the operation of appraisal systems will tend to be subjective, for several reasons:

1 Emotional reaction

The personality of an individual will cloud the assessment of his ability to work effectively. Thus Bill, the gregarious golf-playing boss will tend to prefer Jim, his subordinate and occasional drinking companion, rather than Edwin who is a Mormon.

2 Job content

The nature of the job will vary often within very small areas of a firm's activity. For example, in a public relations department there may be an individual concerned with media contact who is regarded as 'the salesman'. Another employee producing the material essential to this form of salesmanship, may be a member of the publications or information department which, according to the perception of the management, may be regarded as totally different work.

3   Personal attitude

Certain supervisors will tend to regard all their subordinates in a totally favourable light. Others might be wholly negative. Thus the same individual rated by the two extremes would receive differing evaluations.

4   Policy effects

The use to which the organisation puts the appraisal system will obviously have a major influence on the nature of the process. Should it be used primarily to determine the training needs of employees negative aspects of performance may easily be magnified because there is no point in praise, as worthwhile aspects of the employees' performance will not be considered for training needs. These will be ticked-off on the list and most of the time will be spent concentrating on strengthening weakness.

If salary is at stake, the positive will be expanded as negative findings will rebound in the supervisor's evaluation by senior management. The tendency will therefore always be towards the middle ground where the supervisor cannot be criticised by his superior for poor personnel management or asked to support the high ranking of a subordinate. Such a process can be seen within university or college exam marking with the bulk of the marking designed to produce a certain spread of exam results. Attempts to widen the band of marks will often run into problems with the external examiners acting in this instance as the equivalent of senior company executives. Through its hierarchical structure, the organisation will tend to develop a common view of the nature of the personnel within it, a process summarised by Dean Swift:

> So Nat'ralists observe, a Flea,
> Hath smaller Fleas that on him prey,
> And these have smaller Fleas to bite 'em
> And so proceed ad infinitum.

5   Halo effect

Within the actual assessment itself, the ranking of one characteristic can often influence another. Thus the employee will tend to be given more or less the same mark throughout the appraisal regardless of a possible variation in many areas of job performance.

Personnel appraisal techniques

Man is imperfect and we have seen that as long as the species exists there will always be shortfalls in the implementation of any appraisal system. But provided suitable allowance is made for them, the various methods used can still be valuable. The majority of the failings appear to be related to the inability of each supervisor to cope with a variety of personal reactions to the individual reporting to him or her, and the problems imposed by the standardised measurement of performance. These shortcomings can be seen in the variety of systems commonly used for job appraisals:

1   Employee comparison

Under this system the immediate supervisor of a particular department ranks staff in order according to their job performance and importance to the organisation, producing a division into the top, middle and bottom thirds. The problems encountered are that the method makes it impossible to compare across departments and does not identify clearly an individual's training needs – a fundamental requirement of any system of job analysis. The tendency to mark all staff equally can be overcome by specifying that they should be ranked in a particular way. This causes further problems in that those within the organisation will already be an atypical sample due to the selection procedure and any attempt to force a standard distribution onto a non-standard sample is unlikely to be successful.

2   Critical incident or attainment

In this system the main points of an individual's performance are measured either in an unstructured or structured fashion. For the unstructured approach each major decision/action is recorded together with a comment as to how the individual coped with the problem. With this approach the individual is assigned targets in each of the main areas of job activity. Achievement is then measured and compared with the goals set at the previous appraisal period.

The advantage of this system is that it is highly attuned to the needs of the individual and can be very useful for identifying training requirements on a personal basis. As a method of salary assessment and for overall company manpower planning it poses certain problems. First, the nature of the tasks set will be extremely varied. Second, the fundamental strengths of the employee will tend to be ignored. Thus his performance in record keeping or his ability with foreign languages will be masked under the cloak of task-orientated target setting. Lastly, the high performer or the unpopular employee will be given harder jobs than the others, again invalidating the testing procedure.

3   Checklist system

The use of a checklist containing a large number of statements about the nature of the work can accurately measure the level of performance as seen by the supervisor. Each job will contain a different specific series of checks. In consequence the evaluation will again be limited to the stated tasks and will also require a considerable length of time to prepare.

4   Rating scales

This, the most commonly used appraisal system, assigns scores to a number of qualities. For the production employee the attributes could be items such as dependability, quantity and quality of work. For the managerial grade the criteria could be decisiveness, attitude and creative ability. This method obviously suffers from the defects mentioned elsewhere – the lack of objectivity of the supervisor, and whether a high score in one attribute can offset a low one in another. If properly structured, it does offer an approach to the standardisation of appraisal systems across a wide range of managerial and non-managerial grades. It provides the ability to break down widely differing jobs into common elements, determining the importance of these various elements, and then rating each person on this basis.

Eliminating subjectivity

The main hazard of most appraisal systems, the effect of one individual on the evaluation of another, can be improved by the introduction of a supervisory pool into appraisal systems. Here a group of three supervisors each in charge of five individuals would jointly appraise the fifteen individuals beneath them. Where employees have been appraised by a group system with a supervisory pool evaluating all their subordinates, the anomalies of personal assessment largely disappear and the training programme mapped out is often more imaginative than would otherwise be possible. This can only be developed as a company-wide method however if the performance evaluation is sufficiently broad and comprehensive.

The personnel analysis model

The model attempts to provide a framework within which a group approach to personnel evaluation, described in the immediately preceding section, can provide a useful means of maximising the human resources of the organisation, and give a yardstick for the salary and promotion prospects of each staff member.

For each one there are three main areas of performance under consideration: skills, tasks and impact on the organisation. Though the roles of the head porter and the chairman of the board are generally regarded as completely disparate the evaluation of their performance can be obtained in the same fashion though obviously through the completion of different job tasks. The model proposes to take the job description of each person; to weight the importance of various skills, tasks, and the areas where the appraisee can have an impact on the organisation; and finally to measure performance against this evaluation. Thus the difference between the head porter and the chairman of the board will occur on many differing planes and it is on these and these alone that they should be judged and not the fact that one is a porter and the other a senior manager.

A   Skill

1   Physical

Each job will contain a differing level of physical requirements. One extreme will be those jobs requiring high levels of physical attainment. For example, attractiveness – a pleasing physical appearance – may be regarded as essential for someone dealing with the press; or strength, co-ordination and physical training may be requirements for store room staff and skilled manual workers. At the other end are jobs where physical skills are of a lower order but where they may nevertheless affect efficiency, as in the case of documentalists or librarians, clerical assistants, and secretarial staff.

2   General educational

The degree of competence in reading, writing and doing sums and the importance attached to academic attainment are relevant here. There are greater demands in this area on the typing pool supervisor than on the head porter; more still on the senior managers and perhaps even on the chairman of the board.

3   Intelligence

A job encompassing the need to correspond effectively, talk coherently, and deal with a variety of complex data on a day to day and long-term basis will require a higher degree of intelligence than one concerned only with routine tasks with limited daily variation.

4   Emotional adjustment

A major organisational work problem concerns the ability to work amicably in a team. Not only is it crucial to marketing management, practically all aspects of which involve working with other departments and outside bodies, but also in such areas as budget reviews and forward planning, conference management, office management, and public relations. All require close collaboration with others which is often the key to achievement and impact. By contrast there are areas where such an ability to deal with others would not be regarded as essential – academic life is one such example. This heading also includes the ability of the individual to motivate others around them: highly important in most team activities and essential to managers responsible for other staff.

5   Stress survival

Many jobs would be regarded as highly stressful and the individual's ability to cope with this may have an important bearing on the assessment of his or her performance. Thus airline pilots are periodically put through extremes of stress in simulated conditions to ascertain their fitness for their work, whereas parking lot attendants do not need such a high level of stress resistance. Increasingly many companies are insisting that high-level executive staff undergo annual physical check-ups to ensure that the problems of stress are minimised.

6   Technical

The importance of specialised, technical skills to a job and their exact nature needs a degree of thought. For example, a high level of linguistic competence may be necessary, or a high level of knowledge of the biological or chemical sciences or of print production techniques.

B Tasks

A particular job can be broken down into an assessment of tasks that are performed on a given time scale. Thus there will be jobs performed:

1 Daily
2 Weekly
3 Monthly
4 Annually
5 Periodically
6 Unplanned

Employees will have to cope with a different mix of activity depending on their jobs. The filing clerk will have a high proportion of daily tasks to perform, whereas public relations officers and press officers may well claim to have a greater number of unplanned jobs because the nature of the work involves continually responding to changing events which defy forward planning by the organisation.

C Organisational impact

The nature of the job to a large extent will determine the impact of the individual within the organisation. It is in this area above all others that the potential for promotion can best be discerned. The success of the organisation will depend on the ability of individuals to progress beyond their own sphere, to cope with problems that are not strictly their province but which they need to acquire for the firm to progress with maximum speed and efficiency. Borrowing an illustration from history, the success of Wellington in the Napoleonic Wars can be said to be due at least in part to the training and development of the British army under Sir John Moore, in the previous decade. The identification of the individual making a greater impact than his peers on any part of the business is worthy of note and analysis.

1 Routine

Essentially these are the housekeeping tasks of the organisation – the business which must be completed. Thus the individual who develops new approaches to record keeping, diminishing the amount of the employer's time taken to deal with this should be rated highly if his job is restricted to routine matters.

2 Broadly defined

For the marketing manager these would include the classic items in the job description – the development and control of support programmes for their particular brands or products. How competently the individual develops approaches to these problems is obviously important as is the ability to make the event occur.

3   Abstractly defined

These areas are included under the heading of 'furthering the interests of the firm'. Thus the individuals developing new products and new approaches to problems which are not specifically stated in their job description may be vitally important people for the organisation's development. Within an authoritarian structure they may however be regarded as an unnecessary luxury.

Using the personnel analysis model

In Listing 3.1 the *Go To* column tells you the cell number and the cursor position. The next column specifies the spreadsheet option (LO = Label Option; VO = Value Option). The *Type In* column gives you instructions within the inverted commas which you must type in or asks you to supply the necessary data. These commas are not part of the instructions supplied here but beware that some spreadsheets, the *Lotus 1-2-3* for example, enter the Label Option by using the inverted-comma key. Under the *Type In* column the symbols * = multipy and / = divide. R in the *Return* column instructs you to commit the information to memory by pressing the Return key.
Remember: When you have finished, save your model.

Listing 3.1   Personnel analysis model

Go To		Type In	Return
A2/	LO	"PERSONNEL	R
B2/		ANALYSIS"	R
C2			R
E5	LO	"Manager A"	R

Note: This relates to the scores given by one of the supervisors in the supervisory pool to a particular manager. The calculations can be copied across to provide scores for other managers: "Manager B", "Manager C", "Manager D" and so on.

I5	LO	"Manager B"	R

Go To		Type In	Return

You can continue across the spreadsheet, using the correct spacing, to include other managers.

D7	LO	"Small"	R
E7	LO	"Moderate"	R
F7	LO	"Large"	R

Note: the scores assigned by the assessor for each of the skills, tasks, and organisational impact items are spread over cells D7, E7 and F7. Taken together these three must always add up to 1 otherwise the model will not work.

Listing 3.1 *(continued)*

Go To	Type In	Return
C10	LO	"Value"	R

Note: This relates to the value given in the job description to the skills, tasks, and organisational impact areas. Where a job requires a high level of emotional adjustment this should be highly rated in value terms. The total value assigned in each category must add up to 10 otherwise the model will not accept it.

Go To	Type In		Return
A9	LO	"SKILLS"	R
A12	LO	"Physical" refers to the physical attributes required for the job as discussed in the text.	R
C12	VO	Enter value for Physical attributes	R
D12 to F12	VO	Enter assessment of individual scores for physical attributes split across "small", "moderate" and "large"	R

Note: They must add up to one. The assessment of any individual will reveal a spread of ability within even a single attribute. Thus, an individual may be physically competent for 50 per cent of the time but, under pressure for 10 per cent of the time perform badly, and be superb on other occasions. The model is replacing conventional single score systems for a particular attribute as this provides a more realistic assessment of an individual's performance.

Go To	Type In	Return
D13	VO	"C12*2*D12"	R
E13	VO	"C12*E12*5"	

Go To	Type In	Return
F13	VO	"C12*F12*10"	R
A14	LO	"Gen educ" refers to general educational requirement as discussed in the text	R
C14	VO	Insert value for general education see C10 Note	R
D14 to F14	VO	Insert the assessment of general education scores split across small, moderate and large. See Note to D12–F12	R
D15	VO	"C14*2*D14"	R
E15	VO	"C14*E14*5"	R
F15	VO	"C14*F14*10"	R
G12	VO	"IFSUM(D12:F12)=1 THEN1ELSE0"	R
G13	VO	"SUM(D13:F13)/G12"	R
G14	VO	"IFSUM(D14:F14)=1 THEN1ELSE0"	R
G15	VO	"SUM(D15:F15)/G14"	R
A16/	LO	"Intelligence"	R
B16			R
C16	VO	Insert value for intelligence	R
D16 to F16	VO	Enter assessment of individual scores for intelligence as per D12 to F12	R
G16	VO	"IFSUM(D16:F16)=1 THEN1ELSE0"	R
D17	VO	"C16*2*D16"	R
E17	VO	"C16*E16*5"	R
F17	VO	"C16*F16*10"	R
G17	VO	"SUM(D17:F17)/G16"	R

Listing 3.1 *(continued)*

Go To		Type In	Return
A18/	LO	"Emotion	
B18		adj" for emotional adjustment	R
C18	VO	Insert value for emotional adjustment	R
D18 to F18	VO	Insert assessment of scores for emotional adjustment as per D12 to F12	R
G18	VO	"IFSUM(D18:F18)=1 THEN1ELSE0"	R
D19	VO	"C18*2*D18"	R
E19	VO	"C18*E18*5"	R
F19	VO	"C18*F18*10"	R
G19	VO	"SUM(D19:F19)/G18"	R
A20	LO	"Stress"	R
C20	VO	Insert value for stress	R
D20 to F20	VO	Enter assessment of individual scores for emotional adjustment as per D12 to F12	R
G20	VO	"IFSUM(D20:F20)=1 THEN1ELSE0"	R
D21	VO	"C20*2*D20"	R
E21	VO	"C20*E20*5"	R
F21	VO	"C20*F20*10"	R
G21	VO	"SUM(D21:F21)/G20"	R
A22/	LO	"Technical"	R
B22			R
C22	VO	Insert value for technical requirements of job	R
D22 to F22	VO	Enter assessment of individual scores for technical requirements as per D12 to F12	R

Go To		Type In	Return
G22	VO	"IFSUM(D22:F22)=1 THEN1ELSE0"	R
C23	VO	"IFSUM(C12:C22)=10 THEN10ELSE0"	R
D23	VO	"C22*2*D22"	R
E23	VO	"C22*E22*5"	R
F23	VO	"C22*F22*10"	R
G23	VO	"SUM(D23:F23)/G22"	R
G24	VO	"G13+G15+G17+G19 +G21+G23"	R
A26	LO	"TASKS"	R
A28	LO	"Daily"	R
C28	VO	Enter value for daily tasks	R
D28 to F28	VO	Insert assessment of individual scores for daily tasks as per D12 to F12	R
G28	VO	"IFSUM(D28:F28)=1 THEN1ELSE0"	R
D29	VO	"C28*2*D28"	R
E29	VO	"C28*E28*5"	R
F29	VO	"C28*F28*10"	R
G29	VO	"SUM(D29:F29)/G28"	R
A30	LO	"Weekly"	R
C30	VO	Insert value for weekly tasks	R
D30 to F30	VO	Enter assessment of individual scores for weekly tasks as per D12 to F12	R
G30	VO	"IFSUM(D30:F30)=1 THEN1ELSE0"	R
D31	VO	"D30*2*C30"	R
E31	VO	"C30*E30*5"	R

Listing 3.1 *(continued)*

Go To		Type In	Return
F31	VO	"C30*F30*10"	R
G31	VO	"SUM(D31:F31)/G30"	R
A32	LO	"Monthly"	R
C32	VO	Enter value for monthly jobs	R
D32 to F32	VO	Enter assessment of individual scores for monthly tasks as per D12 to F12	R
G32	VO	"IFSUM(D32:F32)=1 THEN1ELSE0"	R
D33	VO	"C32*2*D32"	R
E33	VO	"C32*E32*5"	R
F33	VO	"C32*F32*10"	R
G33	VO	"SUM(D33:F33)/G32"	R
A34	LO	"Annual"	R
C34	VO	Enter value for annual tasks	R
D34 to F34	VO	Enter assessment of individual scores for annual tasks as per D12 to F12	R
G34	VO	"IFSUM(D34:F34)=1 THEN1ELSE0"	R
D35	VO	"C34*2*D34"	R
E35	VO	"C34*E34*5"	R
F35	VO	"C34*F34*10"	R
G35	VO	"SUM(D35:F35)/G34"	R
A36	LO	"Periodic"	R
C36	VO	Enter value for periodic tasks	R
D36 to F36	VO	Enter assessment of individual scores for periodic tasks as per D12 to F12	R

Go To		Type In	Return
G36	VO	"IFSUM(D36:F36)=1 THEN1ELSE0"	R
D37	VO	"C36*2*D36"	R
E37	VO	"C36*E36*5"	R
F37	VO	"C36*F36*10"	R
G37	VO	"SUM(D37:F37)/G36"	R
A38/	LO	"Unplanned"	R
B38			R
C38	VO	Enter values for unplanned tasks	R
D38 to F38	VO	Enter assessment of individual scores for unplanned tasks as per D12 to F12	R
G38	VO	"IFSUM(D38:F38)=1 THEN1ELSE0"	R
G39	VO	"IFSUM(C28:C38)=10 THEN10ELSE0"	R
D39	VO	"C38*2*D38"	R
E39	VO	"C38*E38*5"	R
F39	VO	"C38*F38*10"	R
G39	VO	"SUM(D39:F39)/G38"	R
G40	VO	"G29+G31+G33+G35 +G37+G39"	R
A42/	LO	"ORGANIS.	R
B42		EFFECT"	R
A44	LO	"Routine"	R
C44	VO	Insert value for routine	R
D44 to F44	VO	Enter assessment of individual scores for routine areas as per D12 to F12	R
G44	VO	"IFSUM(D44:F44)=1 THEN1ELSE0"	R
D45	VO	"C44*2*D44"	R

Listing 3.1 *(concluded)*

Go To		Type In	Return	Go To		Type In	Return
E45	VO	"C44*5*E44"	R	G48	VO	"IFSUM(D48:F48)=1 THEN1ELSE0"	R
F45	VO	"C44*10*F44"	R	C49	VO	"IFSUM(C44:C48)=10 THEN10ELSE0"	R
G45	VO	"SUM(D45:F45)/G44"	R				
A46/	LO	"Broadly	R	D49	VO	"C48*2*D48"	R
B46		defined"	R	E49	VO	"C48*5*E48"	R
C46	VO	Insert value for broad-ly defined areas	R	F49	VO	"C48*10*F48"	R
				G49	VO	"SUM(D49:F49)/G48"	R
D46 to F46	VO	Enter assessment of individual scores for routine areas as per D12 to F12	R	G50	VO	"G45+G47+G49"	R
				A52	LO	"Totals"	R
				C52	LO	"Manager A"	R
G46	VO	"IFSUM(D46:F46)=1 THEN1ELSE0"	R	A55	LO	"SKILLS"	R
D47	VO	"C46*2*D46"	R	C55	VO	"G24/C23"	R
E47	VO	"C46*5*E46"	R	A57	LO	"TASKS"	R
F47	VO	"C46*10*F46"	R	C57	VO	"G40/C39"	R
G47	VO	"SUM(D47:F47)/G46"	R	A59	LO	"ORGANIS"	R
A48/	LO	"Abstract	R	C59	VO	"G50/C49"	R
B48		def" for abstractly defined areas	R				

The totals A52 to A59 give the values placed on an individual in each of the categories held in the model.

Go To		Type In	Return
C48	VO	Insert value for abstractly defined areas	R
D48 to F48	VO	Enter assessment of individual scores for abstractly defined areas as per D12 to F12	R

Go To		Type In	Return
A62/	LO	"GRAND"	R
B62		TOTAL"	R
C62	VO	"C55+C57+C59"	R

Personnel analysis commentary

The two examples shown, Example 3.1.1 and Example 3.1.2, apply the model to two managers in the same job and illustrate how the final assessment is reached. In Example 3.1.1 the importance of various attributes as defined in the manager's job description appears in column C. In this instance, the physical demands of the job are not great and a weighting value of 1 (out of the total 10) has been given. Other aspects of the job's skill requirements receive a low score: emotional adjustment and the degree of technical or specialist knowledge

Proforma 3.1   Personnel analysis model

	A	B	C	D	E	F	G
2	PERSONNEL		ANALYSIS				
5					MANAGER A		
7				Small	Moderate	Large	
9	SKILLS						
10			Value				
12	Physical		1	0,5	0,5	0	IFSUM(D12:F12)=1THEN1ELSE0
13				C12*2*D12	C12*E12*5	C12*F12*10	SUM(D13:F13)/G12
14	Gen educ		2	0,8	0,2	0	IFSUM(D14:F14)=1THEN1ELSE0
15				C14*2*D14	C14*E14*5	C14*F14*10	SUM(D15:F15)/G14
16	Intelligence		3	0,1	0,3	0,6	IFSUM(D16:F16)=1THEN1ELSE0
17				C16*2*D16	C16*E16*5	C16*F16*10	SUM(D17:F17)/G16
18	Emotion adj		1	0,3	0,6	0,1	IFSUM(D18:F18)=1THEN1ELSE0
19				C18*2*D18	C18*E18*5	C18*F18*10	SUM(D19:F19)/G18
20	Stress		2	0,2	0,3	0,5	IFSUM(D20:F20)=1THEN1ELSE0
21				C20*2*D20	C20*E20*5	C20*F20*10	SUM(D21:F21)/G20
22	Technical		1	0	0,8	0,2	IFSUM(D22:F22)=1THEN1ELSE0
23			IFSUM(C12:C22)=10THEN10ELSE0	C22*2*D22	C22*E22*5	C22*F22*10	SUM(D23:F23)/G22
24							G13+G15+G17+G19+G21+G23
26	TASKS						
28	Daily		2	0,2	0,8	0	IFSUM(D28:F28)=1THEN1ELSE0
29				C28*2*D28	C28*E28*5	C28*F28*10	SUM(D29:F29)/G28
30	Weekly		2	0,5	0,3	0,2	IFSUM(D30:F30)=1THEN1ELSE0
31				C30*2*D30	C30*E30*5	C30*F30*10	SUM(D31:F31)/G30
32	Monthly		4	0,8	0,1	0,1	IFSUM(D32:F32)=1THEN1ELSE0
33				C32*2*D32	C32*E32*5	C32*F32*10	SUM(D33:F33)/G32
34	Annual		1	0,3	0,3	0,4	IFSUM(D34:F34)=1THEN1ELSE0
35				C34*2*D34	C34*E34*5	C34*F34*10	SUM(D35:F35)/G34
36	Periodic		1	0,2	0,6	0,2	IFSUM(D36:F36)=1THEN1ELSE0
37				C36*2*D36	C36*E36*5	C36*F36*10	SUM(D37:F37)/G36
38	Unplanned		0	1	0	0	IFSUM(D38:F38)=1THEN1ELSE0
39			IFSUM(C28:C38)=10THEN10ELSE0	C38*2*D38	C38*E38*5	C38*F38*10	SUM(D39:F39)/G38
40							G29+G31+G33+G35+G37+G39

Proforma 3.1   *(concluded)*

	A	B	C	D	E	F	G
42	ORGANIS EFFECT						
44	Routine		7	0.8	0.2	0	IFSUM(D44;F44)=1THEN1ELSE0
45				C44*2*D44	C44*5*E44	C44*10*F44	SUM(D45;F45)/G44
46	Broadly defined		3	0.5	0.4	0.1	IFSUM(D46;F46)=1THEN1ELSE0
47				C46*2*D46	C46*E46*5	C46*F46*10	SUM(D47;F47)/G46
48	Abstract def		0	1	0	0	IFSUM(D48;F48)=1THEN1ELSE0
49			IFSUM(C44;C48)=10THEN10ELSE0	C48*2*D48	C48*E48*5	C48*F48*10	SUM(D49;F49)/G48
50							G45+G47+G49
52	Totals						
52			Manager A				
55	SKILLS		G24/C23				
57	TASKS		G40/C39				
59	ORGANIS		G50/C49				
62	GRAND TOTAL		C55+C57+C59				

Notes on the values used in this model are included in the line by line listing.

required. Situations where such low ratings might be relevant are where individuals work on their own or where there is little need to liaise closely with others. More important for this particular job is the ability to cope with stress, the level of general education required and the amount of native intelligence that the post demands.

The values assigned by the job description also show clearly, in this particular instance, that the majority of the tasks that the job demands are of a repetitive nature, some daily, some weekly, with a large element of monthly reporting. Unplanned tasks are not regarded as relevant and are given a zero score.

The areas in which the job affects the organisation are largely a reflection of the tasks the individual performs. Thus, the majority of areas are those of a routine or broadly defined nature, with the undefined areas being regarded as totally unimportant.

Such an evaluation can be carried out for each employee group by the supervisory management team who would agree on the weighting common to the group's job descriptions.

On this backbone of the job description, the supervisor has entered his assessment of how the appraisee (in this case Manager A) meets the requirements of the job. For the physical skills category he considers that the individual does not meet the requirements of the job – he may be frequently ill though this is not

Example 3.1.1 Personnel analysis model

	A	B	C	D	E	F	G
					MANAGER A		
2	PERSONNEL	ANALYSIS					
5					MANAGER A		
7				Small	Moderate	Large	
9	SKILLS						
10			Value				
12	Physical		1	0.5	0.5	0	1
13				1	2	0	3
14	Gen educ		2	0.8	0.2	0	1
15				3.2	1.6	0	4.8
16	Intelligence		3	0.1	0.3	0.6	1
17				0.6	3.6	10.8	15
18	Emotion adj		1	0.3	0.6	0.1	1
19				0.6	2.4	0.6	3.6
20	Stress		2	0.2	0.3	0.5	1
21				0.8	2.4	6	9.2
22	Technical		1	0	0.8	0.2	1
23			10	0	3.2	1.2	4.4
24							40
26	TASKS						
28	Daily		2	0.2	0.8	0	1
29				0.8	6.4	0	7.2
30	Weekly		2	0.5	0.3	0.2	1
31				2	2.4	2.4	6.8
32	Monthly		4	0.8	0.1	0.1	1
33				6.4	1.6	2.4	10.4
34	Annual		1	0.3	0.3	0.4	1
35				0.6	1.2	2.4	4.2
36	Periodic		1	0.2	0.6	0.2	1
37				0.4	2.4	1.2	4
38	Unplanned		0	1	0	0	1
39			10	0	0	0	0
40							32.6

Example 3.1.1 *(concluded)*

	A	B	C	D	E	F	G	□
42	ORGANIS EFFECT							■
44	Routine		7	0.8	0.2	0	1	
45				11.2	0.64	0	11.84	
46	Broadly defined		3	0.5	0.4	0.1	1	
47				3	0.8	0.24	4.04	
48	Abstract def		0	1	0	0	1	
49			10	0	0	0	0	
50							15.88	
52	Totals							
52			Manager A					
55	SKILLS		4					
57	TASKS		3.26					
59	ORGANIS		1.588					
62	GRAND TOTAL		8.848					

apparent in the stress score, or not strong enough for occasional lifting jobs. Similarly, he considers that Manager A's general level of education is low, but this is, to an extent, offset by the higher level of intelligence shown along the A16 line. Remember too that intelligence is rated more highly than physical skills in column C. Within the tasks area, poor performance is clearly shown in both daily and monthly tasks, with heavy emphasis on the 'small' or 'moderate' areas of performance evaluation shown in columns D and E.

The analysis of Manager A's impact on the organisation reveals that even in the important routine areas his performance falls well below accepted levels. The final scores for this individual (8.8 out of a possible grand total of 40) reveal that his performance is substandard in all aspects of his job except that he scores well on intelligence, which is highly rated, and on stress. This suggests a problem in need of attention, lack of motivation or job dissatisfaction perhaps. The input of other managers can easily be compared and major anomalies in the evaluation of this employee's performance considered by the group.

Manager A of Example 3.1.2 is quite a different character. In the same job, this person is performing well in all areas except technical knowledge and general education. The logical decision should be taken by the group (and the author would like to think that all decisions on personnel matters are logical with the exception of the appointment of the chairman of the board!) would be to provide this manager with time off to attend external or internal courses.

Example 3.1.2   Personnel analysis model

	A	B	C	D	E	F	G
2	PERSONNEL		ANALYSIS				
5					MANAGER A		
7				Small	Moderate	Large	
9	SKILLS						
10			Value				
12	Physical		1	0	0.2	0.8	1
13				0	1	8	9
14	Gen educ		2	0.3	0.5	0.2	1
15				1.2	5	4	10.2
16	Intelligence		3	0	0.4	0.6	1
17				0	6	18	24
18	Emotion adj		1	0.1	0.3	0.6	1
19				0.2	1.5	6	7.7
20	Stress		2	0	0.1	0.9	1
21				0	1	18	19
22	Technical		1	0	0.8	0.2	1
23			10	0	4	2	6
24							75.9
26	TASKS						
28	Daily		2	0	0.3	0.7	1
29				0	3	14	17
30	Weekly		2	0	0.3	0.7	1
31				0	3	14	17
32	Monthly		4	0.1	0.2	0.7	1
33				0.8	4	28	32.8
34	Annual		1	0.1	0.5	0.4	1
35				0.2	2.5	4	6.7
36	Periodic		1	0	0.1	0.9	1
37				0	0.5	9	9.5
38	Unplanned		0	1	0	0	1
39			10	0	0	0	0
40							83

Example 3.1.2 *(concluded)*

	A	B	C	D	E	F	G	□
42	ORGANIS EFFECT							■
44	Routine		7	0.1	0.3	0.6	1	
45				1.4	10.5	42	53.9	
46	Broadly defined		3	0.2	0.5	0.3	1	
47				1.2	7.5	9	17.7	
48	Abstract def		0	1	0	0	1	
49			10	0	0	0	0	
50							71.6	
52	Totals							
52			Manager A					
55	SKILLS		7.59					
57	TASKS		8.3					
59	ORGANIS		7.16					
62	GRAND TOTAL		23.05					

References

1 A. Jay, *Management and Machiavelli*, Hodder and Stoughton, 1967.

2 R. Lickert, 'A New Twist to People Accounting', *Business Week*, October 21, 1972, page 67.

3 J.E. Muckley, 'Dear Fellow Shareholders', *Harvard Business Review*, No. 2, 1984, page 46.

4 Export pricing

At some point within the company's development and growth, expansion overseas will inevitably be considered. There are a number of advantages and disadvantages for such a course of action, which will affect different organisations to differing extents, so that the final balance may or may not be in its favour.

Expansion overseas: the credit side

The credit side of the ledger normally reads as follows:

Product factors

1   There will be an increase in volume which should allow economies of scale as described in Chapter 5 on marginal profitability. This raises the issue of whether the product is sufficiently standardised for this exercise to be carried out effectively. Any modification to the product line will mean that different costings need to be applied to the line with additional inventory costs and so on. In consequence the marginal profitability of the product may be considerably different. Such changes would include alterations to packaging, slight or major modifications in product content – for example, differing flavourings.

2   The introduction of the product in overseas markets can significantly strengthen a product's viability. Thus, with a range of countries at differing stages of development, a product that was in demand at one stage can be maintained by overseas sales once the home market moves into another phase of growth. For example, paraffin-powered Aladdin lamps are a product range that would have become extinguished if it had only been for the European market with the practically universal provision of electric light. However, in Third World countries it has been assured of long-term sales due to differing socio-economic levels. But

there is a qualification that must be raised for a number of product fields, the problem of trade mark infringement. Certain countries are notorious for this in certain areas, and a manufacturer may take the view that, in consequence, sales in certain territories should not be attempted. The costs of maintaining and protecting the trade mark of the particular product overseas may be very considerable and are often not considered in the detail that should be devoted to the subject.

3   Exporting can help to smooth out fluctuations in seasonal products. The ice-cream firm that exports to the tropics from the Northern Hemisphere will have a market throughout the year, and the manufacturer of woolly underwear can supply the northern world for six months and the southern world for the remainder of the year.

4   Overseas development can allow a degree of 'dustbin' activity to protect the major markets of the firm. In the case of an out-of-date product where the firm holds large stocks, these can be sold in fringe markets. Such activity can be quite important in fashion industries such as toys where large stocks of a certain line are purchased against a rising trend. Should this reverse, the organisation will need to move these stocks without damaging home sales of other lines.

Strategic factors

1   Once a firm has reached a dominant position in the home market, growth will tend to slow down, and expansion will depend on either the use of standard expertise in other markets or the development of new areas for the established market.

2   Overseas activity makes good strategic sense. Texts on military theory make much of knowing the enemy's intentions and not allowing him secure bases from which to carry out invasions of your territory. In the context of the firm this is obviously relevant to competitive advantage and market intelligence. The company that can meet and match its major competitors on *their* home ground will be far more able to compete effectively on its home ground than might otherwise be so. The results of failure to carry through such a strategy can be clearly seen in the motorcycle industry, now dominated by Japan. New ranges were developed in the Far East by Japanese firms at a time when no European or North American manufacturer was actively involved in motorcycle export development. This inactivity allowed the Japanese to expand from their base and capture the world market, including the home markets of the European and American competition.

   The use of overseas markets in this context is also a very successful way of developing new concepts for core markets (see Chapter 12 on test markets).

3   Expansion overseas can help to reduce the risks inherent in concentration on a single country. There are numerous examples of this working to the benefit of, and several to the detriment of, a wide range of industrial firms. Thus American and European construction firms have benefited considerably from work carried out in

Saudi Arabia, but many have, equally, suffered in the aftermath of the Iranian revolution. For a number of firms the development of overseas activity can do much to overcome the political instability that they experience at home. A striking example of this at present is the flight of capital away from Hong Kong with the imminence of the return of that territory to the People's Republic of China in 1997.

4   Several other ideas can be considered as 'advantages'. It is held by the majority of governments that exporting is good for the 'soul' of the organisation, with well-worn slogans – of the 'export or die' type – often translated into a variety of languages. In many instances this will lead the government to guarantee payment of the money outstanding on export orders, though this does not totally offset the generally higher credit risks of overseas activity.

5   Export is also often regarded as prestigious. For a manufacturer of women's clothes in New Mexico, sales in Paris will be generally regarded as far more worthwhile than sales in Oregon: the reverse being true for the manufacturer in France.

Expansion overseas: the risks

We have seen that the advantages of expansion overseas can be considerable, but each positive point does contain its own pitfalls.

Resources

The main drawback will always lie in the field of resources. Does the organisation have sufficient managerial and financial strength to overcome the problems that involvement in an international environment will cause?

The five Cs

The problems that will be faced can be conveniently summarised under the 5Cs.

1   *Climate*   This covers changes both in physical and political climate. Both of these will tend to cause problems, as has been mentioned in the discussion in this chapter of strategic advantages associated with export.

2   *Custom*   Attitudes will differ in overseas countries, often in surprising ways, and can prove a very difficult barrier to overcome.

3   *Communication*   Languages obviously differ and the way in which items should be visually presented will also vary. Any observer of Japanese and American commercial television will be struck by the major differences in the methods used to promote similar products.

4   *Currency*   Foreign exchange problems, and high inflation rates can all add to the headaches of the firm's financial control systems, making debt control and budgeting far more complex.

5 *Control* Any problem becomes magnified by distance, multiplied by language barriers and compounded by factors such as differing holiday periods throughout the world.

Export channels

The nature of the export channel chosen will have fundamental effects on the development of the business. It will obviously affect pricing, distribution, advertising policy, promotional activity, and new product development. Each level of involvement in overseas markets will influence these areas in differing fashions and it is worth considering each in turn to outline the problems encountered.

1 Export houses

There are a large number of organisations based in the company's home country which are involved in overseas markets.

(a) Wholesalers These act in a similar fashion to home-based wholesalers (and often are one and the same thing) except that a proportion of their business will be done with overseas clients. Normally they specialise by products and territories handled.

(b) Confirming houses These act on behalf of the overseas buyer with varying levels of discretion. Thus a confirming house may be directed towards a specific product and quantity or it may be given general directions within an area. One specific area in which the confirming house differs from the wholesaler is in dealing with countries where tariff or financial barriers are a major problem. In these cases the confirming house may be acting on behalf of governmental bodies as the sole point of contact within the particular overseas country.

(c) Buying offices Japanese department stores for example, maintain wholly owned subsidiaries in the United States and Europe to evaluate and buy merchandise for their home-based operations.

(d) Specialist export firms These organisations provide expertise normally on specific areas of activity in the world. Thus a firm may specialise in South America, Africa, or the Far East. The level of service supplied may vary considerably from a trading function, to developing support packages for product lines in certain overseas markets.

Advantages of export houses The advantages of these differing export houses are considerable. They remove all requirements for export documentation and the costs of insurance or shipping, which for small quantities of product can be considerable.

More important the credit risk is practically eliminated (provided, of course, that the company is wisely chosen), as the export house takes over all relationships with the overseas markets.

Similarly, the export house provides valuable expertise that would be very expensive for the organisation to acquire. This is most true for those countries with tariff barriers, such as many African countries, and Comecon.

Disadvantages of export houses   These are all related to the lack of control that the principal is exerting over the product and the markets in which it appears. In all cases the level of control is practically or totally non-existent.

Crucial to many firms is the long-term stability of their operations both in respect of volume and revenue. Using the export house prevents the firm being able to plan effectively because the level of demand will depend on the criteria of the intermediary rather than the criteria of the consumer. Thus the arrival of a competitive line in any portfolio could mean that the company line will be totally excluded from certain markets irrespective of consumer demand. The intermediaries will tend to consider the products as commodities, not as properties to be developed and nurtured for the future. A buying house could, for example, buy a product from a supplier for a number of years for distribution in their store chain. At the end of this period the senior management of the store group decides for strategic reasons that a group of products will be dropped from their product range. Overnight through no fault of the product a substantial annual sale is lost.

2   Local exclusivity arrangements

(a)   Agencies   These may be defined as any legal relationship between principal and sales company, which also tend to include distributors. The nature of the agreement will again vary from country to country and from product to product. The lowest level of involvement is normally seen in the case of the commission agent who does not hold stocks of the product, merely passing on orders to the principal for which he receives a previously agreed commission percentage. Higher levels of commitment can be seen with the appointment of agents that hold stocks to pass on at agreed levels of on-cost pricing, and agents that provide a level of service at agreed levels of cost.

(b)   Distributors   Though normally included under the agency heading, distributors are slightly different in their relationships with the manufacturer. They can best be seen as locally based wholesalers with exclusivity on a geographical basis. In consequence, the political relationships between distributor and exporter can be more delicate as both are essentially acting as principals within the market.

Advantages and disadvantages of agents   These are similar to those already discussed, with certain additions. For example, the exporter gains an immediate specific market presence which can be protected to an extent from the incursion of competitive lines.

The contractual nature of agency appointment does have a number of implications which should not be overlooked. In many countries the contract will prove to be extremely difficult to change. Thus in many countries in the Middle East agency agreements entered into when the manufacturer was producing a line of babies' rattles will still hold valid if it starts producing home computers.

Advantages and disadvantages of distributors The distributor in common with the export houses will have his own priorities which may be at considerable variance with what is considered acceptable by the exporter. Areas of conflict may develop over distribution policy, pricing, and the level of advertising support necessary to achieve a particular sales target. An example from the author's own experience was an overseas distributor raising prices in a competitive market and in consequence losing volume because the financial controllers of the distributor's parent company were insisting on a certain financial return. This level of financial return could only be achieved by the cross-subsidisation of other areas of activity by the raised price levels of certain product lines.

3 Local sales operations

The level of involvement of the exporter can obviously be increased by the establishment of a branch or local sales office. Though control by the principal is naturally increased there are a number of factors that need to be carefully considered which can mitigate against the full development of this approach. The first is the legal constraints of the host country. Many countries will not permit the establishment of subsidiaries. Others stipulate very different conditions for the employment and dismissal of staff than occurs in the country of the parent company.

More important generally is the concept of 'critical mass'. This idea, borrowed from the world of physics, (enough uranium 235 and there is a nice big bang, less than this and it does not work), means that the local sales operation will require a sufficient level of volume to pay for the sales force/advertising/distribution costs and generate a profit. Below this level the company will continue to be loss-making and unable to create the funds to invest and grow.

Subsidiary sales companies of overseas principals face one other problem not encountered by independent distributors. They find the acquisition of other brands from competitive organisations very difficult to achieve. This is totally understandable in that companies in the same field are wary about the long-term stability of products in a competitor's portfolio and secondly about the entire aspect of new product development security which will be jeopardised by this relationship.

4 Third party manufacture

One can construct a line which relates the level of investment that a company makes overseas to the amount of return that it should expect within that country (see Figure 4.1). A variety of manufacturing arrangements can provide further penetration of overseas markets while stopping short of the final commitment of expenditure which is involved in the creation or acquisition of a local manufacturing base.

Some of these alternatives are applicable as solutions in markets where the remittance of foreign exchange is particularly difficult such as the Indian sub-continent. Here the use of licence agreements is often the only way to gain access to the market. In these agreements the manufacturer in the target market

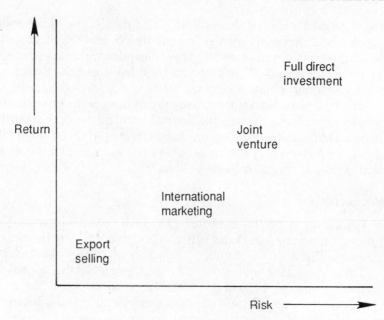

Figure 4.1   Risk and return in overseas business

gains the technology/trade mark of the overseas principal in return for a (small) percentage of total turnover. Problems of several types quite often arise in respect of product quality, payment of royalties, total quantities produced, and so on.

Contract manufacture enables the parent company to become established in the export country without the investment involved in the purchase of plant and machinery. It does still pose control problems though these will now be in the production, rather than in the sales, pricing and distribution areas. The difficulties associated with finding a suitable contract producer in a number of markets can be insurmountable: any producer will inevitably receive a degree of education making him a potential competitor on the cessation of the contract. Additionally, products will tend to have to be purchased in relatively large quantities requiring large inventories and investment in considerable warehouse space.

5   *Equity involvement*

The establishment of a joint venture company or a totally owned subsidiary needs the highest level of investment that the parent company can make overseas. While it provides the greatest risks, it can also lead to the largest return. To take an example, several major companies had attempted to establish themselves in Iran which was in the early 1970s regarded as one of the most interesting growth markets of the future. Entry costs were high but the companies that managed to develop there regarded these as worthwhile. The downfall of the Shah has meant that these wise evaluations have proved practically worthless. The lessons of the past five years in respect of Latin American bank loans is also a case in point. It is therefore crucial that major investments of this nature in, say, Comecon or the People's Republic of China receive hard examination.

In conclusion, the problem facing the firm involved in international trade is how to decide and control the channels that are available for the maximum expansion of overseas trade.

This will involve the evaluation of profitability at each stage of the operation. When organisations such as export houses are used as the intermediary the profitability of the operation will be limited to the margin attainable by the producer. Thus the equation is very similar to any operation within the home market:

$$\text{Volume} \times \text{Price} - \text{Cost of sale} = \text{Gross margin}$$

Once the producer company starts to becomes more involved in the development of sales within the overseas markets other criteria will become important as increasingly the combined profitability of the manufacturer and distributor becomes more and more interrelated.

The concept of through profitability

A company will therefore need to develop approaches to minimise the problems of expansion overseas and maximise the return. Whatever route is chosen, accurate control over costs and return are particularly important.

The manufacturer needs to consider the financial implications of each stage of the operation, developing a system for analysing and controlling each stage. As there will be two sources of profit (or loss) to the organisation, a system that provides an overall calculation of costs and effects of actions taken by the parent company and its overseas arm is needed to provide full information for control of a complex area.

The concept of through profitability considers the costs accrued at each stage of export and the effects of changing investment and pricing at various points along the chain from the parent company to the overseas consumer. The structuring of information in this fashion enables the parent company and the distributor or local manufacturer to determine the most effective means of maximising profit and benefits for both. Classical export profit maximisation largely ignores the impact of local distributors' costs and investment levels on the product in that overseas market.

The export pricing model

A spreadsheet-based computer model is an ideal tool to develop a system whereby interactions of the elements of the principals' and distributors' price structure/volume relationship can be used to develop the best approach for the market place. This aids the establishment of a market-led philosophy. Thus in some price-sensitive markets an aggressive pricing policy can be investigated. Distribution changes might be important in other markets and therefore the model needs to consider the implication of changes in fixed and variable sales overheads. Similarly the interaction of advertising and price should also be evaluated as this again will differ from market to market.

Local manufacture can then be compared with the established export procedure to ascertain whether the proposed change in export channel structure (from direct export to local manufacture) is worthwhile in profitability terms.

The elements of this model can best be described from a base of the supplier's marginal production cost. This links very successfully into the marginal profitability model described elsewhere (see Chapter 5 on marginal profitability).

1   Production cost

2   FOB price   There are a variety of terms used in the export environment of which the most common is *FOB* (free on board). Others are *CIF* (carriage insurance freight), *FAS* (free alongside), *DD* (delivered docks).

3   Freight/insurance   This will obviously vary from country to country. Thus the freight costs to the Middle East will be higher for European countries than export to North America because of distance and frequency of shipping. Similarly, insurance costs will differ according to the value of the product and to a lesser extent the destination.

4   Duty levels   These will depend on the type of product, and remain the final element that comprises the landed cost of the product, which can compare with the manufactured cost should local production be considered.

5   Fixed sales costs   The establishment of a sales force will demand some fixed elements regardless of the volume of goods sold; these could, for example, include the salaries of the sales force.

6   Variable sales costs   These cover all those cost elements which are volume-related, such as the commissions that sales representatives may or may not receive on the total sales. It also involves sales discounts.

7   Fixed support costs   For any product there will be base costs and variable costs in the advertising field. The costs of mounting an advertising campaign can be regarded as fixed in that often the money is totally committed before all the revenue relating to the budget plan has been achieved.

8   Variable support costs   Promotional expenditure can be more easily related directly to volume expenditure.

These items then combine to provide the total ex-warehouse cost, though as is stated elsewhere, this cost is very sensitive to volume changes.

The next elements within the pricing structure include:

9   Wholesaler margin   This is the percentage that wholesalers will add on if they exist within the retail chain though such a factor will not be relevant in organisations selling direct to major retail chains. Further levels would need to be considered in countries such as Japan where more than one wholesaler level exists. However, the typical structure of distribution in the majority of export countries will include one wholesaler level.

10   Retail margin   The final element in the price structure provides the final consumer price.

What we have not considered in this analysis is the question of profit for the distribution company. This will obviously be variable according to the effects of volume on the variable costs within the pricing structure. One method of assessing the effect of advertising is to consider advertising elasticities (discussed in Chapter 11 on media investment). However one of the most immediate interactions is the level of consumer price and the price elasticity operating within the market (see Chapter 13 on price evaluation). In a highly price-sensitive market, small changes in price can have considerable effects on volume with consequent changes in overall variable costs and profitability.

The model, therefore, needs to consider the effects of price and advertising within the overall through profitability of the organisation. Advertising expenditure particularly on the media can be regarded as largely a fixed element as has already been stated (certainly on a yearly basis) whereas changes in pricing will tend to have more immediate effects providing price sensitivity is high.

Given an understanding of the price factors operating within the market, changes in the relative market price should lead to a linear volume response: smooth decreases in price leading to smooth increases in volume. This will be true if there are no other price factors at work in the market (for example, price points, halo effects and so on). The model will provide a picture of this interaction based on the normal price elasticity operating within the market. From that it will provide a combined profitability of both the producing and distribution company from a historical base of the previous year's experience.

The range of market price together with overall profit can be used to evaluate the strategic direction of the company's products within the export market. Would it for example be more profitable to manufacture locally than import? Will raising prices damage or improve overall profitability? Is the local distributor making too high a margin?

Using the export pricing model

The *Go To* column in Listing 4.1 tells you the cell number and the cursor position. The next column specifies the spreadsheet option (LO = Label Option; VO = Value Option). The *Type In* column gives you instructions within the inverted commas which you must type in or asks you to supply the necessary data. These commas are not part of the instructions supplied here and should not be typed in. Beware however that some spreadsheets, the *Lotus 1-2-3* for example, enter the Label Option by using the inverted-comma key. Under the *Type In* column the symbols * = multiply and / = divide. R in the *Return* column instructs you to commit the information to memory by pressing the Return key.
Remember: When you have finished, save your model.

Listing 4.1   Export pricing model

Go To		Type In	Return
D3/	LO	"Export	R
E3/	LO	Pricing	R
F3	LO	Model"	R
D5	LO	"Historic"	R
F5	LO	"Option A"	R

Option A can be described as your "What If" column enabling you to see the effects of possible changes on the factors presented in the model.

Go To		Type In	Return
A8/	LO	"FOB	R
B8	LO	Price($)" per unit	R
A10/	LO	"Freight/	R
B10	LO	Ins($)" for insurance per unit	R
A12	LO	"Duties($)" per unit	R
A14/	LO	"Landed	R
B14	LO	Cost($)" per unit	R
A16/	LO	"%profit	R
B16	LO	on l.cost" for landed cost	R
A18/	LO	"Fixed	R
B18	LO	dist($)" for fixed distribution costs per unit	R
A20/	LO	"Fixed	R
B20	LO	sell($)" for fixed selling costs per unit	R
A22/	LO	"Fixed	R
B22	LO	adv($)" for fixed advertising costs per unit	R
A24/	LO	"Fixed	R
B24	LO	admin($)" for fixed administration costs per unit	R

Go To		Type In	Return
A26/	LO	"Fixed	R
B26	LO	total($)" per unit	R
D26	VO	"SUM(D18:D24)"	R
A28/	LO	"Variable	R
B28	LO	adv($)" for variable advertising costs per unit	R
A30/	LO	"Variable	R
B30	LO	sell($)" for variable selling cost per unit	R
A32/	LO	"Variable	R
B32	LO	dist($)" for variable distribution cost per unit	R
A34/	LO	"Variable	R
B34	LO	total($)" per unit	R
A38/	LO	"COST OF	R
B38	LO	SALE($)" per unit	R
D38	VO	"SUM(D14+D26+D34)"	R
D34	VO	"SUM(D28:D32)"	R
A40/	LO	"Profit	R
B40	LO	margin($)" per unit	R
A42/	LO	"Sale	R
B42	LO	price($)" per unit	R

Note: The sale price is the price to the trade before tax.

Go To		Type In	Return
A44	LO	"Tax($)" per unit	R
A46/	LO	"Selling	R
B46	LO	price($)" per unit	R

Note: The selling price is the price to the trade.

Listing 4.1 *(continued)*

Go To		Type In	Return	Go To		Type In	Return
A48/	LO	"Dist.	R	A69/	LO	"Consumer	R
B48	LO	margin 1($)" distri-		B69/	LO	price	R
		butor's margin per unit	R	C69		fall(%)"	R
A50/	LO	"Dist.	R				
B50	LO	margin 2($)" distri-					
		butor's margin per unit	R				

Note: This tells you what happens if you drop the price in percentage terms. You may be more interested in the effects of a consumer price rise based on the figures you will enter in column D. If this is so insert the price rise percentage figure as a negative value. Remember: if you put in a positive the model will assume you're concerned with a fall in price; negative and it will calculate the effects of a price rise.

Go To		Type In	Return
A52/	LO	"RETAIL	R
B52	LO	PRICE($)" per unit	R
A54	LO	"VOLUME"	R
A55/	LO	"Total	R
B55/	LO	Gross	R
C55	LO	Cont(dist)($)" for total gross contribution of distributor	R
A56/	LO	"Total	R
B56/	LO	Gross	R
C56/	LO	Cont(suppl)($)" for total gross contribution for supplier	R
A70/	LO	"Supplier	R
B70	LO	cost($)" per unit	R
A72/	LO	"Supplier	R
B72	LO	adv($)" for supplier advertising	R
A57/	LO	"Total net	R
B57	LO	profit($)"	R
A74/	LO	"Total fixed	R
B74	LO	cost($)"	R
A60/	LO	"DATA	R
B60	LO	LINES"	R
A76/	LO	"Revised	R
B76/	LO	vol.	R
A62/	LO	"Sales	R
B62	LO	margin(%)" for sales company margins, whether export agents etc	R
C76	LO	index"	R

Note: The revised volume index is a percentage of the original volume. If it is less than one the volume is falling; if it's more the volume will go up.

Go To		Type In	Return
A64/	LO	"Dist.	R
B64		margin 1(%)"	R
A66/	LO	"Dist.	R
B66	LO	margin 2(%)"	R
A68/	LO	"Price	R
B68	LO	Elasticity"	R
D8	VO	Insert FOB price per unit ($)	R
D10	VO	Insert freight insurance per unit($)	R
D12	VO	Insert duties per unit($)	R

Listing 4.1   *(continued)*

Go To		Type In	Return	Go To		Type In	Return
D14	VO	"SUM(D8:D12)"	R	D55	VO	"D40*D54"	R
D16	VO	"(D42/D14−1)*100" gives % profit on land- ed costs	R	D56	VO	"SUM(D8−D70)*D54"	R
				D57	VO	"SUM(D55+D56)−D72"	R
D18	VO	Insert value for fixed distribution cost per unit($)	R	D62	VO	Insert value for % sales margin on cost	R
D20	VO	Insert value for fixed selling cost per unit($)	R	D64	VO	Insert % value for dis- tributor's margin 1 per unit ($)	R
D22	VO	Insert value for fixed advertising cost per unit($)	R	D66	VO	Insert % value for dis- tributor's margin 2 per unit($)	R
D24	VO	Insert value for fixed administration cost per unit($)	R	D68	VO	Insert value for price elasticity	R
D28	VO	Insert value for vari- able advertising cost per unit($)	R	D69	VO	Insert % value for con- sumer price fall	R
D30	VO	Insert value for vari- able selling cost per unit($)	R	D70	VO	Insert value for sup- plier's costs per unit ($)	R
D32	VO	Insert value for vari- able distribution cost per unit($)	R	D72	VO	Insert supplier adver- tising expenditure($)	R
D40	VO	"D42−(D42*1/F62)"	R	D74	VO	"D26*D54"	R
D42	VO	"D38+D40"	R	D76	VO	"(D68*D69)/100+(1)" gives revised volume index	R
D44	VO	Insert value for sales tax per unit ($)	R				
D46	VO	"D42+D44"	R	F8	VO	"F38−(F34+F26+F12 +F10)" gives value of FOB price	R
D48	VO	"D46*(1+D64/100) −D46"	R	F10	VO	Insert value for freight and insurance cost per unit ($)	R
D50	VO	"SUM(D46:D48)* (1+D66/100)− (D46−D48)"	R	F12	VO	Insert value of freight and insurance duties per unit($)	R
D52	VO	"SUM(D46:D50)" gives the retail price in $ per unit	R	F14	VO	"SUM(F8:F12)"	R
				F16	VO	"D16"	R
D54	VO	Insert value for volume in units	R	F18		leave blank	
				F20		leave blank	

Listing 4.1 *(concluded)*

Go To		Type In	Return	Go To		Type In	Return
F22		leave blank		F44	VO	Insert value of sales tax ($) per unit	R
F24		leave blank					
F26	VO	"D74/F54"	R	F46	VO	"F52−F48−F50"	R
F28	VO	Insert value for cost of variable advertising per unit ($)	R	F48	VO	"(F52−F50)∗−(1/F64)+ (F52−F50)"	R
				F50	VO	"F52−(F52∗1/F66)"	R
F30	VO	Insert value for variable selling costs per unit ($)	R	F52	VO	"D52∗(100−D69)/100"	R
				F54	VO	"D54∗D76"	R
F32	VO	Insert value for variable distribution ($)	R	F55	VO	"F40∗F54"	R
				F56	VO	"SUM(F8−D70)∗F54"	R
F34	VO	"SUM(F28:F32)"	R	F57	VO	"SUM(F55∗F56)−D72"	R
F38	VO	"F42−F40"	R	F62	VO	"100/(100−D62)"	R
F40	VO	"F42−(F42∗1/F62)"	R	F64	VO	"100/(100−D64)"	R
F42	VO	"F46−F44"	R	F66	VO	"100/(100−D66)"	R

Export pricing commentary

The model considers changes that may be introduced by the supplier and distributor into the pricing structure of a particular product in an export market, analysing price, volume and profitability.

The current or historic market pricing will consist of a product being shipped at an FOB price subject to freight costs, insurance and duties which together produce the landed cost to the distributor. For any given volume of goods there will be a level of fixed costs that the distributor needs to recover, and in addition for each unit there will be a level of unchanging variable cost as discussed earlier in the section on the model.

As the volume increases the level of fixed cost per unit will obviously decrease though variable costs will remain identical. This can be seen clearly in Example 4.1.1. The distributor will then fix a profit margin either on an on-cost or gross margin basis, which can be entered in one of the data lines (D62 – in this example 20 per cent of gross selling price or 25 per cent on cost). This is the average price at which the product is sold out to the trade, net of any taxes that may or may not be collected at this point. The distributor will either then sell to wholesalers, who sell on in their turn to retailers, or to retailers irect. In either case the model allows for the introduction of one or two levels of distribution margin to be introduced (D64, D66). From these figures the final consumer price

Proforma 4.1 Export pricing model

	A	B	C	D	E	F
3				Export	Pricing	Model
5				Historic		Option A
8	FOB Price($ per unit)			35		F38-(F34+F26+F12+F10)
10	Freight/Ins ($)			5		5
12	Duties($ per unit)			12		12
14	Landed Cost ($per unit)			SUM(D8:D12)		SUM(F8:F12)
16	%Profit on landed cost			(D42/D14-1)*100		D16
18	Fixed distribution cost $ per unit			2		
20	Fixed selling cost $ per unit			2		
22	Fixed advertising cost $ per unit			3		
24	Fixed admin cost $ per unit			2		
26	Fixed total cost $ per unit			SUM(D18:D24)		D74/F54
28	Variable advertising cost $ per unit			1		1
30	Variable selling cost $ per unit			1		1
32	Variable distribution cost per unit			1		1
34	Variable total $ per unit			SUM(D28:D32)		SUM(F28:F32)
38	COST OF SALE $ per unit			SUM(D14+D26+D34)		F42-F40
40	Profit margin $ per unit			D42-(D42*1/F62)		F42-(F42*1/F62)

68

	A / B	C	D	E	F
42	Sale price $ per unit		D38+D40		F46-F44
44	Tax $ per unit		2		2
46	Selling price $ per unit		D42+D44		F52-F48-F50
48	Distributor's margin per unit-1		D46*(1+D64/100)-D46		(F52-F50)*-(1/F64)+(F52-F50)
50	Distributor's margin per unit -2		SUM(D46:D48)*(1+D66/100)-(D46-D48)		F52-(F52*1/F66)
52	Retail Price $ per unit		SUM(D46:D50)		D52*(100-D69)/100
54	VOLUME		28000		D54*D76
55	Total Gross Cont(dist)$		D40*D54		F40*F54
56	Total Gros Cont (suppl)$		SUM(D8-D70)*D54		SUM(F8-D70)*F54
57	Total Net Profit $		SUM(D55+D56)-D72		SUM(F55*F56)-D72
60	DATA LINES				
62	Sales margin%		20		100/(100-D62)
64	Distributor's margin per unit -1		5		100/(100-D64)
66	Distributor's margin per unit - 2		10		100/(100-D66)
68	Price elasticity		2		
69	Consumer price fall%		10		
70	Supplier cost $ per unit		25		
72	Supplier advertising $		150000		
74	Total fixed cost $		D26*D54		
76	Revised volume index		(D68*D69)/100+(1)		

Example 4.1.1 Export pricing model

■ □

	A	B	C	D	E	F
3				Export	Pricing	Model
5				Historic		Option A
8	FOB Price($ per unit)			35		29.2035
10	Freight/Ins ($)			5		5
12	Duties($ per unit)			12		12
14	Landed Cost ($per unit)			52		46.2035
16	%Profit on landed cost			53.8462		53.8462
18	Fixed distribution cost $ per unit			2		
20	Fixed selling cost $ per unit			2		
22	Fixed advertising cost $ per unit			3		
24	Fixed admin cost $ per unit			2		
26	Fixed total cost $ per unit			9		7.5
28	Variable advertising cost $ per unit			1		1
30	Variable selling cost $ per unit			1		1
32	Variable distribution cost per unit			1		1
34	Variable total $ per unit			3		3
38	COST OF SALE $ per unit			64		56.7035
40	Profit margin $ per unit			16.0000		14.1759

	A	B	C	D	E	F
42	Sale price $ per unit			80.0000		70.8794
44	Tax $ per unit			2		2
46	Selling price $ per unit			82.0000		72.8794
48	Distributor's margin per unit-1			4.10000		3.83576
50	Distributor's margin per unit -2			8.61000		8.52390
52	Retail Price $ per unit			94.71000		85.2390
54	VOLUME			28000		33600
55	Total Gross Cont(dist)$			448000		476311
56	Total Gros Cont (suppl)$			280000		141237
57	Total Net Profit $			578000		467540
60	DATA LINES					
62	Sales margin%			20		1.25
64	Distributor's margin per unit -1			5		1.05263
66	Distributor's margin per unit - 2			10		1.11111
68	Price elasticity			2		
69	Consumer price fall%			10		
70	Supplier cost $ per unit			25		
72	Supplier advertising $			150000		
74	Total fixed cost $			252000		
76	Revised volume index			1.2		

Example 4.1.2 Export pricing model

	A	B	C	D	E	F
				Export	Pricing	Model
3						Option A
5				Historic		
8	FOB Price($ per unit)			35		38.4098
10	Freight/Ins ($)			5		5
12	Duties($ per unit)			12		12
14	Landed Cost ($per unit)			52		55.4098
16	%Profit on landed cost			53.8462		53.8462
18	Fixed distribution cost $ per unit			2		
20	Fixed selling cost $ per unit			2		
22	Fixed advertising cost $ per unit			3		
24	Fixed admin cost $ per unit			2		
26	Fixed total cost $ per unit			9		11.25
28	Variable advertising cost $ per unit			1		1
30	Variable selling cost $ per unit			1		1
32	Variable distribution cost per unit			1		1
34	Variable total $ per unit			3		3
38	COST OF SALE $ per unit			64		69.6598
40	Profit margin $ per unit			16.0000		17.4150

	A B C	D	E	F
42	Sale price $ per unit	80.0000		87.0748
44	Tax $ per unit	2		2
46	Selling price $ per unit	82.0000		89.0748
48	Distributor's margin per unit-1	4.10000		4.68814
50	Distributor's margin per unit -2	8.61000		10.4181
52	Retail Price $ per unit	94.71000		104.181
54	VOLUME	28000		22400
55	Total Gross Cont(dist)$	448000		390005
56	Total Gros Cont (suppl)$	280000		300380
57	Total Net Profit $	578000		540475
60	DATA LINES			
62	Sales margin%	20		1.25
64	Distributor's margin per unit -1	5		1.05263
66	Distributor's margin per unit - 2	10		1.11111
68	Price elasticity	2		
69	Consumer price fall%	-10		
70	Supplier cost $ per unit	25		
72	Supplier advertising $	150000		
74	Total fixed cost $	252000		
76	Revised volume index	0.8		

□■

73

is calculated, together with the supplier profit and distributor profit at that particular volume level.

The model will also serve as a useful control for investigating the effects that, for example, an increase in taxation may have on the eventual retail price. The main value however comes in analysing the price and promotional expenditure of both supplier and distributor to arrive at the most advantageous combined level.

The user of the model can choose to introduce a consumer price rise (or fall) and investigate the effects on profitability. In Example 4.1.1 a price decrease of 10 per cent with a price elasticity of 2 in the market, means that the volume would increase from 28 000 units to 33 600 units, and the consumer price would fall from $94 to $85. The model, using the information provided in the current pricing column, will then recalculate backwards from the new consumer price using the same ratios to produce new distributors' mark ups, price to the trade and eventually the FOB price which would be required to produce that 10 per cent drop in consumer price if the same considerations ruling for current pricing still remain true (same level of distributor margin and so on).

Though the per unit return of the distributor would decrease, his overall profit would increase due to the greater volumes and the effects of the declining fixed costs per unit. However, the supplier would face a considerable weakening of his FOB price if the 10 per cent price drop were to be achieved, and in consequence a major drop in profitability. The user can, in this instance, then investigate the effects of changing the distributors' margins, advertising support and so on, to ascertain the most cost effective route to be followed for the planning of product growth in that particular export market.

Changes in the consumer price will lead the model to recalculate the whole structure of the factors contributing to pricing in the market place. Example 4.1.2 illustrates what will happen in the case of a 10 per cent price rise. Putting the price up will improve the supplier's profitability at the expense of the distributors' profitability but the total profit will nonetheless decrease.

Similar exercises can be carried out to compare imports with local manufacture to ascertain the most profitable solution to the expansion of local sales.

5 Marginal profitability

There is a story about a man who set out in a balloon, but because of contrary winds, was driven off his known path, and managed to land in a tree. While he was hanging there in his basket he saw beneath him a man passing by in the lane nearby.

'Where am I?', he enquired.

After a long pause, the man replied, 'You are in a basket hanging under a tree'.

'You must be an accountant.'

'Yes,' answered the man in the lane puzzled at this apparent clairvoyance. 'But how did you know?'

'Simple,' retorted the intrepid aviator, 'the information that you gave me was totally accurate but for practical purposes useless.'

Before this raises an additional movement to go alongside sexism, agism, racism (accountism?) one can accuse marketing management of similar short-sightedness. What it underlines is the point that the management information contained in the accounts should be used not only to provide historic information (including that required by the law) but also to develop an understanding and greater control over the business processes at work.

The marginal profitability concept

The information that is most valuable to selling and marketing is what the true profitability of a particular operation may be, and how this profit will alter in respect of the volume of product sold. In other words the *marginal* price, that is, the price relating to incremental quantities should always be higher than the marginal cost. The difference between the two will be the *marginal profitability* and as volumes will vary from the plan, it will be the true measure of the rate of return on investment over that time period.

The problems of financial reporting

In contrast to this true reflection of operating conditions the first requirement of an accounting system within a business is to produce the overall financial statement of operations, thus:

1   The financial statement in relation to the outside world
2   The overall result, based on profit and loss, of the total business activities

Subdivisions of these two main elements will depend on the legal framework of the country and the amount of 'creative' accounting that is deemed necessary, but in general terms it will include:

What is owing to the business
What is owed by the business
The nature of the profit/loss and its source
What the business owns
The capital employed within the organisation

The problems associated with financial accounts statements are well-known. The first is that they are historic. If the situation within the company is bad, corrective action within the company should have been taken long before final accounts are prepared. Second, the results are presented in the form of a total company statement and lose track of internal elements of the company operation. Thus the overall statement of operations might look something like this:

Sales	$3000
Expenses	$2000
Profit	$1000

The overall profit of 30 per cent might appear reasonable but the split within the product range might be very different:

Product	A	B	C
Sales	1000	1000	1000
Expenses	1200	500	300
Profit	(200)	500	700

Thus product A is being subsidised by the other products within the portfolio. The issue immediately raised by this inaccuracy is the need to develop improved systems to evaluate the different contributions made by each product line.

The requirements of the complex factory producing a wide range of products has led to a great development of cost accounting. This demands the methods to handle the analysis of all the expenses the firm incurs in achieving the final product sale.

At its purest level, the total range of costs could be considered and analysed, from the small addition of grease to the assembly line to the provision of a first-aid kit in the secretaries' office.

As this system is too laborious for the majority of firms, short cuts tend to be developed, and the cost element is divided between *variable* or *direct* (all those items specifically involved in the production process), and *fixed* (all others).

1 Direct/variable costs

This is the area of expenditure which can be conveniently and directly attributed to the particular task in hand.

(a) Labour costs From work or time sheets the number of hours per employee can be obtained and multiplied by the appropriate hourly rate.

(b) Material A product line will consume a quantifiable amount of raw material and energy to produce, and these can be obtained from invoices and analysis of machine operating times.

(c) Expenses These can include the hire of special equipment, or extra travel, or some other factor directly relating to the particular item.

These elements can be *singly* and *directly* attributed to the specific exercise. Another approach is to call this the 'prime' cost.

However there is obviously a large element of cost that cannot be specifically allocated to a particular project, as they are general to the activities of the entire organisation. The whole question is further complicated by the fact that non-specific costs are not evenly spread. Certain departments will be more expensive than others (the computer department will tend to be more costly than the paint shop). Time is often overlooked: the longer a project takes the more expensive it should be.

The general solution to this problem is to divide the overhead within the main administrative areas:

(i) Production overhead

This can be applied to all the general cost elements operating within the production department. Examples of this are depreciation of machinery, supervisory labour, heating, lighting, rent, rates and so on.

These overall costs can then be divided by the total number of hours worked in the production area and an overall hourly cost calculated. This has the weakness that the nature of the production process will not be uniform. For example, one machine may be much more expensive than another and thus a time allocation for a job entailing say five hours will in reality cost far more on one machine than on the other, though an averaging approach would not produce this result.

As a result, organisations have tended towards developing costing areas for as many discrete areas of activity as can be identified within the organisation. There remains the fundamental flaw that the cost element is based on a forecast of time utilisation and is therefore *highly volume sensitive*. This issue will be considered in greater detail, because it is a key to the overall strategic planning of the firm.

(ii)   Administrative overhead

These problems become accentuated when one considers the allocation of other indirect expenses to the various activities within the organisation.

The first of these is the increasing burden of administration. How should the work of the credit control department be allocated across the range of products/services supplied to a host of customers?

One general method is to allocate this in the ratio to the overall prime production cost, on the basis that the higher the cost of production, the greater the level of administration required. As the level of administrative expenses rises with the expansion of automation the percentage of this overhead in relation to total overhead cost will tend to increase and grow as a problem.

(iii)   Sales overhead

Similar problems exist in relation to selling overhead. Although one can differentiate the specific costs of an advertising campaign unless it is for a range of products, it is more difficult when the costs of the salesman are allocated. Should these be in proportion to the time that he takes to sell each item within the range (see production overhead) or in relation to the total value or profitability of the items sold?

In addition, the amount of time that is allocated to the development of new products is rarely properly accounted for – the days at launch conferences, the extra time spent in the field explaining concepts to the customers.

(iv)   Distribution overhead

Distribution costs tend to be more easily attributable to specific lines; though in certain instances it will require more analysis. A product that is restricted in sales to one particular region may, for example, be significantly more profitable on a case-per-case basis than one sold nationally, since transport costs will be lower and only one or two depots will need to stock the product, in contrast to the national position.

2   Fixed costs

While the definition of fixed overhead varies with the organisation, it frequently covers such items as rent/rates which are 'general' to the company. These overheads are also normally allocated by some factor such as floor space. Other items can be similarly treated:

Possible basis	Suitable for
Floor space	Rent/rates/upkeep
Number of employees	Canteen/first aid
Hours worked	Maintenance etc.

Fixed and variable expenses are then combined to produce the total costs relating to that product in respect of the way the firm defines the different factors.

Various features of this system are likely to cause problems, the main objection being the rigidity it imposes with regard to changing volumes. Should the firm commence selling either considerably more, or less, than planned, the information that such a system provides on line-by-line profitability becomes more and more suspect.

Over-reliance on such costing figures can and does lead to disaster. Once the costs are regarded as accurate it is often assumed that the sum of the sales of individual lines each of which is generating a 'cost profit' will lead to an overall company profit. The reason why this is not so can be due to two factors, one more important than the other. It may be that exceptional costs such as redundancy/closure costs are not sufficiently included, or it may be due to interest on major loans. The inclusion of these items should not be beyond the majority of organisations, and is not an insurmountable obstacle. The major hurdle is the effect of under- or over-recovery of costs on company profitability.

The chapter on pricing strategy discusses the over reliance on pricing by cost build-up instead of a method of market pricing which ensures maximum profitability. The price build-up method tends to set what is regarded by management as a 'reasonable' level of profit, which often means one that provides a bare return to the organisation. Should anything occur to interfere with this achievement the effect on overall survival will often be very poor. Better control over the return that a product makes to the company at varying levels of price will allow a more sophisticated view of pricing strategy to be developed.

Overhead recovery difficulties will be encountered in two main areas, one in connection with costing and the other with volume. The effects of errors in costing can be projected in a straightforward example:

Estimate of overhead:	$5000
Estimate hours production:	500
Overhead/hour estimated recovery:	$10
Actual overhead:	$6000
Hours of production:	400
Overhead/hour estimate recovery:	$15

Each unit actually costs $5 more than was projected in the initial planning exercise.

The effect of pricing changes can be clearly shown in a simple illustration where one can see the evolution of cost with volume:

Output(units)	200	300	600
Fixed expenses	$ 400	400	400
Variable expenses	$ 400	600	1200
Cost per unit	$ 4	3.3	2.6

In a graphical form (Figure 5.1) the gap between the combined fixed and variable

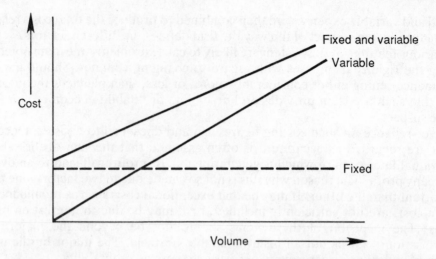

Figure 5.1 Changes in slope of fixed and variable costs as volume changes

cost line will narrow as volumes increase, leading to one of the tablets of stone of modern marketing wisdom: the economy of scale. It is often forgotten that this only relates to mass-marketed goods with low profit margins, and for specialised products with high margin levels different criteria will need to be applied.

The problem still remains how the financial accounting demands can best be integrated with the internal demands of the marketing department, how the company's internal costing system can best be developed to produce a coherent planning system to maximise the market possibilities for the product range.

The important problem that any control system needs to address is the interplay between price and 'real' variable costs while maintaining a close watch over the fixed element in the product costing to ensure maximum flexibility and profitability.

The marginal profitability model

The use of a spreadsheet system which allows the maximum control over the variables involved in the costing procedure needs to take account of the direct and variable cost problems associated with each particular product line. Using the spreadsheet system model can aid the development of a system in which profit is the most important element in the equation, and not the recovery of overhead. The aims are to produce a *profit and loss statement* for each product line.

The first necessity is to evaluate the level of costs which are always incurred by a particular product at any level of activity. For example, the production of powder detergents demands the use of a blowing tower, so whatever happens the cost of maintaining that plant item will always be incurred by the powder detergent company.

Costs for a particular product as volume increases will not move in a linear fashion but tend to be a compound of a series of different factors (Figure 5.2). Materials tend to become cheaper as volume utilisation increases, labour unit costs remain linear, as do energy costs. Some other costs may increase in step fashion as each new level of volume brings in a complete unit of additional resource.

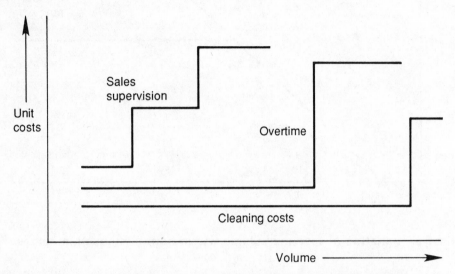

Figure 5.2   Non-linear changes in certain costs as volume increases

The summation of these lines occurs naturally within any company as demand either increases or decreases. Thus the company will have produced for each product line a graph of costs over a particular volume range (Figure 5.3). Regression analysis of this line will cross the cost line at a particular point, which can be termed the basic activity cost which would be analogous to the costs continuing to be incurred during a strike (Figure 5.4)

As well as the specific base costs of a particular product there may be a series of expenditures which are general to the product range and can only be allocated on that basis. To carry the analogy of the detergent powder further, packaging line costs can be specific, blowing tower depreciation would be general.

For a profit and loss account these items should be included as below the line activities as they are standard expenses not relating to any particular activity level.

Similar considerations should apply to the development of advertising support, promotional activity, and finally any research and development expenditure relating to the specific product line.

Once these two areas have become established it is possible to consider specific areas of volume related pricing:

1   Trade discounts   These can be an important loss maker if margins are slim and total discounts are not controlled.

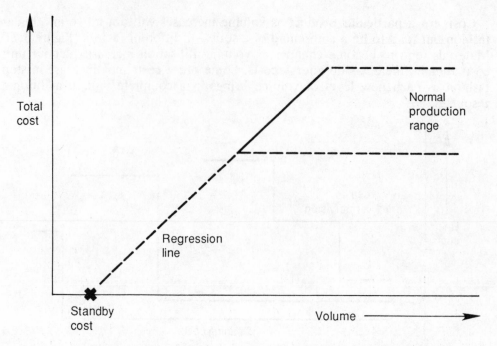

Figure 5.3   Variation of cost and volume within normal production ranges

Plant financing   Distribution costs

Administrative staff salaries/pensions   Insurance

Security costs   ·   Raw material financing

Company cars   Finished goods financing

Taxes

Figure 5.4   Standby/strike costs

2   Commissions   Similarly, control over the amount of money that is being
expended in commissions is important in the overall brand profitability.

3   Distribution costs   These will be particularly relevant if they constitute a large
number of separate deliveries to customers and will require an individual line in
any evaluation.

4   Direct materials   Here all the material cost relating to the product line should
be included.

5 *Direct labour* As in point 4 immediately preceding.

6 *Manufacturing expense* All the variable expenses associated with the production of the product.

7 *Commercial expense* This category includes all the overheads associated with the credit control department, personnel function and so on. These figures will provide the total variable production cost directly relating to the particular product line.

8 *Base costs* Those costs relating to the product at a shutdown level of activity, both at a general and specific level.

9 *Line expenditure* This covers all advertising and research and development expenditure relating either in a general or specific fashion.

10 *Capital employed* One of the important aspects of this model is to enable the manager to gain an understanding of the level of capital employed for each particular product line. This should be provided as an input for calculation, to develop the overall profit analysis as a return on capital employed and not in comparison with the budgeted figures of the previous year or a return on sales. This may reveal that a certain product while being highly profitable in isolation is requiring a high level of capital investment whereas other items in the range may easily show a higher return on investment albeit with a lower profit margin on sales price.

The major advantages that this system has are two-fold. First, it enables the budgeting to be simply changed without a total re-evaluation of the underlying basic costs in the product costings as these are fixed at all levels of production. Second, the model concentrates on the return on capital employed, which the majority of analyses tend to ignore, but which is crucial to profit planning.

This model escapes the problems faced by overhead recovery systems, in that problems can be quickly identified and acted upon. It also avoids the difficulties of direct costing systems which do not include sufficient information concerning the basic costs that the company must continue to carry.

The main advantage to the manager is that he is presented with a level of cost at any level of output which enables decisions to be reached easily without the complexity of coping with variations of cost at varying levels of demand. The model provides an easy way of calculating the likely return on capital employed of any particular pricing policy, increasingly important in many companies with budgets based on rates of internal return. The model can also help in the determination of component costing for the finished article. Management can analyse the effect of buying in components against the cost of producing them in-house, allowing for all the research and development costs separately from the production cost.

The integration of these elements in one complete model allows the manager to decide:

1 The level of capacity that is most profitable to the organisation
2 The most profitable level of volume/base cost/line cost

3   The closest approximation to the 'true' cost to the company of any new development

Using the marginal profitability model

The *Go To* column in Listing 5.1 tells you the cell number and the cursor position. The next column specifies the spreadsheet option (LO = Label Option; VO = Value Option). The *Type In* column gives you instructions within the inverted commas which you must type in or asks you to supply the necessary data. These commas are not part of the instructions supplied here and should not be typed in. Beware that some spreadsheets, the *Lotus 1-2-3* for example, enter the Label Option by using the inverted-comma key. Under the *Type In* column the symbols *= multiply and / = divide. R in the *Return* column instructs you to commit the information to memory by pressing the Return key.
Remember: When you have finished, save your model.

Listing 5.1   Marginal profitability model

Go To		Type In	Return	Go To		Type In	Return
B4/	LO	"Marginal	R	E12	VO	Enter actual sales volume for product Line A	R
C4/D4	LO	Profitability	R				
E4/F4	LO	Control"	R	F12	VO	"E12–D12"	R
C10/	LO	"Company	R	G12	VO	Enter planned sales volume for product Line B	R
D10	LO	Line A"	R				
E10	LO	"Actual"	R	H12	VO	Enter actual sales volume for product Line B	R
F10	LO	"Variance"	R				
G10	LO	"Line B"	R	I12	VO	"H12–G12"	R
H10	LO	"Actual"	R	A13	LO	"Unit Price"	R
I10	LO	"Variance"	R	D13	VO	Enter planned unit price of product Line A	R
K10/	LO	"Company	R				
K11	LO	revised"	R	E13	VO	Enter actual unit price of product Line A	R
L10/	LO	"Company	R				
L11	LO	variance"	R	F13	VO	"E13–D13"	R
A12	LO	"Volume"	R	G13	VO	Enter planned unit price of product Line B	R
D12	VO	Enter planned sales volume for product Line A in units	R	H13	VO	Enter actual unit price of product Line B	R

Listing 5.1 *(continued)*

Go To		Type In	Return
I13	VO	"H13−G13"	R
A14	LO	"Sales"	R
C14	VO	"D14+G14"	R
D14	VO	"D12∗D13"	R
E14	VO	"E12∗E13"	R
F14	VO	"D14−E14" (variance value)	R
G14	VO	"G12∗G13"	R
H14	VO	"H12∗H13"	R
I14	VO	"H14−G14"	R
K14	VO	"E14+H14"	R
L14	VO	"K14−C14"	R
A16/	LO	"Variable	R
B16	LO	Costs"	R
A18	LO	"Discount"	R
C18	VO	"D18+G18"	R
D18	VO	Insert planned value for discounts on Line A	R
E18	VO	Insert actual value for discounts	R
F18	VO	"D18−E18"	R
G18	VO	Insert planned value for discounts on Line B	R
H18	VO	Insert actual value for discounts	R
I18	VO	"G18−H18"	R
K18	VO	"E18+H18"	R
L18	VO	"C18−K18"	R
A20/	LO	"Commissions"	R
B20	LO		R
C20	VO	"D20+G20"	R
D20	VO	Insert value for planned commissions on Line A	R

Go To		Type In	Return
E20	VO	Insert value for actual commissions	R
F20	VO	"D20−E20"	R
G20	VO	Insert value for the planned commissions on Line B	R
H20	VO	Insert value for actual commissions on Line B	R
I20	VO	"G20−H20"	R
K20	VO	"E20+H20"	R
L20	VO	"C20−K20"	R
A22/	LO	"Distribution"	R
B22	LO		R
C22	VO	"D22+G22"	R
D22	VO	Insert value for planned distribution cost on Line A	R
E22	VO	Insert value for actual distribution cost on Line A	R
F22	VO	"D22−E22"	R
G22	VO	Insert value for planned distribution cost on Line B	R
H22	VO	Insert value for actual distribution cost on Line B	R
I22	VO	"G22−H22"	R
K22	VO	"E22+H22"	R
L22	VO	"C22−K22"	R
A24	LO	"Material"	R
C24	VO	"D24+G24"	R
D24	VO	Insert value for planned material on Line A	R
E24	VO	Insert value for actual costs on Line A	R

Listing 5.1 *(continued)*

Go To		Type In	Return	Go To		Type In	Return
F24	VO	"D24−E24"	R	K28	VO	"E28+H28"	R
G24	VO	Insert planned value for Line B	R	L28	VO	"C28−K28"	R
H24	VO	Insert actual value for Line B	R	A30/	LO	"TOTAL	R
				B30	LO	VARIABLE"	R
I24	VO	"G24−H24"	R	C30	VO	"SUM(C18:C28)"	R
K24	VO	"E24+H24"	R	D30	VO	"SUM(D18:D28)"	R
L24	VO	"C24−K24"	R	E30	VO	"SUM(E18:E28)"	R
A26	LO	"Labour"	R	F30	VO	"SUM(F18:F28)"	R
C26	VO	"D26+G26"	R	G30	VO	"SUM(G18:G28)"	R
D26	VO	Insert planned value for labour for Line A	R	H30	VO	"SUM(H18:H28)"	R
F26	VO	"D26−E26"	R	I30	VO	"SUM(I18:I28)"	R
E26	VO	Insert actual value for labour for Line A	R	K30	VO	"SUM(K18:K28)"	R
				L30	VO	"SUM(L18:L28)"	R
G26	VO	Insert planned value for labour costs on Line B	R	A31	LO	"COST"	R
				A33/	LO	"TOTAL	R
H26	VO	Insert actual value for labour costs on Line B	R	B33	LO	VARIABLE"	R
				A34	LO	"PROFIT"	R
I26	VO	"G26−H26"	R	C33	VO	"C14−C30"	R
K26	VO	"E26+H26"	R	D33	VO	"D14−D30"	R
L26	VO	"C26−K26"	R	E33	VO	"E14−E30"	R
A28	LO	"Manufacture"	R	F33	VO	"F14+F30"	R
C28	VO	"D28+G28"	R	G33	VO	"G14−G30"	R
D28	VO	Insert value for planned manufacturing costs for Line A	R	H33	VO	"H14−H30"	R
				I33	VO	"I14+I30"	R
				K33	VO	"K14−K30"	R
E28	VO	Insert value for actual cost for Line A	R	L33	VO	"L14+L30"	R
F28	VO	"D28−E28"	R	A36/	LO	"BASE	R
G28	VO	Insert planned values for Line B	R	B36	LO	COSTS"	R
				A38	LO	"Specific" i.e. base costs	R
H28	VO	Insert actual values for Line B	R	A39	LO	"General" i.e. base costs	R
I28	VO	"G28−H28"	R				

Listing 5.1 *(continued)*

Go To		Type In	Return	Go To		Type In	Return
C38	VO	"D38+G38"	R	E44	VO	Insert value for actual Line expenditure	R
D38	VO	Insert values for planned base costs Line A	R	F44	VO	"D44−E44"	R
E38	VO	Insert values for actual base costs Line A	R	G44	VO	Insert value for planned Line expenditure	R
F38	VO	"D38−E38"	R	H44	VO	Insert value for actual Line expenditure	R
G38	VO	Insert values for planned base costs Line B	R	I44	VO	"G44−H44"	R
H38	VO	Insert value for actual costs Line B	R	K44	VO	"E44+H44"	R
I38	VO	"G38−H38"	R	L44	VO	"C44−K44"	R
K38	VO	"E38+H38"	R	C45	VO	"D45+G45"	R
L38	VO	"C38−K38"	R	D45	VO	Insert value for planned general expenditure	R
A39	LO	"General"					
C39	VO	"D39+G39"	R	E45	VO	Insert value for actual expenditure	R
D39	VO	Insert value for planned general base costs Line A	R	F45	VO	"D45−E45"	R
E39	VO	Insert actual value of general base cost	R	G45	VO	Insert values for planned Line expenditure	R
F39	VO	"D39−E39"	R	H45	VO	Insert values for actual Line expenditure	R
G39	VO	Insert value for planned general base costs Line B	R	I45	VO	"G45−H45"	R
H39	VO	Insert value for actual base costs Line B	R	K45	VO	"E45+H45"	R
I39	VO	"G39−H39"	R	L45	VO	"C45−K45"	R
K39	VO	"E39+H39"	R	A48/	LO	"TOTAL	R
L39	VO	"C39−K39"	R	B48	LO	PROFIT"	R
A42	LO	"LINE EXP" for line expenditure	R	C48	VO	"D48+G48"	R
A44	LO	"Specific"	R	D48	VO	"D33−SUM(D38:D45)"	R
A45	LO	"General"	R	E48	VO	"E33−SUM(E38:E45)"	R
C44	VO	"D44+G44"	R	F48	VO	"F33+SUM(F38:F45)"	R
D44	VO	Insert value for planned Line expenditure	R	G48	VO	"G33−SUM(G38:G45)"	R
				H48	VO	"H33−SUM(H38:H45)"	R
				I48	VO	"I33+SUM(I38:I45)"	R
				K48	VO	"K33−SUM(K38:K45)"	R

Listing 5.1   *(concluded)*

Go To		Type In	Return
L48	VO	"L33+SUM(L38:L45)"	R
A50	VO	"CAPITAL	R
A51	VO	EMPLOYED"	R
C50	VO	"D50+G50"	R
D50	VO	Enter value for planned capital employed	R
E50	VO	Enter value for actual value of capital employed	R
F50	VO	"E50−D50"	R
G50	VO	Enter value for planned capital employed on Line B	R
H50	VO	Enter value for actual capital employed	R
I50	VO	"H50−G50"	R
K50	VO	"E50+H50"	R
L50	VO	"K50−C50"	R
A53/	LO	"RETURN	R
B53	LO	ON CAP"	R
A54	LO	"EMPLOYED"	R
C53	VO	"C48/C50−1"	R
D53	VO	"D48/D50−1"	R
E53	VO	"E48/E50−1"	R

Go To		Type In	Return
G53	VO	"G48/G50−1"	R
F53	VO	"IF(E53>D53)THEN(10) ELSE(0)"	R

Note: If you score 10 this shows that your profitability is improving, if you score 0 you are failing.

Go To		Type In	Return
H53	VO	"H48/H50−1"	R
I53	VO	"IF(H53>G53)THEN(10) ELSE(0)"	R
K53	VO	"K48/K50−1"	R
L53	VO	"IF(K53>C53)THEN(10) ELSE(0)"	R
A/B55	LO	"Gross mg/unit" for gross margin per unit	R
D55	VO	"D33/D12"	R
E55	VO	"E33/E12"	R
G55	VO	"G33/G12"	R
H55	VO	"H33/H12"	R
A/B56	VO	"Break even"	R
D56	VO	"SUM(D38:D45)/D55"	R
E56	VO	"SUM(E38:E45)/E55"	R
G56	VO	"SUM(G38:G45)/G55"	R
H56	VO	"SUM(H38:H45)/H55"	R

Marginal profitability commentary

Example 5.1 shows how the marginal profitability approach will work in practice. The model is set up to provide a company total in column C and then a series of individual product assessments in columns D–I of this example but which can be extended to the full width of the spreadsheet. For the moment we are however concerned with only two cases: that of Line A and Line B.

Each line of input shows the planned figure in columns D and G, what was actually achieved in columns E and H, and the variance between the two in columns F and I. Cell F14 for Product Line A shows that sales have fallen below target for the period, a drop of $450 000. Because the volumes are lower there has however been an improvement in the variable costs such as material and labour – cells D24–F24 and D26–F26; manufacturing costs (D28–F28) show a worrying increase even on diminished volume and would need further investigation. Because of diminished variable costs the product variable profitability is very close to the planned figure. The expenditure on line-related activities has however increased considerably (cells D44–F44 and D45–F45) – the media budget might have been increased or more money spent on sales force promotional activity. This together with the high level of capital employed to manufacture this product dramatically reduces the return on capital employed – cells D50–F50 and cells D53–F53.

By contrast sales on Line B have increased (cells G14–I14) leading to a rise in variable production costs (G30–I30). Nevertheless, there is an overall increase in total variable profitability (G33–I33). Higher line expenditure (G44–I44 and G45–I45) has the effect of decreasing overall profitability compared with the plan (G53–I53). It can be seen in this approach that Line B is a more effective investment for the company because the return on investment that it achieves is greater than on Line A: compare results shown in cell E53 for Line A with cell H53 for Line B. Profit margins calculated in the traditional way would show that the gross margins of the two are very similar.

Using this system the manager can investigate changes in capital investment on a line by line basis and more easily identify major problem areas in the business.

The model also allows the manager to analyse the break-even point for each product; where the marginal profit generated by the sales passes the level of fixed costs. It will analyse the effects of decreasing the unit price, and increasing the levels of discounts and other factors upon this figure. The break-even point is a very important figure for many businesses, particularly small businesses that are greatly concerned with covering their fixed and variable costs.

Proforma 5.1 Marginal profitability model

A/B	C	D	E	F	G
4 Marginal	Profitability	Control			
10	Company	Line A	actual	variance	Line B
11					
12 Volume		300000	277500	E12-D12	200000
13 Unit price $		20	20	E13-D13	20
14 Sales $	D14+G14	D12*D13	E12*E13	D14-E14	G12*G13
16 Variable costs					
18 Discount$	D18+G18	250000	240000	D18-E18	300000
20 Commissions$	D20+G20	205000	230000	D20-E20	150000
22 Distribution$	D22+G22	40000	35000	D22-E22	35000
24 Material$	D24+G24	2500000	2200000	D24-E24	1500000
26 Labour$	D26+G26	800000	720000	D26-E26	450000
28 Manufacture$	D28+G28	125000	168000	D28-E28	100000
30 TOTAL VARIABLE	SUM(C18:C28)	SUM(D18:D28)	SUM(E18:E28)	SUM(F18:F28)	SUM(G18:G28)
31 COST$					
33 TOTAL VARIABLE	C14-C30	D14-D30	E14-E30	F14+F30	G14-G30
34 PROFIT$					
36 BASE COSTS					
38 Specific	D38+G38	750000	750000	D38-E38	450000
39 General	D39+G39	230000	230000	D39-E39	125000
42 LINE EXP $					
44 Specific	D44+G44	230000	345000	D44-E44	150000
45 General	D45+G45	112000	122000	D45-E45	42000
48 TOTAL PROFIT $	D48+G48	D33-SUM(D38:D45)	E33-SUM(E38:E45)	F33+SUM(F38:F45)	G33-SUM(G38:G45)
50 CAPITAL	D50+G50	500000	500000	E50-D50	405000
51 EMPLOYED					
53 RETURN ON CAP	C48/C50-1	D48/D50-1	E48/E50-1	IFE53)D53THEN10ELSE0	G48/G50-1
54 EMPLOYED					
55 Gross mg/unit		D33/D12	E33/E12		G33/G12
56 Break even		SUM(D38:D45)/D55	SUM(E38:E45)/E55		SUM(G38:G45)/G55

Proforma 5.1 *(concluded)*

	H	I	K	L	□■
4					
10	actual	variance	company	company	
11			revised	variance	
12	200000	H12-G12			
13	21	H13-G13			
14	H12*H13	H14-G14	E14+H14	K14-C14	
16					
18	240000	G18-H18	E18+H18	C18-K18	
20	165000	G20-H20	E20+H20	C20-K20	
22	35000	G22-H22	E22+H22	C22-K22	
24	1550000	G24-H24	E24+H24	C24-K24	
26	475000	G26-H26	E26+H26	C26-K26	
28	150000	G28-H28	E28+H28	C28-K28	
30	SUM(H18:H28)	SUM(I18:I28)	SUM(K18:K28)	SUM(L18:L28)	
31					
33	H14-H30	I14+I30	K14-K30	L14+L30	
34					
36					
38	450000	G38-H38	E38+H38	C38-K38	
39	125000	G39-H39	E39+H39	C39-K39	
42					
44	230000	G44-H44	E44+H44	C44-K44	
45	65000	G45-H45	E45+H45	C45-K45	
48	H33-SUM(H38:H45)	I33+SUM(I38:I45)	K33-SUM(K38:K45)	L33+SUM(L38:L45)	
50	430000	H50-G50	E50+H50	K50-C50	
53		IF(H53>G53)THEN(10)ELSE(0)	K48/K50-1	IF(K53>C53)THEN(10)ELSE(0)	
54	H48/H50-1				
55					
56	H33/H12				
	SUM(H38:H45)/H55				

Notes on the values used in the model are given in the line by line listing.

Example 5.1 Marginal profitability model

■□

A/B		C	D	E	F
4	Marginal	Profitability	Control		
10		Company	Line A	actual	variance
12	Volume		300000	277500	-22500
13	Unit price $		20	20	0
14	Sales $	1.E7	6000000	5550000	-450000
16	Variable costs				
18	Discount$	550000	250000	240000	10000
20	Commissions$	355000	205000	230000	-25000
21	Distribution$	75000	40000	35000	5000
24	Material$	4000000	2500000	2200000	300000
26	Labour$	1250000	800000	720000	80000
28	Manufacture$	225000	125000	168000	-43000
30	TOTAL VARIABLE	6455000	3920000	3593000	327000
31	COST$				
33	TOTAL VARIABLE	3545000	2080000	1957000	-123000
34	PROFIT$				
36	BASE COSTS				
38	Specific	1200000	750000	750000	0
39	General	355000	230000	230000	0
42	LINE EXP $				
44	Specific	380000	230000	345000	-115000
45	General	154000	112000	122000	-10000
48	TOTAL PROFIT $	1456000	758000	510000	-248000
50	CAPITAL	905000	500000	500000	0
51	EMPLOYED				
53	RETURN ON CAP	0.60884	0.516	0.02	0
54	EMPLOYED				
55	Gross mg/unit		6.93333	7.05225	
56	Break even		190673	205183	

Example 5.1   *(concluded)*

	G	H	I	K
4				
10	Line B	actual	variance	company
11	200000			revised
12	20	200000	0	
13	4000000	21	1	
14		4200000	200000	9750000
16	300000			
18	150000	240000	60000	480000
20	35000	165000	-15000	395000
22	1500000	35000	0	70000
24	450000	1550000	-50000	3750000
26	100000	475000	-25000	1195000
28	2535000	150000	-50000	318000
30		2615000	-80000	6208000
31	1465000			
33		1585000	120000	3542000
34				
36	450000			
38	125000	450000	0	1200000
39		125000	0	355000
42	150000			
44	42000	230000	-80000	575000
45	698000	65000	-23000	187000
48	405000	715000	17000	1225000
50		430000	25000	9300000
53	0.72346	0.66279	0	0.31720
54				
55	7.325	7.925		
	104710			

Note that this print out does not include column L

6 Promotional techniques

The development of promotional techniques has accompanied the growth of modern retailing. In the majority of Western consumer markets the percentage of trade handled by the supermarket/hypermarket has steadily increased. In France for example it now accounts for 60 per cent of total grocery turnover, in Belgium it is nearly 70 per cent. With the fundamental change in the nature of retailing, demands have arisen for sales promotion techniques that harmonise with the needs of the store. The importance of promotions in certain outlets can hardly be understated; in one French hypermarket chain it has been claimed that around 85 per cent of a certain product line is bought on promotion, either of price or some other special offer.

The promotions environment

The enhanced strength of the retailer places the manufacturer under more and more pressure particularly in competitive consumer markets with a wide range of alternative brands. The effective blackmail that takes place in negotiations between large store groups and the key account sales force of the producer is very hard to resist. If the demands of the retailer are not met an increasingly large percentage of market share will be lost as the retailer retaliates by the removal of the product from the shelf. The reaction of most major firms has been to both cut prices and to raise spending on promotions, leading to inevitable drops in profitability. Return on capital employed within the food manufacturing industry has fallen over the last twenty years by a substantial factor (1).

The inevitable conclusion is that this pressure will increase as retailing becomes more and more concentrated. The manufacturer's reaction is predictable: margins will be continuously strained as the demands of the retailer increase. Greater circumspection will be required of the manufacturer in pricing, and in the development and control of promotional expenditure.

From the viewpoint of the manufacturer promotions are crucial to the survival of products: the maintenance or improvement of market share, securing the market against competitors, long-term acceptability and viability. Together such factors underline the need for continual experimentation and innovation.

Promotions can provide valuable additional ways in which the product can be kept alive and prevented from possible decline. Thus the promotion can have short-term benefits by improving sales as well as improving the consumer's awareness of the product and its likely benefits. Within the past few years there has been increasing evidence that the success rate of new product introductions has been declining as markets become more fragmented and the competition for retail shelf space grows.

Another important issue is that the rate of economic growth attained by the majority of industrialised countries continues to fluctuate in the short term, with unemployment an unceasing problem. These combine to suggest that in many areas of business activity, stability rather than growth will be the dominant aim, using resources in the key cash generating areas to the maximum effect while developing new product diversification strategies. The holding operation for the established brands will inevitably mean a growth in promotional expenditure.

Some key issues

The higher percentage of the firm's resources being given over to promotions raises a number of questions:

1   How much should the company spend on promotions in total?
2   What is the best type and form that the promotion can take?
3   What should the frequency of the promotions be for greatest effectiveness?

These questions largely remain unanswered but the first can be dealt with through the application of investment appraisal techniques to the annual expenditure level. In the majority of firms the pattern of return on expenditure probably is very similar in shape, though not in absolute terms, with a rising level of return, a peak, and then a rapid decline (Figure 6.1).

The company should aim at looking at this expenditure in a commercial context and attempt to maximise the return on the promotional investment that is being made. Obviously in practical terms this is difficult. Promotions are generally regarded as short-term measures budgeted for in outline during the year, but quite often reactive in effect. Thus manufacturer A, seeing manufacturer B carrying out a test market for a new product in a certain area, may implement a promotion to confuse the results. The promotion will most often be used as a means of achieving a budgeted volume target.

The main weakness in the commercial application of promotions is the lack of accurate information on the effectiveness of promotions compared with the normal product on offer. As the time span of promotions is normally short, the use of the normal measures of sales achievement is not normally applicable, for two reasons. The first is that the audit, such as those carried out by Nielsen or Intercor, does not identify any special pack or promotional item (unless in certain cases

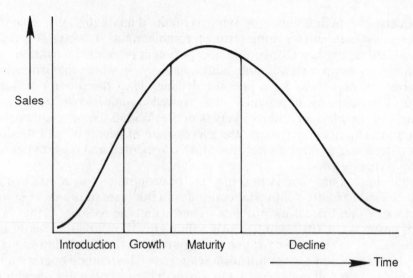

Figure 6.1   The classic product 'life cycle'

when a new size of pack is being used – but not even in all these instances). Second, an audit carried out every two months will not sufficiently isolate promotional effects lasting four or six weeks. Even if the promotion runs for two months – a long time for the majority of promotions – the data will be restricted to three observations: before, during and after. Statistically, this is quite inadequate for any assessment of the accuracy of the promotional effect, and in consequence the organisation is obliged to investigate other methods of promotional evaluation.

Techniques of promotional evaluation

A variety of techniques are commonly employed to derive information about the value of promotional items. They are broadly divided into opinion-based and sales-based techniques.

Consumer-based techniques

1   'Hall' testing   The 'hall' test (so named because it is based on a central location into which consumers are invited to give their opinions) is often used to provide information on a wide range of consumer promotions such as on-pack premiums, free offers, and self-liquidating items.

The prospective consumer is given the range of alternatives and asked to rank them in order of acceptability. The testing needs to be carefully controlled in a number of areas to provide a useful qualitative insight into likely successes and failures. The items must be limited in number – ideally not more than six – otherwise the consumer cannot rank the items with any degree of accuracy. They should be of similar cost and 'value'. In this instance value relates to whether the items have the same utility – glasses and cutlery would be similar but the comparison of calendars and glasses may produce test anomalies. The hall test also needs to ensure that the correct group of consumers is being questioned – it is obviously senseless to ask consumers who never buy your product – and to ensure that all the products are ranked.

The problem with this test is that it fails to quantify the likely performance of the alternatives on offer. Provided a control item is included in the test about which there has been previous experience, some indication of the likely market performance can be obtained. Its most obvious attraction is as a filter to identify total failures and items which might be highly successful – but it cannot separate the middle ground.

2   Consumer surveys   The use of consumer surveys can also identify areas where promotional expenditure would be effective, providing an answer to the likely appeal of any particular item, its potential consumer, as well as any major shortcomings that the material has.

Sales-based techniques

1   Store test   Small-scale shop tests can do much to overcome the lack of quantifiable data available in the other methods. They are particularly useful when money-off and other types of price cutting are considered, and any on-pack or branded pack promotion. The promotion is run on a side-by-side basis, the promotional pack being sold alongside the standard, in a closely controlled group of stores which provide the fullest co-operation and accurately record the results.

2   Display checks   Specialised personnel can be used to record the amount of display space that is taken up by the promoted item; or the sales force, if properly briefed, can record a large element of this information. Methods such as these will continually face problems in the control of the store panels, and in the design and maintenance of the data recording system.

The promotional analysis model

The best system from these various promotional evaluation alternatives would appear therefore to be a method by which the store sales can be compared within a statistical framework which takes into account the small numbers used in the method, as sales analyses provide the only realistic method of assessment for what still remains, for the majority of firms, a short-term tactical operation.

The model compares the sales of products placed in a series of stores side-by-side over a short period, on a week-by-week basis. For any given number of shops and weeks of sales there will be a probability that the difference in the achieved level of offtake can be explained by chance. The longer the test and the wider the test areas, the greater the chance that any result seen will be repeated in a more wide-scale use of the particular technique. This is also relevant in test marketing techniques considered elsewhere.

A simple example will illustrate this. No one would claim that a sales difference of 5 per cent in one store over the period of a month between two products is particularly significant, whereas a 55 per cent variation in a Nielsen region over a year would be considered differently.

Smaller test regions and time periods are more complex to evaluate, and it is these grey areas that require more detailed investigation. Each organisation will have different criteria for judging the level of risk faced by any particular action. For some, the result that a particular event could have appeared by chance one in twenty times (5 per cent level of probability) will be sufficient, others will demand higher levels of one in a hundred (1 per cent) or one thousand (0.1 per cent).

The design of the test is therefore fairly straightforward. A dozen shops are chosen in one or (ideally) more regions for testing. This can be particularly important with certain promotions where there will be strong regional differences in uptake. For example, the number of entrants in competitions tends to be significantly higher in the North of England than the South. In the case of each shop the actual sales in units of the two items placed side-by-side will be collected each week. Strictly, the position of each item should be rotated at the end of the week to ensure that positional bias is removed; in the majority of large stores this is unlikely to be a problem.

The model can also be used to investigate the effectiveness of using promotions in small shops compared with supermarkets or hypermarkets. Practical experience would suggest that the amount of brand switching that takes place in the larger stores is considerably higher than the level in the corner store, but research in this area is limited.

From the sales data the model then calculates from this small sample of shops whether the sales difference between the two products is statistically significant.

Using the promotional analysis model

In Listing 6.1 the *Go To* column tells you the cell number and the cursor position. The next column specifies the spreadsheet option (LO = Label Option; VO = Value Option). The *Type In* column gives you instructions within the inverted commas which you must type in or asks you to supply the necessary data. These commas are not part of the instructions supplied here and should not be typed in. Beware however that some spreadsheets, the *Lotus 1-2-3* for example, enter the Label Option by using the inverted-comma key. Under the *Type In* column the symbols * = multiply and / = divide. R in the *Return* column tells you to enter the information into the computer's memory by pressing the Return key.
Remember: When you have finished, save your model.

Promotional analysis commentary

Example 6.1 shows the model analysing the sales of two products, A and B, over a two-week period in 12 stores. Then it determines whether the difference in the sales level of the two products is significant statistically.

Listing 6.1 Promotional analysis model

Go To		Type In	Return	Go To		Type In	Return
C4/	LO	"PROMOTIONAL	R	R7	LO	"Prod. B"	R
D4/		ANALYSIS"	R	S7	LO	"Prod. A"	R
E4			R	T7	LO	"Prod. B"	R
C6	LO	"Store 1"	R	U7	LO	"Prod. A"	R
E6	LO	"Store 2"	R	V7	LO	"Prod. B"	R
G6	LO	"Store 3"	R	W7	LO	"Prod. A"	R
I6	LO	"Store 4"	R	X7	LO	"Prod. B"	R
K6	LO	"Store 5"	R	Y7	LO	"Prod. A"	R
M6	LO	"Store 6"	R	Z7	LO	"Prod. B"	R
O6	LO	"Store 7"	R	A9/	LO	"SALES	R
Q6	LO	"Store 8"	R	B9		(units)"	R
S6	LO	"Store 9"	R	A10	LO	" week 1"	R
U6	LO	"Store 10"	R	C10	VO	Insert value of sales of	
W6	LO	"Store 11"	R	to		products A and B in	
Y6	LO	"Store 12"	R	Z10		week 1, in units, across	
C7	LO	"Prod. A" for product				the spreadsheet	R
		A	R	C11	VO	"LOG10(C10)"	R
D7	LO	"Prod. B" for product		D11	VO	"LOG10(D10)"	R
		B	R	E11	VO	"LOG10(E10)"	R
E7	LO	"Prod. A"	R	F11	VO	"LOG10(F10)"	R
F7	LO	"Prod. B"	R	G11	VO	"LOG10(G10)"	R
G7	LO	"Prod. A"	R	H11	VO	"LOG10(H10)"	R
H7	LO	"Prod. B"	R	I11	VO	"LOG10(I10)"	R
I7	LO	"Prod. A"	R	J11	VO	"LOG10(J10)"	R
J7	LO	"Prod. B"	R	K11	VO	"LOG10(K10)"	R
K7	LO	"Prod. A"	R	L11	VO	"LOG10(L10)"	R
L7	LO	"Prod. B"	R	M11	VO	"LOG10(M10)"	R
M7	LO	"Prod. A"	R	N11	VO	"LOG10(N10)"	R
N7	LO	"Prod. B"	R	O11	VO	"LOG10(O10)"	R
O7	LO	"Prod. A"	R	P11	VO	"LOG10(P10)"	R
P7	LO	"Prod. B"	R	Q11	VO	"LOG10(Q10)"	R
Q7	LO	"Prod. A"	R	R11	VO	"LOG10(R10)"	R

Listing 6.1 *(continued)*

Go To		Type In	Return	Go To		Type In	Return
S11	VO	"LOG10(S10)"	R	V12	VO	"V11*V11"	R
T11	VO	"LOG10(T10)"	R	W12	VO	"W11*W11"	R
U11	VO	"LOG10(U10)"	R	X12	VO	"X11*X11"	R
V11	VO	"LOG10(V10)"	R	Y12	VO	"Y11*Y11"	R
W11	VO	"LOG10(W10)"	R	Z12	VO	"Z11*Z11"	R
X11	VO	"LOG10(X10)"	R	AA12	VO	"SUM(C12:Z12)"	R
Y11	VO	"LOG10(Y10)"	R	A13	LO	" week 2"	R
Z11	VO	"LOG10(Z10)"	R	C13 to Z13	VO	Insert value of sales of product A and product B in week 2, in units, across the spreadsheet	R
AA11	VO	"SUM(C11:Z11)"	R				
AB11	VO	"C11+E11+G11+I11 +K11+M11+O11+Q11 +S11+U11+W11+ Y11"	R	C14	VO	"LOG10(C13)"	R
				D14	VO	"LOG10(D13)"	R
C12	VO	"C11*C11"	R	E14	VO	"LOG10(E13)"	R
D12	VO	"D11*D11"	R	F14	VO	"LOG10(F13)"	R
E12	VO	"E11*E11"	R	G14	VO	"LOG10(G13)"	R
F12	VO	"F11*F11"	R	H14	VO	"LOG10(H13)"	R
G12	VO	"G11*G11"	R	I14	VO	"LOG10(I13)"	R
H12	VO	"H11*H11"	R	J14	VO	"LOG10(J13)"	R
I12	VO	"I11*I11"	R	K14	VO	"LOG10(K13)"	R
J12	VO	"J11*J11"	R	L14	VO	"LOG10(L13)"	R
K12	VO	"K11*K11"	R	M14	VO	"LOG10(M13)"	R
L12	VO	"L11*L11"	R	N14	VO	"LOG10(N13)"	R
M12	VO	"M11*M11"	R	O14	VO	"LOG10(O13)"	R
N12	VO	"N11*N11"	R	P14	VO	"LOG10(P13)"	R
O12	VO	"O11*O11"	R	Q14	VO	"LOG10(Q13)"	R
P12	VO	"P11*P11"	R	R14	VO	"LOG10(R13)"	R
Q12	VO	"Q11*Q11"	R	S14	VO	"LOG10(S13)"	R
R12	VO	"R11*R11"	R	T14	VO	"LOG10(T13)"	R
S12	VO	"S11*S11"	R	U14	VO	"LOG10(U13)"	R
T12	VO	"T11*T11"	R	V14	VO	"LOG10(V13)"	R
U12	VO	"U11*U11"	R	W14	VO	"LOG10(W13)"	R

Listing 6.1 *(continued)*

Go To		Type In	Return	Go To		Type In	Return
X14	VO	"LOG10(X13)"	R	C16	VO	"C11+D11+C14+D14"	R
Y14	VO	"LOG10(Y13)"	R	D16	VO	"C16*C16"	R
Z14	VO	"LOG10(Z13)"	R	E16	VO	"E11+F11+E14+F14"	R
AA14	VO	"SUM(C14:Z14)"	R	F16	VO	"E16*E16"	R
AB14	VO	"C14+E14+G14+I14+ K14+M14+O14+Q14+ S14+U14+W14+Y14"	R	G16	VO	"G11+H11+G14+H14"	R
				H16	VO	"G16*G16"	R
C15	VO	"C14*C14"	R	I16	VO	"I11+J11+I14+J14"	R
D15	VO	"D14*D14"	R	J16	VO	"I16*I16"	R
E15	VO	"E14*E14"	R	K16	VO	"K11+L11+K14+L14"	R
F15	VO	"F14*F14"	R	L16	VO	"K16*K16"	R
G15	VO	"G14*G14"	R	M16	VO	"M11+N11+M14+N14"	R
H15	VO	"H14*H14"	R	N16	VO	"M16*M16"	R
I15	VO	"I14*I14"	R	O16	VO	"O11+P11+O14+P14"	R
J15	VO	"J14*J14"	R	P16	VO	"O16*O16"	R
K15	VO	"K14*K14"	R	Q16	VO	"Q11+R11+Q14+R14"	R
L15	VO	"L14*L14"	R	R16	VO	"Q16*Q16"	R
M15	VO	"M14*M14"	R	S16	VO	"S11+T11+S14+T14"	R
N15	VO	"N14*N14"	R	T16	VO	"S16*S16"	R
O15	VO	"O14*O14"	R	U16	VO	"U11+V11+U14+V14"	R
P15	VO	"P14*P14"	R	V16	VO	"U16*U16"	R
Q15	VO	"Q14*Q14"	R	W16	VO	"W11+X11+W14+ X14"	R
R15	VO	"R14*R14"	R				
S15	VO	"S14*S14"	R	X16	VO	"W16*W16"	R
T15	VO	"T14*T14"	R	Y16	VO	"Y11+Z11+Y14+Z14"	R
U15	VO	"U14*U14"	R	Z16	VO	"Y16*Y16"	R
V15	VO	"V14*V14"	R	AA16	VO	"D16+F16+H16+J16+ L16+N16+P16+R16+ T16+V16+X16+Z16"	R
W15	VO	"W14*W14"	R				
X15	VO	"X14*X14"	R	A18/	LO	"Total log	R
Y15	VO	"Y14*Y14"	R	B18		Sales"	R
Z15	VO	"Z14*Z14"	R	B19	VO	"AA11+AA14"	R
AA15	VO	"SUM(C15:Z15)"	R	A20/	LO	"Corrected	R

Listing 6.1 *(continued)*

Go To		Type In	Return	Go To		Type In	Return
B20		Sales"	R	G37		Final"	R
B21	VO	"B18*B18/48"	R	B38	LO	"SHOPS"	R
B23	VO	"AA12+AA15"	R	D38	VO	Insert value for degrees of freedom relating to the 12 shops	R
A24/	LO	"Net	R				
B24		effect"	R				

As there are 12 shops the value for this model is 11; if there were 24 it would be 23 and so on.

Go To		Type In	Return	Go To		Type In	Return
B25	VO	"B23−B21"	R	E38	VO	"B27/D38"	R
A26/	LO	"Shop sum of	R	F38	VO	"B27/E44"	R
B26		squares"	R	B40	LO	"WEEKS"	R
B27	VO	"AA16/4−B21"	R	D40	VO	Insert value for degrees of freedom for weeks one and two	R
A28/	LO	"Week	R				
B28		squares"	R				

In this model it's one as there are two weeks.

Go To		Type In	Return	Go To		Type In	Return
B29	VO	"(AA11−AA14)*(AA11−AA14)/48	R	E40	VO	"B29/D40"	R
A30/	LO	"Prom.	R	F40	VO	"F40/E44"	R
B30		sqrs." for sum of promotions squares	R	B42/	LO	"PROMOTIONS"	R
C30	LO	"A"	R	C42			R
D30	LO	"B"	R	D42	VO	Insert value for degree of freedom for promotions	R
E30	LO	"net diff." for net difference	R				

In this model two options are being tested so the value is one.

Go To		Type In	Return	Go To		Type In	Return
C31	VO	"AA11+AA14−AB11−AB14"	R	E42	VO	"F31/D42"	R
D31	VO	"AA11+AA14−C31"	R	F42	VO	"E42/E44"	R
E31	VO	"D31−C31"	R	B44	LO	"RESIDUAL"	R
F31	VO	"E31*E31/48"	R	D44	VO	Insert value for degree of freedom for residual factors	R
A32/	LO	"Residual	R				
B32		square"	R				
B33	VO	"B25−B27+B29+F31"	R				
A36/	LO	"PROBABILITY	R				
B36/		VALUES"	R				
C36			R				
F37/	LO	"Prob. value	R				

Listing 6.1 *(concluded)*

Go To	Type In	Return	Go To	Type In	Return
This is the total number of observations: 12 shops multiplied by 4 observations = 48; or 47 degrees of freedom minus the degrees of free-			dom of shops, weeks and promotions: $47 - 11 - 2 = 34$.		
			E44	VO	"B33/D44"	R

The two products can either be two promotions or more effectively, the standard product and one on promotion. The promotion chosen can either be money-off, on-pack items or competitions: the model can be used to evaluate any number of possibilities.

Reading across Example 6.1 from cells C10 and C13 to cells Z10 and Z13 you will see how the sales data from the 12 stores have been entered under the appropriate headings for product and week. In cells E38–40 the model provides the results of calculations of the various factors involved, namely the effects of the number of stores, the number of weeks, and the number of promotions being considered. The number of weeks, stores, and promotions will all affect the probability of any event occurring by chance. In general terms, the larger the number of observations the more accurate the final result will be (or the less subject it will be to statistical error). At the end of the calculation one is left with a probability value for shops, weeks and promotions (column F, cells 38–40). This relates to the likelihood of the data evaluation occurring by chance. Followers of the roulette wheel would expect a single zero to appear 36 occasions out of every 1000 turns of the wheel. The model will tell you whether the difference between the two sales levels is due to chance or to a successful promotional effort.

The resulting value for promotions can be looked up in standard probability tables. Should the value of the promotions figure be greater than that on the probability chart this will indicate that the promotion is significantly better than the other item. In the example given, the value for the promotion's probability is 3.8 (cell F42) which falls well within the category of differences which could be explained by chance. Therefore, the conclusion one would draw is that the product on promotion does not offer any advantage over the standard item.

The advantages of this method are obvious: it enables the manager to carry out a large range of promotional research for extremely low outlay. It is also a very rapid means of determining response to any proposed action. Furthermore, the demonstration of the results of such a test do help in convincing the distribution outlets, particularly supermarkets and hypermarkets, of the value of your promotional planning. Finally, it ensures that the increasing amount of resource that is being put into the promotional area will be cost-effectively spent.

Proforma 6.1 Promotional analysis model

	A	B	C	D	E	F	G	H
4			PROMOTIONAL	ANALYSIS				
6			Store 1		Store 2		Store 3	
7			Product A	Product B	Product A	Product B	Product A	Product B
9	Sales (units)							
10	Week 1		450	300	450	420	34	67
11			LOG10(C10)	LOG10(D10)	LOG10(E10)	LOG10(F10)	LOG10(G10)	LOG10(H10)
12			C11*C11	D11*D11	E11*E11	F11*F11	G11*G11	H11*H11
13	Week 2		347	380	340	450	56	89
14			LOG10(C13)	LOG10(D13)	LOG10(E13)	LOG10(F13)	LOG10(G13)	LOG10(H13)
15			C14*C14	D14*D14	E14*E14	F14*F14	G14*G14	H14*H14
16			C11+D11+C14+D14	C16*C16	E11+F11+E14+F14	E16*E16	G11+H11+G14+H14	G16*G16
18	Total log sales							
19		AA11+AA14						
20	Corrected sales							
21		B18*B18/48						
23		AA12+AA15						
24	Net effect							
25		B23-B21						
26	Shop sum of squares							
27		AA16/4-B21						
28	Week squares							
29		(AA11+AA14)*(AA11-AA14)/48						
30	Sum of promotions squares		A	B	Net difference			
31			AA11+AA14-AB11-AB14	AA11+AA14-C31	D31-C31	E31*E31/48		
32	Residual square							
33		B25-B27+B29+F31						
36	PROBABILITY VALUES							
37						Prob.value-final		
38		SHOPS		11	B27/D38	B27/E44		
40		WEEKS		1	B29/D40	F40/E44		
42		PROMOTIONS		1	F31/D42	E42/E44		
44		RESIDUAL		34	B33/D44			

Proforma 6.1 *(concluded)*

	AA	AB		☐■
4				
6				
7				
9				
10				
11	SUM(C11:Z11)	C11+E11+G11+I11+L11+N11+P11+R11+T11+V11+X11+Z11		
12	SUM(C12:Z12)			
13				
14	SUM(C14:Z14)	C14+E14+G14+I14+L14+N14+P14+R14+T14+V14+X14+Z14		
15	SUM(C15:Z15)			
16	D16+F16+H16+J16+L16+N16+P16+R16+T16+V16+Z16			

This model is spread across 28 columns. The figures inserted on the spreadsheet for stores 4 to 12 are given in the full print out in Example 6.1. Since the calculations on lines 11,12, 14,15 and 16 of columns C-Z follow an easily discernible pattern this Table, in two parts, shows the data inserted for three stores and the calculations in lines 18-44 and in columns AA and AB. If you're in doubt about the sequence on the missing lines consult the line by line listings which must in any case be consulted for guidance on the degree of freedom concept used.

Example 6.1   Promotional analysis model

■□□□□□□

	A	B	C	D
4			PROMOTIONAL	ANALYSIS
6			Store 1	
7			Product A	Product B
9	Sales (units)			
10	Week 1		450	300
11			2.65321	2.47712
12			7.03954	6.13613
13	Week 2		347	380
14			2.54033	2.57978
15			6.45327	6.65528
16			10.2504	105.072
18	Total log sales			
19		103.466		
20	Corrected sales			
21		223.027		
23		236.848		
24	Net effect			
25		13.8217		
26	Shop sum of squares			
27		11.5750		
28	Week squares			
29		0.00724		
30	Sum of promotions squares		A	B
31			49.8881	53.5782
32	Residual square			
33		2.53764		
36	PROBABILITY VALUES			
37				
38		SHOPS		11
40		WEEKS		1
42		PROMOTIONS		1
44		RESIDUAL		34

Example 6.1 *(continued)*

	E	F	G	H	I	
4						□■□□□□□
6	Store 2		Store 3		Store 4	
7	Product A	Product B	Product A	Product B	Product A	
9						
10	450	420	34	67	560	
11	2.65321	2.62325	1.53148	1.82607	2.74819	
12	7.03954	6.88144	2.34543	3.33455	7.55254	
13	340	450	56	89	342	
14	2.53148	2.65321	1.74819	1.94939	2.53403	
15	6.40839	7.03954	3.05616	3.80012	6.42129	
16	10.4612	109.436	7.05513	49.7749	10.3921	
18						
19						
20						
21						
23						
24						
25						
26						
27						
28						
29						
30	Net difference					
31	3.69007	0.28368				
32						
33						
36						
37		Prob.value-final				
38	1.05227	155.085				
40	0.00724	0.09702				
42	0.28368	3.80083				
44	0.07464					

Example 6.1   *(continued)*

☐☐■■☐☐☐

	J	K	L	M
4				
6		Store 5		Store 6
7	Product B	Product A	Product B	Product A
9				
10	230	23	89	157
11	2.36173	1.36173	1.94939	2.19590
12	5.57776	1.85430	3.80012	4.82197
13	560	12	54	238
14	2.74819	1.07918	1.73239	2.37658
15	7.55254	1.16463	3.00119	5.64812
16	107.996	6.12269	37.4874	9.46568

☐☐☐☐■☐☐

	R	S	T	U
4				
6		Store 9		Store 10
7	Product B	Product A	Product B	Product A
9				
10	128	45	22	33
11	2.10721	1.65321	1.34242	1.51851
12	4.44033	2.73311	1.80210	2.30588
13	452	34	34	45
14	2.65514	1.53148	1.53148	1.65321
15	7.04976	2.34543	2.34543	2.73311
16	64.2512	6.05859	36.7066	6.70727

☐☐☐☐☐☐■

	Z	AA	AB
4			
6			
7	Product B		
9			
10	345		
11	2.53782	51.4384	26.8504
12	6.44053	116.793	
13	239		
14	2.37840	52.0279	26.7278
15	5.65678	120.055	2.73311
16	96.4715	938.407	47.8771

Example 6.1 *(concluded)*

	N	O	P	Q				☐☐☐■☐☐☐
4								
6		Store 7		Store 8				
7	Product B	Product A	Product B	Product A				
9								
10	230	1234	890	56				
11	2.36173	3.09132	2.94939	1.74819				
12	5.57776	9.55623	8.69890	3.05616				
13	340	1432	999	32				
14	2.53148	3.15594	2.99957	1.50515				
15	6.40839	9.95998	8.99739	2.26548				
16	89.5992	12.1962	148.748	8.01569				

	V	W	X	Y				☐☐☐☐☐■☐
4								
6		Store 11		Store 12				
7	Product B	Product A	Product B	Product A				
9								
10	44	23	236	234				
11	1.64345	1.36173	2.37291	2.36922				
12	2.70094	1.85430	5.63071	5.61318				
13	78	34	45	344				
14	1.89209	1.53148	1.65321	2.53656				
15	3.58002	2.34543	2.73311	6.43413				
16	44.9875	6.91933	47.8771	9.82199				

Note on statistical technique

This test is a standard analysis of variance:

1   The sales in each shop are converted to logarithms to remove bias.
2   A correction factor is produced by squaring the total sales and dividing by the total number of observations.
3   The squares of the individual sales are then totalled and the correction factor subtracted.
4   The model then derives the shops sums of squares by summing the squares of the totals, dividing by the number of observations per shop, and subtracting the correction factor.
5   The weeks and promotions sums of squares are found by finding the difference between the two weeks and dividing by the total of events.
6   The residual sum of squares is then found by subtracting the total of the sum of squares for shops, weeks and promotions from the corrected total sum of squares.
7   The degrees of freedom are derived by the number of sources minus one.
8   The mean square for each source is derived by dividing the source sum of squares by the source degrees of freedom.
9   The F value for each of the sources is found by dividing the source mean square by the residual mean square.
10 The significance of the F value can be arrived at by comparing the results with the appropriate tables.

Reference

1   K. Davies, C. Gilligan, C. Sutton, 'The Changing Competitive Structure of British Grocery Retailing', *Quarterly Review of Marketing*, Vol. 10, No.1, October 1984.

7 Sales productivity

One of the major problems confronting the majority of firms involved in direct sales of one form or another is how to control and maximise the effectiveness of their sales forces.

The costs and rewards of so doing are not small, as a substantial element of the firm's expenditure may be tied up in the maintenance of the field team. For example, in France the cost of a 35-strong hypermarket/supermarket sales force for a distributor of alcoholic drinks is 6 per cent of net sales price; the costs had been even higher for salesmen based in the major towns dealing with the traditional liquor shops (1). Such levels of cost are not unusual, and in consequence they form a crucial area of business management which has not been sufficiently controlled. It would appear that sales force costs are, throughout the economy, approximately triple the money expended on advertising (2).

As in other fields of activity, the organisation must set the objectives for the way in which it approaches the market place. All the major textbooks contain lists of ways in which the sales operation can be performed (3). Broadly they see a variety of job functions being carried out ranging from van selling (physical delivery of the product) to the sale of intellectual products such as religion (emotional delivery of the product).

Measurement of the output criteria is the first difficulty encountered when trying to analyse the effectiveness of the sales force. The van salesman may be measured on purely physical attributes such as the weight of coal removed from the back of the lorry. Within the evangelical organisation the parameter will be entirely different, consisting perhaps of redeemed souls.

Evaluating sales productivity

The first stage must be to analyse the variety of tasks that the organisation expects the sales force to complete, and to determine their relative importance.

In many firms this is not carried out in any systematic way and in consequence conflict can rapidly develop between sales force and commercial or marketing management.

Criteria for sales achievement

The elements of the sales achievement that are regarded as important will vary from organisation to organisation but can generally be included under:

1 Sales volume
2 Sales value
3 Gross margin
4 Callage rate
5 Repeat business
6 New business development
7 Credit control
8 Merchandising
9 Public relations
10 Record keeping

1 Sales volume   This tends to be the first measure that the majority of firms choose for evaluation. The reasoning is that the job of the sales representative, customer contact personnel, or whatever the department is named, is to provide the maximum potential inflow of work to maintain the existence of the organisation. It is particularly appropriate where the products are similarly priced, for differing values would make this an inappropriate measure.

2 Sales value   Where there is considerable variation in pricing between product lines the development of a value system will become more important as the number of product lines increases.

3 Gross margin analysis   Within the overall mix of products sold it is possible to combine the total gross margin and evaluate the sales force on this basis. One factor that must be taken into account however is the cost of distribution. From the two extremes – that of the salesmen who take a small number of large orders and those gaining a large number of small orders – there may not be an overall difference in gross margin. There would however be a substantial variation in the net return to the company if the costs of handling the two series of transactions were fully evaluated. Many companies overcome this particular problem by some variation of a minimum order system. This can limit the client to either a minimum order, or the order can be delivered differently depending on size. This is at best, however, an approximation and within a company with a widely differing product range where very high-margin products rub shoulders with low-margin items, it is often not the most profitable route for the organisation to follow.

The nature of the accounts that a salesman approaches will have an important influence on the gross profit. A sale to a supermarket may net considerable gross volume but low margin as the discount provided would have to be considerable.

4   Callage rate   Many firms judge the fitness of their sales force at least in part by the callage rate, the amount of sales calls that are completed during the day. This can obviously lead to anomalies within the system with sales representatives filling the day with unproductive calls just to achieve the necessary quota.

5   Repeat business   The stability of the company obviously depends on the nature of its customers and how they are maintained over time, and the degree of repeat business that is achieved. In many industries this is regarded as a prime sales task, though in some instances the repeat business generation moves away from the sales force to some other section such as a telephone sales division. The loss or gain of accounts over time can be a particularly important element in the development of repeat business to give a measure of the account stability; or the amount of business that can be reasonably relied upon in the next business period. Should there be a considerable loss of customer base from one period to another the degree of confidence in any forecasting process must be considerably blunted.

6   New business development   As a component of any sales representative routine the introduction of new products is often regarded as highly important by certain elements within the organisation. Time spent in this area, however, often has deleterious effects on the repeat business achievement as the development of new products is time consuming.

7   Credit control   Many sales forces are used to determine and monitor credit within their areas, collecting overdue payments and acting as an agent for the accounting and finance function. This is especially true within the export sphere where clients are outside the home territory legal framework which can often accentuate the credit control problems.

8   Merchandising   One of the sales force tasks in many companies is the control of local advertising activity. Frequently they are required to be present at national and local exhibitions; to control the work of sales demonstrators; to maintain shelves; to put up point-of-sale material and so on.

   In addition, regional sales representatives can be expected to supervise the activities of local distributors, dealing with a different market sector. All these tasks obviously consume large elements of time which must be considered in any evaluation of the sales performance.

9   Public relations   As well as the standard tasks, the representative often sorts out distribution problems and is normally the first to receive customer complaints, acting as the frontline individual between the organisation and the consumer.

10   Record keeping   The sales force are expected to maintain accurate records not only of total business but also of mileage, expenses, callage rate, administrative time, competitive activity, pricing, merchandising and so on.

In addition to these largely quantifiable output criteria there may also be a number of more intangible but important aspects of the sales representative's job. Thus knowledge of the company and its products are factors difficult to quantify, as are attitudes (how co-operative the individual is and so on), and the ability to overcome objections and effectively conclude the sale. In some firms, factors such as appearance and smartness may be regarded as important aspects of evaluating sales force performance.

Training

Many of these criteria are thought to be influenced by training. There are numerous psychological studies in existence commenting on the nature of the learning curve (4, 5). Thus any individual in any new environment takes in data rapidly in the early days and this uptake of information levels off over time (Figure 7.1).

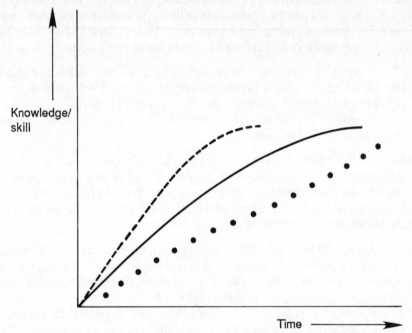

Figure 7.1   The learning curve – differences in knowledge acquisition

It is quite clear therefore that a new sales representative will be less effective than one who has been long established in the job. This problem is particularly acute in firms with high sales force turnover operating in areas of insurance/personal savings and office equipment. The training element in any evaluation of sales force ability is therefore crucial.

One of the most valuable concepts in this area is the idea of *effective head count* covering sales force development over time. It provides for the fact that a newly recruited salesman will be less effective than one who has worked for a period of time with that particular firm and that particular industry, often in a new part of the country. Management therefore has to consider the length of time needed to fully train the newcomer to maximum effectiveness. A number of studies suggest that upwards of twelve months is necessary for an individual to achieve maximum efficiency at a complex task (6, 7). Though the rate of improvement is not linear, the use of a training or the effective head count concept will provide the organisation with some form of in-built insurance to analyse sales force productivity. This will be especially true in cases of high sales force turnover, or sales force expansion.

It can be seen that the evaluation of the sales force can take place on a number of levels and it is important for the organisation to be clear as to what is actually involved.

For example, one sales force statistic much used for calculating output is the *callage rate*. This can be divided by the frequency of success to produce the 'batting average'. In the opinion of the author and several other commentators these concepts are practically meaningless for a number of reasons. The most important is that concentration on such criteria does not yield much useable data on the value of the sales individual to the organisation in terms of balance sheet return, which any control system should attempt to achieve. Such an approach is used by a number of companies to develop sales areas as profit centres whereby goods are 'sold' to the sales office at a transfer price (8). The office then controls the sales team as a distribution company, and is measured on the profitability that is generated. Most manufacturers in home markets would not be over-concerned if one of their overseas distributor's sales force spent every other day playing golf *provided* they were performing effectively. Similar leniency in the home market may cause major problems when dealing with directly employed personnel, but surely what is important to any organisation is largely the end result – and profit – achieved. Should this be obtained by working schedules regarded by the remainder of the firm as 'non-standard', so be it.

In the final analysis what should matter to the firm is the return on capital employed achieved by the sales representatives for the firm. Should tasks such as debt collection or merchandising be regarded as important to the organisation they should be allowed for, and accounted for, as part of the contribution made by the sales force. Should the sales force be required to be present at exhibitions, for example, suitable allowance should be made in the analysis of productivity when comparisons are made between representatives.

The organisation of sales activity

The way the firm organises sales activity will also have a considerable impact on any standardised approach for sales productivity.

1 Physical organisation

The first basic factor is the structural organisation of the sales force. The market is normally split into specific areas which are defined to:

(a) Ensure proper coverage of the market by assigning responsibilities
(b) Improve customer relations and the interest/motivation of the sales force

(c)   Provide a basis for comparison and evaluation

The most normal division is a geographical one, with the country divided into broadly equal areas within which the salesmen operate. Equality should determine the nature of these territories, with each containing broadly similar industry (sales revenue) potential; even so there will inevitably arise complications. A rural territory containing the same industrial potential as an urban area will naturally involve the salesmen in substantially different amounts of travelling. Secondly, the strength of the product or market share in each individual area will also have a bearing on the likely effectiveness of the sales representative. Thus maintenance of a 50 per cent market share in one area will inevitably mean double the sales achieved in another region with 25 per cent.

Geographical divisions can also be reflected in the number of accounts – for example hypermarkets may be much more prevalent in one part of the country – and relations with the trade. Within this category can be included the sales force expenses, especially those relating to entertainment. Various sections of the trade may develop attitudes towards entertainment totally different from another area.

Similar structural constraints exist in slightly different ways with other sales force organisational systems. Apart from geographical criteria, companies can divide the market place by product specialisation, customer specialisation, or a mixture of these methods in some form of national accounts system. Product specialisation obviously occurs within an extensive product range – for example within wholesalers. Customer specialisation is often a feature of the industrial sector with a combination of a high degree of required technical expertise and customers with widely differing needs and expectations. Thus Xerox divides its sales force to deal with differing levels of company requirements within the photocopying market. Lastly, national accounts systems have been developed to deal with major customers who contribute a major proportion of the company's turnover and therefore expect a greater level of service from the sales force in terms of advertising, promotion and price.

Sales support

The level of support that the sales force is receiving will have a major impact on the overall performance in any area.

1   Advertising

The effect of advertising on sales is one of the most hotly debated issues in the whole marketing arena (see Chapter 11 on media investment). Yet there is general agreement that advertising increases sales. Put another way, there is an effect of advertising on the demand curve of any product in question, which some authors describe as the advertising elasticity (9). The overall effect of advertising is to increase demand or make the sales representative's job easier: depending on the particular point of view prevailing in the company at the time. As a result, the sales area receiving a high level of media support should be more productive than one in which it is lacking. High levels of competitive advertising will however lower demand for the companies' products.

2 Pricing

Similar arguments can be applied to the effect of price (see Chapter 13 on price evaluation). Demand for the product will be determined to an extent by the price elasticity operating within the market and the current pricing position of the product within different market areas. In highly competitive environments this can make a substantial difference in the sales force performance, where a product has locally become over-priced. With the expansion of large national and multinational retailing and industrial organisations this is not such a substantial problem as price becomes more and more standardised.

3 Promotional expenditure

In addition to price and advertising there are the effects of promotional activity to consider. Within each area the amount of money being spent by the competition can vary considerably with effects on resulting sales. Elasticities due to the effects of promotion are probably much more varied than those of price and advertising, though it is an area which has received scant attention.

The development of information in these areas will enable the organisation to acquire greater control over existing potential in one particular area compared with another. From that it should be able to produce a control system to evaluate the return the individual is *actually* making rather than one which may be fortuitously happening due to changes in the external environment.

The sales productivity analysis model

The model aims to evaluate the performance of different sales force personnel, taking relevant factors into consideration to arrive at an objective assessment of their effectiveness and the rate of return on the investment which the company is making. In consequence all the inputs are value related.

Industry factors

The first range of data relates to the background against which the sales force is working – industry factors.

1 Industry potential   For any given territory there will be a total potential which will be arrived at by studying industry figures or maket research and netting off any involvement of national accounts structures. The important question to answer at the initial stage is the period over which the sales productivity is to be analysed. Most of the sales statistics available are for an annual period and this will largely overcome any seasonality factor which might produce anomalous results when studied over a shorter time period. For the purposes of the model the figure should be entered in value terms, not volume.

2   Market share   Again this would be available from rough calculation (company sales/total industry) or from audit data of some description.

3   Total number of accounts   In many industries there will be a distinction between total accounts and total 'available' accounts. To take an example from the catering trade one could include all bars, restaurants and cafes within the account base for a liquor salesman. Should the smaller customers be dealt with by a distributor/wholesaler these should not be double counted within the sales force territory. Similar comments apply to the interaction of national accounts.

4   Company advertising   Regional breakdowns for television, radio, press, will often be available, though regional poster expenditure will be more difficult to obtain.

5   Competitive advertising

6   Advertising elasticity   This is the measure of how responsive the particular product area and product type is to advertising. Within the consumer goods section there is some evidence that for major products elasticities lie between 1/3 and 1/8. Low levels of advertising will be disregarded by the model as having no effect on sales.

7   Regional price position   It is possible to determine for each region the relative price position on a base 100. Obviously for a large percentage of companies this will be standard particularly if major chains of retailers exist throughout the country, but in several markets there may be considerable price variation.

8   Price elasticity   Estimates of this can be achieved from the use of audit data over time or by past experience of the effects of price rises in the market.

9   Competitive promotional expenditure   Input in this area will largely flow from market intelligence as published sources are inadequate.

10   Company promotional expenditure

11   Promotional elasticity   This in common with the advertising elasticity is the degree to which expenditure on promotions can shift the demand curve. The promotion elasticities can be determined from internal company research or 'guesstimated' with industry averages of 1/5 to 1/20 depending on the effectiveness of the promotion.

These eleven factors will determine the total background against which the efforts of the local sales representative can be judged. Again it should be stressed that this analysis will be in terms of value and not volume.

Personnel factors

Next to be considered are those points which concern the sales representative and the nature of the business that he is generating:

1   Level of training – effective head count concept   The average percentage level achieved during the time period under consideration should be entered. Should the individual have joined the firm at the beginning of the year and the training period for full effectiveness is twelve months, he could be considered as 50 per cent effective over the period.

The rate of return on sales force training is outside the scope of this model, but it should be an important consideration for any company with a major sales force or planning significant sales force expansion.

2   Days in field   This input figure is used in the final analysis of the productivity figure to yield a per day assessment of the individual's performance. To arrive at this figure some of the following calculations will need to be made:

Total days in year	365
Weekends (unless worked)	−104
Public holidays	−10
Company holidays	−20
Sales meetings	−12
Exhibitions	− 5
Varied support work	−10
Illness	− 4
Total effective year	*200*

Should the sales representative be involved in significant non-selling activity such as merchandising, supervising distributor sales forces and so on this will be clearly apparent and suitable adjustments can then be made.

3   Total account base   At the point at which the analysis is performed there will be a mixture of old accounts and new clients, figures concerning which are both important for the calculation of the stability of the customer base and for the future development of the business. This factor has considerable implications for marketing policy. Should the account base be rapidly changing a large effort will need to be devoted to gaining new outlets; should there be substantial stability, emphasis can then be placed on expanding business within the outlet.

4   Customers lost in the accounting period   For most practical purposes the model calculates on an annual basis – but obviously shorter time periods can be used.

5   Customers gained

6   Total value of orders obtained   As has been stated earlier, the model functions for the widest use on value only; all sales data should be converted to this.

7   Average gross profit margin   There is no short cut way of producing this as each company will have different product mixes and differing delivery costs. For example, the distribution of perfume (high margin, low mass) will be very different from a steel stockholder's business (low margin, high mass). Even within these broad categories product mix will have considerable effects. The concentration of the sales effort in certain areas is naturally a feature of the overall company objectives, nevertheless over-concentration on one particular line would have significant effects on the organisational profitability in other areas such as inventory levels.

8 Expense levels These are one of the standard input items that can show considerable variations due to working environment: rural/urban split and so on. Ideally the figures should include an allocation of the office overhead, in addition to the standard operating expenses, such as car, entertaining, and other travel.

9 Salary level This can vary considerably within the sales force and is quite often not included in any consideration of sales force productivity.

Using the sales productivity analysis model

The *Go To* column in Listing 7.1 tells you the cell number and the cursor position. The next column specifies the spreadsheet option (LO = Label Option; VO = Value Option). The *Type In* column gives you instructions within the inverted commas which you must type in or asks you to supply the necessary data. These commas are not part of the instructions supplied here and should not be typed in. Beware however that some spreadsheets, the *Lotus 1-2-3* for example, enter the Label Option by using the inverted-comma key. Under the *Type In* column the symbols * = multiply and / = divide. R in the *Return* column instructs you to commit the information to memory by pressing the Return key.
Remember: When you have finished, save your model.

Listing 7.1 Sales productivity analysis model

Go To		Type In	Return

The model is designed so that if advertising on promotion is very small in relation to the total market turnover the effects of either or both are disregarded.

C1/F1	LO	"Sales Productivity	
		Analysis"	R
A4/	LO	"Industry	R
B4		factors"	R
D4	LO	"Area A"	R

By replicating the formula from column D across the spreadsheet all

Go To		Type In	Return

salesmen can be compared. This listing gives column D only; to continue across the spreadsheet into columns E, F etc. simply substitute 'D' in the calculations with the appropriate alternative letter (see Proforma 7.1).

A6/	LO	"Potential	R
B6		$ mill"	R
D6	VO	Insert estimated value of area sales potential	R
A8/	LO	"Market	R
B8		share %"	R
D8	VO	Enter estimated market share in %	R

Listing 7.1 *(continued)*

Go To		Type In	Return
D9	VO	"IF D6>D15*15	
		THEN0ELSED6"	R
A10/	LO	"No	R
B10		accounts"	R

A10/B10 refers to total number of accounts in region.

Go To		Type In	Return
D10	VO	Insert total no. of accounts in area	R
A12/	LO	"Company adv	R
B12		$ mill" for company advertising	R
D12	VO	Insert value of company advertising in area	R
A14/	LO	"Compet adv	
B14		$ mill" for competitive advertising	R

Note that both A12/B12 and A14/B14 refer to advertising in the region.

Go To		Type In	Return
D14	VO	Insert value of competitive advertising in area	R
D15	VO	"D12+D14"	R
A16/	LO	"Adv.	R
B16		elasticity" for advertising elasticity	R
D16	VO	Insert estimated value for advertising elasticity	R
A18/	LO	"Co. prom.	R
B18	LO	$ mill" for company promotion	R

Go To		Type In	Return
D18	VO	Insert value of expenditure on company promotion in the area	R
A20/	LO	"Compet.	R
B20		prom. $ mill" for competitive promotional expenditure for area	R
D20	VO	Insert value of competitive promotion in the area	R
D21	VO	"D18+D20"	R
A22/	LO	"Prom.	R
B22		elasticity" for promotional elasticity	R
D22	VO	Insert promotional elasticity value	R
A24/	LO	"Price	R
B24		position"	R
D24	VO	Insert value for price position	R

Note: Average price in market = 100. A 5% price premium would therefore be 105 and a 5% discount would be 95.

Go To		Type In	Return
A26/	LO	"Price	R
B26		elasticity"	R
D26	VO	Insert value of price elasticity	R

Note: If a 1% increase in relative price leads to a 2% drop in sales, elasticity is 2; a 1% increase in price leading to a 3% drop in sales is an elasticity of 3.

Listing 7.1 *(continued)*

Go To		Type In	Return
A29/	LO	"Historic	R
B29		potential"	R
D29	VO	"D6*D8/100"	R
A31/	LO	"Market	R
B31		adv. eff" for market advertising effect	R

Note: This refers to the theoretical expansion of the market taking account of overall advertising expenditure and advertising elasticity. The model calculates this for you.

Go To		Type In	Return
D31	VO	"D9*(D12+D14)*D16* (D8/100)+D6"	R
A33/	LO	"Share of	R
B33		voice"	R

This is the effect of the amount of money the company is spending on advertising in relation to the competition.

Go To		Type In	Return
D33	VO	"D31−D9*(D12/D15)"	R
A35/	LO	"Revised	R
B35		share"	R
D35	VO	"D33*D8/100"	R
A37/	LO	"Promotion	R
B37		effect"	R
D37	VO	"IFD6 > D21*20THEN0 ELSED6*D21*22−1+ D6"	R
A39/	LO	"Share of	R
B39		promotion"	R
D39	VO	"D37−D21*(D18/D20)"	R
A41/	LO	"Revised	R
B41		share"	R
D41	VO	"D39*D8/100"	R

Go To		Type In	Return
A43/	LO	"Net prom/	R
B43		adv" for net promotion on advertising effect calculated by the model	R
D43	VO	"D35+D41−D29"	R
A45/	LO	"Price	R
B45		effect"	R
D45	VO	"D26*(100/D24)−1"	R
A47/	LO	"Net	R
B47		market"	R
D47	VO	"D43*D45"	R
A50/	LO	"Sales	R
B50/		force	R
C50		factors"	R
A52/	LO	"Level of	R
B52		training"	R
D52	VO	Insert value for level of training	R

Note: 1.0 indicates that salesmen are fully trained.

Go To		Type In	Return
A54/	LO	"Days in	R
B54		the field"	R
D54	VO	Insert total days of representative in the field for the area	R
A56/	LO	"Total	R
B56/		account	R
C56		base"	R
D56	VO	Insert total numbers of accounts at end of accounting period	R
A58/	LO	"Customers	R
B58		lost"	R

Listing 7.1 *(concluded)*

Go To		Type In	Return
D58	VO	Insert total number of customers lost during accounting period	R
A60/	LO	"Customers	R
B60		gained"	R
D60	VO	Insert total number of customers gained during accounting period	R
A62/	LO	"Total	R
B62/		order value	R
C62		$mill"	R
D62	VO	Insert total value of orders gained during accounting period	R
A64/	LO	"Gross	R
B64		profit %"	R
D64	VO	Insert figure for average profit margin for orders taken	R
A66/	LO	"Expenses	R
B66		$000"	R
D66	VO	Insert value of expenses in $000 in accounting period	R
A68/	LO	"Salary	R
B68		$000"	R
D68	VO	Insert salary costs during accounting period in $000	R
A70/	LO	"Effective	R
B70		days"	R

Note: This is a measure of the number of days in the field by the level of expertise the salesman has and is calculated by the model.

Go To		Type In	Return
D70	VO	"D52*D54"	R
A72/	LO	"G.P. per	R
B72		day" for gross profit per day	R
D72	VO	"D62*D64*10000/D70"	R
A74/	LO	"Net profit/	R
B74		day $" for net profit per day	R
D74	VO	"D72−(D66+D68/D70)"	R
A76/	LO	"Total	R
B76		prod" for total productivity	R
D76	VO	"D62*D64/(D47*D64*D52*D54)"	R
A78/	LO	"Total	R
B78		prof" for total annual profit in $	R
D78	VO	"D62*D64*10000−(D66+D68)"	R
A80/	LO	"Net	R
B80		prod"	R
D80	VO	"D78/(D47*D64*D52*D54)"	R
A82/	LO	"Prof. per	R
B82		account" for profitability per account ($)	R
D82	VO	"D78/D56"	R
A84/	LO	"Account	R
B84		stability" is a measure of how many customers are gained and are being lost as calculated by the model	R
D84	VO	"(D60−D58)/D56"	R

Note: The lower this figure is the more stable the account base will be.

Proforma 7.1 Sales productivity analysis model

A/B/C	D	E	F
	Productivity	Analysis	
Sales	Area A	Area B	Area C
4 Industry factors	5	5	5
6 Potential $ mill	20	30	10
8 Market share %			
9	IFD6>D15*15THENOELSED6	IFE6>E15*15THENOELSEE6	IFF6>F15*15THENOELSEF6
10 No.accounts	2000	3000	4000
12 Company adv $ mill	0.1	0.1	0.1
14 Compet adv $ mill	1	1.5	1.8
15	D12+D14	E12+E14	F12+F14
16 Adv. elasticity	1.125	1.125	1.125
18 Co. promotion $ mill	0.05	0.05	0.05
20 Compet.prom.$mill	0.25	0.3	0.3
21	D18+D20	E18+E20	F18+F20
22 Prom. elasticity	1.2	1.2	1.2
24 Price position	105	108	110
26 Price elasticity	2	2	2
29 Historic potential	D6*D8/100	E6*E8/100	F6*F8/100
31 Market adv. eff	D9*(D12+D14)*D16*(D8/100)>D6	E9*(E12+E14)*E16*(E8/100)+E6	F9*(F12+F14)*F16*((F8/100)+F6
33 Share of Voice	D31-D9*(D12/D15)	E31-E9*(E12/E15)	F31-F9*(F12/F15)
35 Revised share	D33*D8/100	E33*E8/100	F33*F8/100
37 Promotion effect	§§	§§	§§
39 Share of promotion	D37-D21*(D18/D20)	E37-E21*(E18/E20)	F37-F21*(F18/F20)
41 Revised share	D39*D8/100	E39*E8/100	F39*F8/100
43 Net prom/adv	D35*D41-D29	E35*E41-E29	F35*F41-F29

A/B/C	D	E	F
45 Price effect	D26*(100/D24)-1	E26*(100/E24)-1	F26*(100/F24)-1
47 Net market	D43*D45	E43*E45	F43*F45
50 Salesforce factors			
52 Level of training	0.8	1	1
54 Days in field	205	220	186
56 Total account base	300	250	340
58 Customers lost	35	56	79
60 Customers gained	65	54	120
62 Total order value $mill	0.7	1.2	1.5
64 Gross profit %	30	30	30
66 Expenses $000	12	23	22
68 Salary $000	20	25	30
70 Effective days	D52*D54	E52*E54	F52*F54
72 G.P. per day	D62*D64*10000/D70	E62*E64*10000/E70	F62*F64*10000/F70
74 Net profit/day	D72-(D66+D68/D70)	E72-(E66+E68/E70)	F72-(F66+F68/F70)
76 Total prod	D62*D64/(D47*D64*D52*D54)	E62*E64/(E47*E64*E52*E54)	F62*F64/(F47*F64*F52*F54)
78 Total prof	D62*D64*10000-(D66+D68)	E62*E64*10000-(E66+E68)	F62*F64*10000-(F66+F68)
80 Net prod	D78/(D47*D64*D52*D54)	E78/(E47*E64*E52*E54)	F78/(F47*F64*F52*F54)
82 Prof. per account $	D78/D56	E78/E56	F78/F56
84 Account stability	(D60-D58)/D56	(E60-E58)/E56	(F60-F58)/F56

§§ The formula for these cells are as follows:
D37 IFD6>D21*20THENOELSED06*D21*22-1+D6
E37 IFE6>E21*20THENOELSEE6*E21*22-1+E6
F37 IFF6>F21*20THENOELSEF6*F21*22-1+F6

Example 7.1 Sales productivity analysis model

A/B/C		D	E	F
1	Sales	Productivity	Analysis	
		Area A	Area B	Area C
4	Industry factors			
6	Potential $ mill	5	5	5
8	Market share %	20	30	10
9		5	5	5
10	No.accounts	2000	3000	4000
12	Company adv $ mill	0.1	0.1	0.1
14	Compet adv $ mill	1	1.5	1.8
15		1.1	1.6	1.9
16	Adv elasticity	1.125	1.125	1.125
18	Co promotion $ mill	0.05	0.05	0.05
20	Compet prom $mill	0.25	0.3	0.3
21		0.3	0.35	0.35
22	Prom elasticity	1.2	1.2	1.2
24	Price position	105	108	110
26	Price elasticity	2	2	2
29	Historic potential	1	1.5	0.5
31	Market adv eff	6.2375	7.7	6.06875
33	Share of voice	5.78295	7.3875	5.80559
35	Revised share	1.15659	2.21625	0.58056
37	Promotion effect	5.8	6.1	6.1

A/B/C	D	E	F
39 Share of promotion	5.74	6.04167	6.04167
41 Revised share	1.148	1.8125	0.60417
43 Net prom/adv	2.30459	4.02875	1.18473
45 Price effect	0.90476	0.85185	0.81818
47 Net market	2.08511	3.43190	0.96932
50 Salesforce factors			
52 Level of training	0.8	1	1
54 Days in the field	205	220	186
56 Total account base	300	250	340
58 Customers lost	35	56	79
60 Customers gained	65	54	120
62 Total order value $mill	0.7	1.2	1.5
64 Gross profit %	30	30	30
66 Expenses $000	12	23	22
68 Salary $000	20	25	30
70 Effective days	164	220	186
72 G.P. per day	1280.49	1636.36	2419.35
74 Net profit/day	1268.37	1613.25	2397.19
76 Total prod	0.00205	0.00159	0.00832
78 Total prof	209968	359952	449948
80 Net prod	20.4673	15.8916	83.1880
82 Prof per account $	699.893	1439.81	1323.38
84 Account stability	0.1	-0.008	0.12059

127

Sales productivity analysis commentary

Example 7.1 shows the model applied to three salesmen. In each case the industrial potential is similar at $5 million (D6–F6). The market share in each area, however, differs as does the level of company and competitive advertising, company and competitive promotion and the relative price position in each area. The effect of company promotion and advertising is to both expand the market and increase brand share; competitive activity will tend to lower brand share. Similarly, the price position in each area will affect the level of demand according to the price elasticity operating for that particular product. The model will only take account of relatively high levels of advertising and promotional expenditure –low levels are ignored as being unlikely to have any significant effect.

The combination of these factors both negative and positive will create a *theoretical* available market against which the sales force performance can be judged. This is the effect of all those factors mentioned in the chapter which will either expand or contract the available market. In the example given, the effect of high advertising and promotional expenditure is to increase the theoretical size of the market from that historically recorded. Lower levels of advertising expenditure and an adverse price position may reduce the available market.

The sales force factors such as training, the number of days in the field, total account base, total order value, and changes in account base provide a series of factors which can be used for the evaluation of sales force performance. These include standard analyses of total profit, gross and net profit per day. In addition two indexes are provided: sales productivity and account stability.

The index of sales productivity provides an assessment of the individual in respect of the total profit that is being generated by the sales representative in relation to the total theoretical industry potential, the number of days in the field, and the level of training the individual has achieved. For an individual who is achieving a high level of sales from a small potential the productivity analysis will yield a higher figure (Area C) than lower orders from a larger territory (Area B). It can be seen that the lower level of training of the Area A representative offsets his lower gross profit achievement compared with Area B, together with greater sales in proportion to the theoretical market size than in the other areas.

The account stability provides a measure of the ability of the representative to hold onto accounts – the higher the figure, the lower the account turnover will be.

References

1   Remy Associés – personal communication, 1984.

2   W.J. Stanton, R.H. Buskirk, *Management of the Sales Force*, Richard D. Irwin, 6th edition, 1967.

3   R.N. McMurry, 'The Mystique of Super-Salesmanship', *Harvard Business Review*, No. 2, 1961.

4 A.D. Baddeley in P.C. Dodwell (ed.), *New Horizons in Psychology*, Penguin, 2nd edition, 1972.

5 D.E. Broadbent, *Perception and Communication*, Pergamon, 1958.

6 J.B. Biggs, *Information and Human Learning*, Cassell, 1968.

7 E.A. Lunzer, J.F. Morris, *Development in Human Learning*, Staples 1968.

8 E. Korn, *Profit Centre Sales Management*, Business Books, London, 1968.

9 P. Kotler, *Marketing Management*, Prentice Hall, 4th edition, 1980.

8 Packaging dilemmas

'If business is a war, packaging is a minefield.'

In any business the marketing problems created by packaging are very considerable. The history of the discipline is littered with examples of packaging successfully working against all predictions contrasted with expensively designed containers which have proved to be dramatic failures. Immense opportunities can be created by good packaging, opening new markets and reaching new consumers. Lord Lever saw that the standard block of soap would be far more appealing when individually wrapped, and from that initial discovery grew the multinational Unilever.

The many faces of packaging

Approaches to the problem vary from the 'blaze a trail' strategy – either dying or gloriously succeeding in crossing the minefield; or 'let's probe the ground' – a cautious forward exploratory process which tends to lead to minimal change.

Without a clear view of why the packaging should be changed, the result of the exercise will tend to be haphazard and ill-defined. In addition changes to packaging can often be considered total solutions when fundamental changes in the marketing mix are in reality necessary, and in consequence the concentration on packaging masks the underlying malaise.

In a company with which the author worked, the final days before bankruptcy were filled with discussions on whether the company logo should be round, oval or square and it was perhaps a consolation to the workforce that there appeared to be as many pack designs as there were creditors when the company collapsed.

The role of packaging should not be underestimated. According to one writer, packaging in Europe accounts for around 2.25 per cent of Gross Domestic Product, significantly higher than the amount of money spent on media expenditure (1).

What the packaging is achieving is therefore of major importance to the majority of companies, apart from those producing basic industrial commodities. Coal is coal, and no one would claim that attractive packaging could gain new, large industrial consumers. However, when one considers the domestic buyer, smart packaging may enable a coal producer to widen distribution – selling for example through garage forecourts; and also to gain new end-users who will carry clean, bright, coloured plastic sacks across woollen carpets which they would not do if the product was only available in large, dirty, jute bags.

Packaging also affects the whole question of long-term product survival, and is one avenue open to the manufacturer to maintain sales levels in a changing market (see Chapter 1 on product viability).

One feature of the packaging or re-packaging exercise is meeting the objectives set by the organisation in this whole area. The issues that confront the firm tend to receive scant attention. For example, it is interesting how seldom marketing textbooks comment on the role of packaging in the marketing mix. Indeed, in several major textbooks, there is no index entry on packaging. Because of this lack of attention, the objectives that tend to be set will often be confused and occasionally contradictory.

Packaging criteria

One can identify three main elements of packaging that need to be considered: brand-related, product-related, and consumer-related. To give a simple example of a fizzy drink, the nature of the product demands that it be contained within an airtight, relatively tough, exterior layer: glass, tin, or thick plastic, rather than a polythene bag. The consumer requires not only a hygienic, pleasant product but also an increasing quantity of information about calorie levels, contents, volume, and manufacturer's name.

Whereas the nature of the container and the information on it are largely predetermined, the demands of the brand may be quite different. First, it is held that the brand name should bear some relevance to the product type – *Softlan*, *Downy*, and *Comfort* for fabric conditioners have the right connotation – and should be easily remembered. There are of course numerous exceptions to this ideal – Japanese car names such as *Sunny, Cherry, Violet* – nevertheless, the underlying concept appears sound. For example, would the washing powder *Tide* have been so successful if it had been called *Swamp*?

Secondly, the use of different colours is held to have a fundamental effect on consumer attitudes (2). Some of the associations put forward are:

Blue: coolness, distinction
Red: heat, excitement
Purple/gold: royalty, richness
Orange: warmth, movement

There is a strong association between the interpretation of colour and culture. White and black have reversed implications in many Eastern cultures – black being a colour of rejoicing and white a colour of mourning among the Chinese.

Thirdly, numbers may or may not have consumer connotations. A car manufacturer such as Renault produces models typed as 5, 9, 11, 12, 14, 16, 18, but never a Renault 13 which would probably be considered unlucky.

Shape can also have important influences on pack design. Over and above the functional aspects – cans produced in a certain way, meaning that if you want a can it must be cylindrical – there are behavioural and traditional factors to be considered. The introduction of table wine in lined paper containers has been slow not only because of the technical problems associated with it but also as a result of consumer resistance. Wine should come in bottles not in orange juice containers: or so the consumer thinks. Finally, one can define a number of interrelated social factors which may have an impact on the buying decision:

1 Cultural group
2 Social class
3 Economic circumstances
4 Age/'life-style'
5 Experience: education, learning, attitudes

These factors interact with other influences to produce the final buying decision, of which the most important are the consumer's tastes or preferences and his (or her) particular 'needs'. Hypothetical structures which explain consumer buying behaviour have been widely developed. Thus Maslow, the most quoted author on the subject suggests that a 'hierarchy of needs' exists (see Figure 8.1) (3).

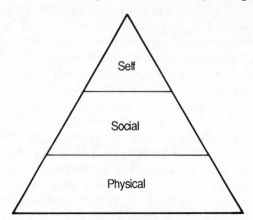

Figure 8.1   Hierarchy of needs (after Maslow)

In common with the use of colour as a means to differentiate humanity, psychological divisions can, at *best*, only offer the broadest divisions, which can provide far from hard and fast guidelines to aid the practical manager attempting to produce suitable packaging. Other approaches can be found in the wealth of psychological/philosophical literature produced since the early 1900s. Any reader in this field will be deluged by vast collections of often contradictory information none of which is much help. Freud, Jung, Adler, Skinner and Pavlov do not, for example, provide much insight into the worldwide success of

Coca-Cola. The Coca-Cola concept has proved acceptable to people of widely differing cultures, living in very different social and economic circumstances.

Research on the broad field of packaging design tends to be limited due to the difficulties of separating pack, product, price, advertising, and promotion. Yet given the importance of packaging to large consumer goods firms this is somewhat surprising.

Minimising the problems of change

Specific studies abound as each manufacturer (specifically within the consumer goods sector, but many industrial producers face similar problems) researches the acceptability of his own pack within the market place, regarding it as an essential part of the interaction between the consumer and himself. Extensive reading of these case studies tends to suggest a number of guidelines that should be followed to minimise the problems that packaging changes can cause.

The first and obvious factor is when an important change is made to the product which will be perceived by the end user, creating an improvement which should be signalled to the consumer. The degree of alteration to the product will vary from minimal 'cosmetic' alterations to major changes. Obviously the introduction of new products can be considered in the light of major changes in the product range.

It is important to realise that changes in the product do not completely alter its nature. Thus a whistle will always remain a whistle even if it has a new metal case and gold mouthpiece.

Secondly, over a period of time a large amount of money will have been spent in building up the consumer's familiarity with the product. Dramatic changes in the structure of the pack may therefore negate this investment. Finally, if the packaging is regarded as purely a cosmetic device it will need to be continually updated with resulting high costs that the company will incur. This is one of the key elements that any organisation must consider: the cost/benefit ratio involved in any packaging exercise.

The updating of the pack can also have important implications for consumer usage and the distribution path that is being chosen. There are a number of examples of packaging successes that have introduced a new application method increasing the *convenience* of the item. The example of Lux toilet soap shows where the introduction of individually wrapped soap superseded the hand-cut block soap.

Disasters also occur: the DeLorean sports car suffered from the fact, apparently forgotten by the designers, that passenger doors opening sideways rather than upwards (the gull wing door) are necessary in modern parking lots with narrow distances separating cars. In consequence several owners (accompanied by the obligatory blonde personal assistant) were unable to get into their extremely expensive motor cars until the neighbouring cars departed.

The nature of the pack can also lead to either its easy acceptance within the trade or considerable resistance. Thus a particular variety of Metaxa, the Greek brandy, has failed to get into wide distribution for the simple fact that the bottle is too elongated for the average shelf. In contrast the provision of specialised spice racks by distribution companies has ensured the considerable expansion of spice distribution in a number of world markets.

Technical reliability of the packaging and the cost constraints under which the whole project goes forward also need to be evaluated. Will, for example, the effects of excessive heat in export markets cause any problems? Could a less expensive material be used to gain the same effect?

Production problems also require careful analysis. An example of this occurred in the production of frosted bottles by a distiller in Europe. The frosting process led to the production of large amounts of fine glass which acted as an abrasive within the filling line area with a resulting large increase in the cost of repair.

The interaction of consumer, distribution, technical and production factors means that the final decision on a particular packaging development will never be objective, relying as it does on the skills of the manager to interpret the importance of the various elements and to determine how the problems can best be overcome.

An outline for change

Any packaging proposal should therefore pass through a number of stages:

1 The development of a detailed rationale as to why the packaging should be changed.
2 The production of a design brief which should include all costing implications.
3 Appraisal of the design proposals that are put forward by the external or internal team, via the use of a structured assessment of the various factors relevant to that particular product.
4 The development of a research programme to test the pack effectiveness, and its evaluation.

The packaging model

The structuring of the decisions necessary to appraise and therefore minimise the problems that may be encountered with new packaging are ideally suited for spreadsheet analysis, as the factors can be listed and multiplied in the weighted fashion that the manager requires.

1 Consumer elements

(a) Mandatory information The amount of information that is required on the pack will vary from country to country. In some an EPOS or bar code will be necessary together with full ingredients, contents, and the manufacturer's name.

(b)   Visibility   The demands of a particular product will vary: for a consumer product it may be that high visibility is required, the ability to differentiate your pack from others from the end of a supermarket aisle.

(c)   Distinctiveness   This may be different from the concept of visibility – the level to which the product stands out from its competitors. It also covers the question of memorability – will the package be remembered by the consumer?

(d)   Display   It is important that the package offers the ability to provide effective mass displays in certain product fields.

(e)   Apparent size   It may be important that the package gives the impression of size consistent with other products in the same area. In the toy market for example the size of packaging is often regarded as synonymous with price, the larger the item, the higher the price.

(f)   Brand identity   The high visibility of brand name and logo is normally considered as one of the more important aspects of packaging development.

(g)   Information   There are a number of items of information that may or may not be important to include on the pack. Full and clear instructions in the case of many products will be crucial, as part of the underlying selling story that should be as self-evident as possible.

(h)   Consistency   There are two important elements that are included under the heading of consistency. The package should reflect as closely as possible any media or promotional investment, ideally by expanding or complementing the media theme. Secondly, is the package consistent with the company 'style'? This may involve the use of particular colours or photographic techniques, but in certain instances will also be required to reflect 'integrity', 'responsibility' or other attitudes that are important for the company's relationship with its consumers.

(i)   Simplicity   The fewer the elements of design on the package, the more effective it is likely to be. Examples include the simplicity of the pack design of Coca-Cola, Colgate toothpaste and McDonald's stores.

(j)   Convenience   It is important that the packaging can be opened and closed easily by the consumer and the in-use product can be stored without difficulty wherever it is in use.

2   Distribution factors

The co-operation of the retailer and wholesaler is crucial to the acceptance of any new introduction and their views in certain areas will be very important (some of these factors are relevant to the development of totally new products – see Chapter 9 on product diversification).

(a)   Display   The crucial factor of shelf display has already been commented on in the case of Metaxa. It is mainly important for non-standard products which will not fit into the normal retail space available.

(b) Packing standardisation The development of different pack styles may make it difficult for the product to be included in a standard outer carton.

(c) Handling The packaging should meet the criteria of all stages of the distribution process. Thus the outer packaging should be designed with the requirements of palletisation and containerisation in mind.

(d) Retailer information The pack should give all the retail information necessary, such as whether a special offer is being made and the date of its completion. It should also give the retailer some date information to allow correct stock rotation, and contain the instructions for the correct opening of the carton.

(e) Simplicity The outer carton again should have the minimum information necessary for the retailer. The use of many colours in the outer cartons for example may need to be justified when a one- or two-colour approach may be as effective.

3 Production factors

The most simple design can easily cause problems in the filling, capping, printing or assembly. These problems are far more easily dealt with before they occur as corrective treatment will be extremely expensive both in money and time.

(a) Efficiency Does the design use the most efficient machinery possible or must it be produced on a slower and therefore more expensive machine?

(b) Shape Will the package pass through the current system without causing breakage, and at a satisfactory speed? This again will be a problem with non-standard packaging for those associated with standard designs will have been previously encountered.

(c) Strength Will the pack stand up to the rigours of mechanical mishandling and can it cope with the effects of heat, moisture, and sunlight? The last is particularly relevant in the choice of printing inks as some will fade badly on exposure to sunlight. Another consideration that is important in this context is whether this packaging will last the life of the product without degradation of the contents. Thus carbonated drinks can be kept in the new PET (plastic derivative) bottles provided the shelf life is reasonably short. For wine or other products with a slower rotation, this packaging would be inadequate.

(d) Components It is important for certain operations that the components can be easily pre-assembled, and that the sealing operations can be easily achieved mechanically. The interaction of the filling mechanism with the system chosen for sealing the pack is another vital factor in any assessment of whether the product can be easily produced.

(e) Cost effectiveness The relevance of this item will obviously vary from product to product. Within mass market items questions such as the nature of the

material used become crucial, and whether savings can be achieved by the use of differing material or a thinner container wall.

(f)   Print surface   The nature of the surface available for the print will also vary in importance from product to product and the degree of print finish necessary. Surface irregularities may also deserve consideration and the ability of the printer to achieve correct register, the combination of colours in a multi-colour process.

Using the packaging model

In Listing 8.1 the *Go To* column tells you the cell number and the cursor position. The next column specifies the spreadsheet option (LO = Label Option; VO = Value Option). The *Type In* column gives you instructions within the inverted commas which you must type in or asks you to supply the necessary data. These commas are not part of the instructions supplied here but beware that some spreadsheets, the *Lotus 1-2-3* for example, enter the Label Option by using the inverted-comma key. Under the *Type In* column the symbols * = multiply and / = divide. R in the *Return* column instructs you to commit the information to memory by pressing the Return key.
Remember: When you have finished, save your model.

Listing 8.1   Packaging model

Go To		Type In	Return
C4/	LO	"PACKAGING	R
D4/		DEVELOPMENT"	R
E4			R
A7	LO	"AREAS"	R
C7	LO	"VALUE"	R
E7	LO	"POOR"	R
F7	LO	"AVERAGE"	R
G7	LO	"EXCELLENT"	R
A10	LO	"CONSUMER"	R
A12/	LO	"Mandatory	R
B12		Information"	R
C12	VO	Enter value for importance given to Mandatory Information for a particular product	R

Go To		Type In	Return
Note: The values assigned in cells C12–C30 must together add up to 25.			
E12 to G12	VO	Insert weighting for likelihood of the event taking place: whether the prospects are Poor, Average or Excellent of the packaging fulfilling the end in view in the area of Mandatory Information	R
The values assigned in E12–G12 must add up to 1.			
H12	VO	"IFSUM(E12:G12)=1 THEN1ELSE0"	R

Listing 8.1   *(continued)*

Go To		Type In	Return
E13	VO	"C12*E12*2"	R
F13	VO	"C12*F12*5"	R
G13	VO	"C12*G12*8"	R
H13	VO	"SUM(E13:G13)/H12"	R
A14/	LO	"Visibility"	R
B14			R
C14	VO	Enter weighting value for product's Visibility	R
E14 to G14	VO	Enter weighting value as per E12–G12 for Visibility	R
H14	VO	"IFSUM(E14:G14)=1 THEN1ELSE0"	R
E15	VO	"C14*E14*2"	R
F15	VO	"C14*F14*5"	R
G15	VO	"C14*G14*8"	R
H15	VO	"SUM(E15:G15)/H14"	R
A16/	LO	"Distinctiveness"	R
B16			R
C16	VO	Enter weighting value for product's Distinctiveness	R
E16 to G16	VO	Enter weighting value for Distinctiveness as per E12–G12	R
H16	VO	"IFSUM(E16:G16)=1 THEN1ELSE0"	R
E17	VO	"C16*E16*2"	R
F17	VO	"C16*F16*5"	R
G17	VO	"C16*G16*8"	R
H17	VO	"SUM(E17:G17)/H16"	R
A18	LO	"Display"	R
C18	VO	Enter weighting value for Display characteristics	R

Go To		Type In	Return
E18 to G18	VO	Enter weighting value for Display as per E12–G12	R
H18	VO	"IFSUM(E18:G18)=1 THEN1ELSE0"	R
E19	VO	"C18*E18*2"	R
F19	VO	"C18*F18*5"	R
G19	VO	"C18*G18*8"	R
H19	VO	"SUM(E19:G19)/H18"	R
A20/	LO	"Apparent	R
B20		size"	R
C20	VO	Enter weighting value for Apparent size for product	R
E20 to G20	VO	Enter weighting value for Apparent size as per E12–G12	R
H20	VO	"IFSUM(E20:G20)=1 THEN1ELSE0"	R
E21	VO	"C20*E20*2"	R
F21	VO	"C20*F20*5"	R
G21	VO	"C20*G20*8"	R
H21	VO	"SUM(E21:G21)/H20"	R
A22	LO	"Branding"	R
C22	VO	Enter Branding weighting value for product	R
E22 to G22	VO	Enter weighting value for Branding as per E12–G12	R
H22	VO	"IFSUM(E22:G22)=1 THEN1ELSE0"	R
E23	VO	"C22*E22*2"	R
F23	VO	"C22*F22*5"	R
G23	VO	"C22*G22*8"	R

Listing 8.1 *(continued)*

Go To		Type In	Return
H23	VO	"SUM(E23:G23)/H22"	R
A24/	LO	"Usage	R
B24		data"	R
C24	VO	Enter Usage data weighting value for product	R
E24 to G24	VO	Insert weighting value for Usage data as per E12–G12	R
H24	VO	"IFSUM(E24:G24)=1 THEN1ELSE0"	R
E25	VO	"C24*E24*2"	R
F25	VO	"C24*F24*5"	R
G25	VO	"C24*G24*8"	R
H25	VO	"SUM(E25:G25)/H24"	R
A26/	LO	"Consistency"	R
B26			R
C26	VO	Enter Consistency weighting value for product	R
E26 to G26	VO	Insert weighting value for Consistency as per E12–G12	R
H26	VO	"IFSUM(E26:G26)=1 THEN1ELSE0"	R
E27	VO	"C26*E26*2"	R
F27	VO	"C26*F26*5"	R
G27	VO	"C26*G26*8"	R
H27	VO	"SUM(E27:G27)/H26	R
A28/	LO	"Simplicity"	R
B28			R
C28	VO	Enter Simplicity weighting value for product	R

Go To		Type In	Return
E28 to G28	VO	Enter weighting value for Simplicity as per E12–G12	R
H28	VO	"IFSUM(E28:G28)=1 THEN1ELSE0"	R
E29	VO	"C28*E28*2"	R
F29	VO	"C28*F28*5"	R
G29	VO	"C28*G28*8"	R
H29	VO	"SUM(E29:G29)/H28"	R
A30/	LO	"Convenience"	R
B30			R
C30	VO	Enter Convenience weighting value	R
E30 to G30	VO	Enter weighting value for Convenience as per E12–G12	R
H30	VO	"IFSUM(E30:G30)=1 THEN1ELSE0"	R
C31	VO	"IFSUM(C12:C30)=25 THEN25ELSE0"	R
E31	VO	"C30*E30*2"	R
F31	VO	"C30*F30*5"	R
G31	VO	"C30*G30*8"	R
H31	VO	"SUM(E31:G31)/H30"	R
H32	VO	"SUM(H13:H31)−9"	R
A34/	LO	"DISTRIBUTION"	R
B34			R
A36	LO	"Display"	R
C36	VO	Enter weighting value for importance given to Display factors	R

Note: The values assigned to C36–C44 must together add up to 25.

Listing 8.1 *(continued)*

Go To		Type In	Return	Go To		Type In	Return
E36 to G36	VO	Enter weighting value for Display as per E12–G12	R	A42/ B42	LO	"Retailer info"	R R
H36	VO	"IFSUM(E36:G36)=1 THEN1ELSE0"	R	C42	VO	Enter weighting value for Retailer informa- tion	R
E37	VO	"C36*E36*2"	R	E42 to G42	VO	Enter weighting value for Retailer informa- tion as per E12–G12	R
F37	VO	"C36*F36*5"	R				
G37	VO	"C36*G36*8"	R				
H37	VO	"SUM(E37:G37)/H36"	R	H42	VO	"IFSUM(E42:G42)=1 THEN1ELSE0"	R
A38/	LO	"Standardisation"	R				
B38			R	E43	VO	"C42*E42*2"	R
C38	VO	Enter weighting value for Standardisation factors	R	F43	VO	"C42*F42*5"	R
				G43	VO	"C42*G42*8"	R
E38 to G38	VO	Enter weighting value for Standardisation as per E12–G12	R	H43	VO	"SUM(E43:G43)/H42"	R
				A44/	LO	"Simplicity"	R
H38	VO	"IFSUM(E38:G38)=1 THEN1ELSE0"	R	B44			R
E39	VO	"C38*E38*2"	R	C44	VO	Enter weighting value for Simplicity	R
F39	VO	"C38*F38*5"	R	E44 to G44	VO	Enter weighting value for Simplicity as per E12–G12	R
G39	VO	"C38*G38*8"	R				
H39	VO	"SUM(E39:G39)/H38"	R	H44	VO	"IFSUM(E44:G44)=1 THEN1ELSE0"	R
A40	LO	"Handling"	R				
C40	VO	Enter weighting value for.Handling factors	R	C45	VO	"IFSUM(C36:C44)=25 THEN25ELSE0"	R
E40 to G40	VO	Enter weighting value for Handling as per E12–G12	R	E45	VO	"C44*E44*2"	R
				F45	VO	"C44*F44*5"	R
				G45	VO	"C44*G44*8"	R
H40	VO	"IFSUM(E40:G40)=1 THEN1ELSE0"	R	H45	VO	"SUM(E45:G45)/H44"	R
				H46	VO	"SUM(H37:H45)–4"	R
E41	VO	"C40*E40*2"	R	A48/	LO	"PRODUCTION"	R
F41	VO	"C40*F40*5"	R	B48			R
G41	VO	"C40*G40*8"	R	A50/	LO	"Efficiency"	R
H41	VO	"SUM(E41:G41)/H40"	R	B50			R

Listing 8.1 *(continued)*

Go To		Type In	Return		Go To		Type In	Return
C50	VO	Enter weighting value of importance given to Efficiency	R		H55	VO	"SUM(E55:G55)/H54"	R
					A56/	LO	"Components"	R
E50 to G50	VO	Enter weighting value for Efficiency as per E12–G12	R		B56			R
					C56	VO	Enter weighting value for Components	R
H50	VO	"IFSUM(E50:G50)=1 THEN1ELSE0"	R		E56 to G56	VO	Enter weighting value for Components as per E12–G12	R
E51	VO	"C50*E50*2"	R					
F51	VO	"C50*F50*5"	R		H56	VO	"IFSUM(E56:G56)=1 THEN1ELSE0"	R
G51	VO	"C50*G50*8"	R					
H51	VO	"SUM(E51:G51)/H50"	R		E57	VO	"C56*E56*2"	R
A52	LO	"Shape"	R		F57	VO	"C56*F56*5"	R
C52	VO	Enter weighting value for Shape	R		G57	VO	"C56*G56*8"	R
					H57	VO	"SUM(E57:G57)/H56"	R
E52 to G52	VO	Enter weighting value for Shape as per E12–G12	R		A58/	LO	"Cost	R
					B58		effectiveness"	R
H52	VO	"IFSUM(E52:G52)=1 THEN1ELSE0"	R		C58	VO	Enter weighting value for Cost effectiveness	R
E53	VO	"C52*E52*2"	R		E58 to G58	VO	Enter weighting value for Cost effectiveness as per E12–G12	R
F53	VO	"C52*F52*5"	R					
G53	VO	"C52*G52*8"	R					
H53	VO	"SUM(E53:G53)/H52"	R		H58	VO	"IFSUM(E58:G58)=1 THEN1ELSE0"	R
A54	LO	"Strength"	R					
C54	VO	Enter weighting value for Strength	R		E59	VO	"C58*E58*2"	R
					F59	VO	"C58*F58*5"	R
E54 to G54	VO	Enter weighting value for Strength as per E12–G12	R		G59	VO	"C58*G58*8"	R
					H59	VO	"SUM(E59:G59)/H58"	R
H54	VO	"IFSUM(E54:G54)=1 THEN1ELSE0"	R		A60/	LO	"Print	R
					B60		surface"	R
E55	VO	"C54*E54*2"	R		C60	VO	Enter weighting value for Print surface	R
F55	VO	"C54*F54*5"	R					
G55	VO	"C54*G54*8"	R					

Note that values assigned from C50–C60 must add up to 25.

Listing 8.1 *(concluded)*

Go To		Type In	Return	Go To		Type In	Return
E60 to G60	VO	Enter weighting value for Print surface as per E12–G12	R	H62	VO	"SUM(H51:H61)–5"	R
H60	VO	"IFSUM(E60:G60)=1 THEN1ELSE0"	R	A64	LO	"SUMMARY"	R
				A66	LO	"CONSUMER"	R
C61	VO	"IFSUM(C50:C60)=25 THEN25ELSE0"	R	C66	VO	"H32/C31"	R
E61	VO	"C60*E60*2"	R	A68/ B68	LO	"DISTRIBUTION"	R R
F61	VO	"C60*F60*5"	R	C68	VO	"H46/C45"	R
G61	VO	"C60*G60*8"	R	A70/ B70	LO	"PRODUCTION"	R R
H61	VO	"SUM(E61:G61)/H60"	R	C70	VO	"H62/C61"	R

Proforma 8.1   Packaging model

A/B	C	E	F	G	H
4	PACKAGING	DEVELOPMENT			
7 AREAS	VALUE	POOR	AVERAGE	EXCELLENT	
10 CONSUMER					
12 Mandatory info	5	0	0,6	0,4	IFSUM(E12:G12)=1THEN1ELSE0
13		C12*E12*2	C12*F12*5	C12*G12*8	SUM(E13:G13)/H12
14 Visibility	2	0,3	0,7	0	IFSUM(E14:G14)=1THEN1ELSE0
15		C14*E14*2	C14*F14*5	C14*G14*8	SUM(E15:G15)/H14
16 Distinctiveness	2	0	0,5	0,5	IFSUM(E16:G16)=1THEN1ELSE0
17		C16*E16*2	C16*F16*5	C16*G16*8	SUM(E17:G17)/H16
18 Display	4	0,6	0,4	0	IFSUM(E18:G18)=1THEN1ELSE0
19		C18*E18*2	C18*F18*5	C18*G18*8	SUM(E19:G19)/H18
20 Apparent size	4	0,3	0,5	0,2	IFSUM(E20:G20)=1THEN1ELSE0
21		C20*E20*2	C20*F20*5	C20*G20*8	SUM(E21:G21)/H20
22 Branding	4	0,2	0,5	0,3	IFSUM(E22:G22)=1THEN1ELSE0
23		C22*E22*2	C22*F22*5	C22*G22*8	SUM(E23:G23)/H22
24 Usage data	2	0,8	0,2	0	IFSUM(E24:G24)=1THEN1ELSE0
25		C24*E24*2	C24*F24*5	C24*G24*8	SUM(E25:G25)/H24
26 Consistency	1	0,4	0,2	0,4	IFSUM(E26:G26)=1THEN1ELSE0
27		C26*E26*2	C26*F26*5	C26*G26*8	SUM(E27:G27)/H26
28 Simplicity	0	0,7	0,3	0	IFSUM(E28:G28)=1THEN1ELSE0
29		C28*E28*2	C28*F28*5	C28*G28*8	SUM(E29:G29)/H28

Proforma 8.1 *(concluded)*

A/B	C	E	F	G	H		
30 Convenience	1	0,3	0,5	0,2	IFSUM(E30;G30)=1THEN1ELSE0	□	■
31	IFSUM(C12;C30)=25THEN25ELSE0	C30*E30*2	C30*F30*5	C30*G30*8	SUM(E31;G31)/H30		
32					SUM(H13;H31)-9		
34 DISTRIBUTION							
36 Display	15	0	0,5	0,5	IFSUM(E36;G36)=1THEN1ELSE0		
37		C36*E36*2	C36*F36*5	C36*G36*8	SUM(E37;G37)/H36		
38 Standardisation	5	0,2	0,5	0,3	IFSUM(E38;G38)=1THEN1ELSE0		
39		C38*E38*2	C38*F38*5	C38*G38*8	SUM(E39;G39)/H38		
40 Handling	3	0,1	0,7	0,2	IFSUM(E40;G40)=1THEN1ELSE0		
41		C40*E40*2	C40*F40*5	C40*G40*8	SUM(E41;G41)/H40		
42 Retailer info	1	0,3	0,5	0,2	IFSUM(E42;G42)=1THEN1ELSE0		
43		C42*E42*2	C42*F42*5	C42*G42*8	SUM(E43;G43)/H42		
44 Simplicity	1	0	0,1	0,9	IFSUM(E44;G44)=1THEN1ELSE0		
45	IFSUM(C36;C44)=25THEN25ELSE0	C44*E44*2	C44*F44*5	C44*G44*8	SUM(E45;G45)/H44		
46					SUM(H37;H45)-4		
48 PRODUCTION							
50 Efficiency	9	0	0,2	0,8	IFSUM(E50;G50)=1THEN1ELSE0		
51		C50*E50*2	C50*F50*5	C50*G50*8	SUM(E51;G51)/H50		
52 Shape	4	0	0,4	0,6	IFSUM(E52;G52)=1THEN1ELSE0		
53		C52*E52*2	C52*F52*5	C52*G52*8	SUM(E53;G53)/H52		
54 Strength	3	0,3	0,2	0,5	IFSUM(E54;G54)=1THEN1ELSE0		
55		C54*E54*2	C54*F54*5	C54*G54*8	SUM(E55;G55)/H54		
56 Components	3	0,3	0,5	0,2	IFSUM(E56;G56)=1THEN1ELSE0		
57		C56*E56*2	C56*F56*5	C56*G56*8	SUM(E57;G57)/H56		
58 Cost effective	3	0	0,1	0,9	IFSUM(E58;G58)=1THEN1ELSE0		
59		C58*E58*2	C58*F58*5	C58*G58*8	SUM(E59;G59)/H58		
60 Print surface	3	0	0,5	0,5	IFSUM(E60;G60)=1THEN1ELSE0		
61	IFSUM((C50;C60)=25THEN25ELSE0	C60*E60*2	C60*F60*5	C60*G60*8	SUM(E61;G61)/H60		
62					SUM(H51;H61)-5		
64 SUMMARY							
66 CONSUMER	H32/C31						
68 DISTRIBUTION	H46/C45						
70 PRODUCTION	H62/C61						

Example 8.1   Packaging model

A/B	C	E	F	G	H
4	PACKAGING VALUE	DEVELOPMENT POOR	AVERAGE	EXCELLENT	
7 AREAS					
10 CONSUMER					
12 Mandatory info	5	0	0.6	0.4	1
13		0	15	16	31
14 Visibility	2	0.3	0.7	0	1
15		1.2	7	0	8.2
16 Distinctiveness	2	0	0.5	0.5	1
17		0	5	8	13
18 Display	4	0.6	0.4	0	1
19		4.8	8	0	12.8
20 Apparent size	4	0.3	0.5	0.2	1
21		2.4	10	6.4	18.8
22 Branding	4	0.2	0.5	0.3	1
23		1.6	10	9.6	21.2
24 Usage data	2	0.8	0.2	0	1
25		3.2	2	0	5.2
26 Consistency	1	0.4	0.2	0.4	1
27		0.8	1	3.2	5
28 Simplicity	0	0.7	0.3	0	1
29		0	0	0	0
30 Convenience	1	0.3	0.5	0.2	1
31	25	0.6	2.5	1.6	4.7
32					111.9
34 DISTRIBUTION					
36 Display	15	0	0.5	0.5	1

A/B	C	E	F	G	H
37		0	37.5	60	97.5
38 Standardisation	5	0.2	0.5	0.3	1
39	3	2	12.5	12	26.5
40 Handling	3	0.1	0.7	0.2	1
41	1	0.6	10.5	4.8	15.9
42 Retailer info	1	0.3	0.5	0.2	1
43		0.6	2.5	1.6	4.7
44 Simplicity	1	0	0.1	0.9	1
45	25	0	0.5	7.2	7.7
46					152.3
48 PRODUCTION					
50 Efficiency	9	0	0.2	0.8	1
51		0	9	57.6	66.6
52 Shape	4	0	0.4	0.6	1
53		0	8	19.2	27.2
54 Strength	3	0.3	0.2	0.5	1
55		1.8	3	12	16.8
56 Components	3	0.3	0.5	0.2	1
57		1.8	7.5	4.8	14.1
58 Cost effective	3	0	0.1	0.9	1
59		0	1.5	21.6	23.1
60 Print surface	3	0	0.5	0.5	1
61	25	0	7.5	12	19.5
62					167.3
64 SUMMARY					
66 CONSUMER	4.796				
68 DISTRIBUTION	6.092				
70 PRODUCTION	6.692				

□ ■

145

Packaging commentary

The model provides a decision framework within which the various elements of the packaging problem can be evaluated. In Example 8.1 the manager has introduced a series of subjective values to the elements of the packaging mix – how important branding may be, for example, for the final pack design compared with factors such as visibility or display.

Distribution and production factors are similarly weighted in each case out of a total of 25. The probability of each element being achieved is then entered under the three headings – poor, average and excellent – whether the factor is likely to be met by the pack design that is under evaluation.

The model then calculates the totals for each of the sectors enabling comparisons to be made between this and other products in the company. For the product in question, the distribution and production criteria are being well met by the particular pack under consideration – the consumer effectiveness is questionable and would require re-evaluation and perhaps redesign to ensure that the maximum possible benefit can be obtained from the new pack.

References

1   R.N. Theodore in M. Rines, *Marketing Handbook*, Gower, 1981.

2   R.C. Teevan and R.C. Birney, (ed), *Colour Vision*, Van Nostrand, 1961.

3   A.H. Maslow, *Motivation and Personality*, Harper and Row, 1954.

9 Product diversification

There is a saying in the North of England, 'Clogs to clogs in three generations', which means that the money made by a first generation of family entrepreneurs is squandered by the second and third, eventually returning the family to the poverty from whence it came.

The history of business is often very similar, with the statement that a stagnant business is a dying business, generally proving accurate. Several studies confirm this point showing quite clearly that a company must evolve to continue to prosper (1, 2). Survival of the fittest, a major plank in evolutionary theory, also holds true in the world of marketing. Examples of this ability to adapt to change being at the root of success are very instructive, as indeed are details of failure. Thus we can see one side of the issue in the recent expansion of Olivetti. From a base in mechanical office equipment, such as manual typewriters and copiers, it has progressed with outstanding success into the area of the electronic office, specifically word processors and computers, with consequent increases in overall profitability and market position (3).

The reverse image can be seen in the ever-growing problems of the Distillers Company, owners of Johnny Walker Whisky and Gordon's Gin. Increasingly their markets are threatened by a number of factors: the most important being the decline in spirits consumption in the majority of the Western World; and lack of foreign exchange in Third World markets. It will be interesting to see whether the problems of Distillers, in what is still, overall, a growth market in many countries – based on total alcohol consumption – can be resolved to the satisfaction of the investment groups owning the majority of the equity, in the same dramatic style as Olivetti.

Adapting to change

The firm will need to adapt its products to changes in the environment (see

147

Chapter 1 on product viability) and there are two broadly defined ways in which this can be achieved:

1   Development using internal resources   Examples of this obviously include: expansion both by increased market share (using existing client base), or new market exploitation (development of export sales); the transfer of a standard product into a new market sector; and minor alterations within the current product/market structure.

2   The introduction of new approaches internally and externally.   This will enable the company to bring itself into line with the total business environment. Included under this heading would be the acquisition of other organisations with skills in different market sectors.

These are obviously not mutually exclusive and each tends to interrelate to the other over a period of time. Thus a firm could expand by concentrating on the components that make up a current product, establishing a presence in a separate sector. From these it may develop laterally into some totally new enterprise from the initial business. The British firm, Spillers, initially produced bread. By-products of milling are traditionally used for animal feed; animal feed products are allied to pet food. Spillers over the years of its existence, before its acquisition by Dalgety, had become active in bread, animal feed and pet food.

Ideas for new products or activities can be gained from a number of sources each requiring evaluation. Salesmen can provide subjective ideas from the customer base, together with comments on inherent weaknesses in either one's own or competitors' lines. Similar contributions can be made by repair or service personnel. Sophisticated market research techniques such as factor or cluster analysis can draw attention to gaps in the market place, or reveal changing consumer attitudes (4, 5). Valuable extra ideas can be received from freelance contributors, including the burgeoning area of new product consultancies. Lastly, research and development departments will be producing new approaches based on current technology or applying new technology to current problems. Differing departments can be given different responsibilities in the various areas (Figure 9.1).

Sales Department	*Production dept*	*Marketing dept*
Competitors' products	Research	Market research
Customer needs	Competitive product	Freelance consultants
	Evaluation	Product testing

Figure 9.1   Defining roles for new product idea generation and testing

Planning for change

The development of totally new approaches does however require a considerably greater investment, both in time and money than the expansion of current activities, in practically all areas of company operations.

It is the wise company that does, in fact, develop a plan based on the structured development of current assets together with the conception of products for the future. One company that has been very competent at maintaining core business while expanding into new fields has been Unilever. Founded by the eccentric Lord Lever in the 1860s on a backbone of soap, and buttressed by its merger with Dutch margarine interests at the turn of the century, it has continued to prosper. A great deal of this continues to come from both soap and margarine, though the products actually sold nowadays differ substantially from their forebears. Unilever has proceeded from this base to develop businesses in frozen food, industrial cleaning, animal feed, distribution, canned food, toiletries, and packaging.

Assessing change

One can simply graph the financial performance of any company in terms of *activities* (Figure 9.2). Put quite simply, the declining activity (line 1) must be balanced by contributions from growing curves (lines 2,3,4). Should the net contribution be positive, the firm will grow, negative and the firm will decline. The intermeshing of current activities with development demands the use of forecasting techniques, some approaches to which are covered elsewhere (see Chapter 10 on forecasting).

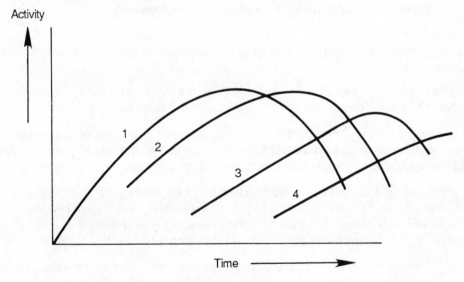

Figure 9.2   Activities of a firm over time

There are three prime problem areas that any forecasting system needs to consider:

1 Industry factors These include growth trends, alterations in competitive structure, changes in the nature of the consumer (this applies whether the firm is

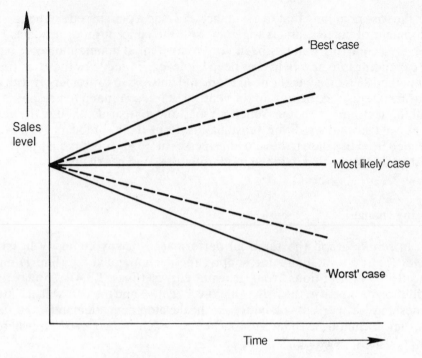

Figure 9.3   Sales levels on various assumptions

involved in selling industrial goods or in the personal sector), pricing, distribution factors, and so on.

2   Fiscal factors   These cover the level of taxation, government policy with respect to raw materials, levels of employment and relevant social issues.

3   Internal factors   The ability of current personnel to cope with current and future problems – a very important consideration in any dramatically new venture; and physical factors such as machinery, and factory layout.

A graphical analysis based on these criteria can be developed to show the likely progress of the firm over the next few years, which will inevitably include a number of levels of activity based on various assumptions (Figure 9.3). The 'major change' lines indicate the likely impact on the company of such actions as:

(a)   Successful product diversification based on access to new markets or new technology ('Best' case)
(b)   Expansion to new geographical or strategic areas
(c)   The demise of a major competitor
(d)   Substantial changes in government policy ('Best' or 'Worst' case)
(e)   Substantial changes in consumer tastes ('Best' or 'Worst' case)

The 'best case' lines indicate the outcome under a generally stable set of conditions, external, internal, and fiscal.

The 'worst case' line indicates the effect of major changes in a negative sense and are largely the mirror image of the items on the 'major change' line. Included under this heading one would need to consider adverse changes in consumer tastes, detrimental changes in the fiscal environment and so on.

The majority of business planning tends to limit the scope under consideration to 'best fit' solutions based on historical performance, and rarely consider the worst case and the consequences.

The worst case may not be a rapid decrease in sales – a rapid increase can often be as damaging to the organisation's chances of success, leading to over-trading and major cash flow problems.

Examples of problems caused by rapid decline are still with us in many forms and fashions: the inability of the majority of engineering firms to cope with the combination of the worldwide recession caused by the rise in oil prices and vastly altered work practices because of the introduction of microprocessors.

The underestimates of IBM, one of the most sophisticated marketing firms in the world, in respect of demand for the IBM PC, is also instructive as an example of undervaluing the potential market. In a company with fewer financial resources than IBM, this might have caused severe funding problems, but fortunately all it can do is to provide some consolation to the marketing manager whose forecasts have proved erroneous!

The elements of planning

The business forecast has to allow for the interaction of current business with the external environment, both industrial and fiscal, combined with the new activities in which the firm is engaged and their total effect on the internal resources of the company.

The prime object of this business plan should be to set objectives. These have two main elements:

1 Growth

Traditionally the first and often single element would have been growth, restricted to an increase in volume. A later and more sophisticated approach was obviously to consider some measure of profitability such as return on capital employed. Any single measure can, however, present problems, even for the most successful firm. Mars, the household name in both the confectionery world, and within the petfood market (Pedigree Petfoods), have failed to diversify beyond these core businesses. It is tempting to see the reason for the failure or partial failure of the company's ventures into toys (Uncle Remus) and catering (Klix, Vendepac) as consequences of a very strict adherence to a concept of rate of internal return, which works for both chocolate and dog food, but not in other industries. In this instance the company may become established in growth industries but because of internal factors be unable to capitalise on them, a reflection of management objectives.

2 Survival

This becomes very important in rapidly changing environments and may indeed mitigate against growth. To continue with the Mars example, one could, in a flight of fancy, see dramatic declines in the chocolate market caused by the increasing awareness of the over-reliance on fat in the Western diet, and in pet food (perhaps a fashion of donating the food used in the upkeep of pets to certain underdeveloped countries). In such a situation, the Mars philosophy of maximising internal return would have little relevance.

The combined plan for a business will therefore have to take a number of factors into account for evaluation:

(a)   Together the performance of the old and new business will not necessarily be a sum of the two component parts. There may easily be a synergistic effect with the newly combined product range being substantially stronger than the old. Classic examples can be found with distribution companies. The collection of individually weak products can produce a range which enables them to achieve acceptance from the major retailing outlets, which the products could not aspire to by themselves.

(b)   The performance will vary considerably over time, according to the effects of the fiscal/industrial environment, and the lag factors operating within any changing system.

It can be seen clearly from the preceding comments that a large element of these forecasts will therefore be *subjective*: they will depend on the value judgements of the executives in charge of that element of the plan. The future for any firm will be very similar to a poker hand in which you do not even see your *own* hand very clearly, in addition to not even having the vaguest idea as to what the other players have been dealt. This is particularly true of any diversification that the firm is involved in. The exercise that the organisation needs to carry out in this area is to consider all the relevant factors involved in the way new activities interrelate with old and how effective an addition they will be.

The product diversification model

The model, split into two, provides a framework for identifying and minimising the principal areas of uncertainty, namely the suitability of any new product within the current activity of the company; and secondly, its effect on the overall profitability, both in the short and long term.

There appears to be general unanimity in the literature that the concentration of resources in a small number of areas (the rifle approach) is more effective than the production of a wide range of alternative possibilities, and in consequence each opportunity requires as much detailed investigation as possible to improve the chance of success. The initial stage should consider the factors that are important to the company for the development of new products, and for the organisation to assign them an importance for the particular product field in which the firm is operating. Secondly, the manager needs to decide on the probability of such an event taking place. For example good packaging may be regarded as vital in a specific market, and there is a good chance that the product will meet this criteria.

Such a product would be more valuable to the organisation than one which failed to meet this criteria.

The main factors which are important to the majority of firms can be summarised as follows:

1 Market dynamics   Questions such as: How unique is the product? Will there be lots of consumers? are naturally of prime importance to any new product development.

2 Product position   Questions such as: Will the product fit in with current distribution strategy? Will it complement or conflict with the current product range?

3 Long-term factors   Included in this section are all the problems that must be faced by any new product over time, such as whether the item is patentable or not, and whether it will be able to maintain its market position.

4 Management   Of great importance to the success of new product ventures is whether the internal personnel resources of the company can maximise the potential of the new departure. This is often a crucial factor overlooked by any product development team. A project may appear financially to be one of the soundest ever investigated, but if the company does not have the management available to handle the new factors it is often a sure recipe for disaster. The conglomerate boom of the mid 1960s and 1970s produced several notable casualties of this nature.

5 Production factors   These will include all major aspects of the problems that any new product will cause. Factors that could be considered important include the availability of raw materials, components and expertise. Many projects fail to consider these vital ingredients. Cement requires coal, water, and chalk for production. The cement factory built to the south of Khartoum in the Sudan lacked both chalk and coal though granted there was a ready supply of water. Once the railway system began to founder the project inevitably collapsed.

The model will therefore provide an analysis under all these headings of how well the new activity or product will fit into the overall company objectives, and can obviously be compared and contrasted with current products in the range.

The evaluation will be in terms of indexed figures for the strength and weakness of the market dynamics, product position, long-term factors, management compatibility and ability of the organisation to cope with the production problems that the new activity will cause.

Within each major sector there will be a series of subdivisions which will be considered.

1 Market dynamics

(a) Consumer presence   The availability of consumers for the particular product should ideally be as large as possible. Thus placing a high probability on the event taking place would imply that a wide audience is available.

(b)   Uniqueness   Does the product have a technical edge which will allow it to maintain a position for a substantial period of time before competition can become established? This is a very important element of any introduction into the market place – the competitive grace period – how long and how well the product can become established.

(c)   Fashion   Does the product coincide with the attitudes of the end consumer? This does not apply to consumer goods only – research has shown that attitudes of industrial buyers are also very important in purchase decisions.

(d)   Profitability   Will the product have a sufficiently high margin which could be re-invested to exclude competitors from the market place? There is ample evidence from a wide range of product innovative successes that the first product in the market place can rapidly establish a supremacy in that sector in such a fashion – Colgate toothpaste, Nescafe coffee, Xerox photocopiers, Sellotape.

2   Product position

(a)   Interaction with present products   Ideally, unless the benefits in other areas are highly significant, the product should help the sale of the current product range. If it does not do so, it will lead to a diversion of resources.

(b)   Number of sizes/grades   The smaller this is the fewer the problems associated with distribution chains and inventory levels.

(c)   Packaging   Does the product fit into current display systems, and current methods of distribution? Two examples are relevant here. First is the firm that introduces a range of spices that require special racking. This may easily limit its acceptability in major outlets wanting complete control over all their sales space. Secondly, a firm using the mail for despatch produces a product which is outside the acceptable size criteria, leading to the necessity of using new distribution systems.

(d)   Quality/price relationship   In order to establish a strong market position, quality/price relationships should be close to that of the competition. Should the product be overpriced the resulting outlook for the product would be poor (see Chapter 13 on price evaluation).

(e)   Distribution compatibility   Does the product fit in with current distribution channels? Examples of the problems that this can cause are innumerable. Within the Airfix group, manufacturing a variety of toys and games including brand leading construction kits, the decision was taken to produce plastic household ware, mirrors, ashtrays and other goods. Though the technology was very similar the distribution outlets were totally different. As a result the decision caused major problems within the group.

3 Long-term factors

(a) Fluctuation resistance There are several markets which have shown considerable growth, followed by very steep decline and often, subsequent renewed growth. One recent example of this can be seen in the problems faced by Warner Brothers and their Atari subsidiary. For a period this division made very healthy profits for their parent division, but once the market went into decline, the situation was reversed, and losses mounted.

(b) Market niche The product will ideally always have a position in the market place allowing return on investment over a long period of time.

(c) Patentable For the product to maximise its potential, a patented process can establish a separate property for the particular item. The more effective the patent, the better the exclusivity.

4 Management

(a) Personnel Any new development will place severe demands on personnel; it is essential that sufficient individuals are available to handle the new project. For example it is necessary that any labour relations problems are considered and planned for. Will the factory workforce accept the new product?

(b) Skills Product diversification leads companies into new areas of activity which demand new knowledge and expertise. Any company embarking on this course requires a high level of flexibility to cope with the new problems that they will face, or will require to initiate a training programme to cope with the anticipated shortfall in skills.

5 Production

(a) Ready availability of equipment The fewer the problems involved in the integration of the new product with current capacity, the more successful the innovation will be from the viewpoint of productive capacity.

(b) Ready availability of components Variety and security of supply are important to ensure the smooth production of any new introduction.

(c) Ready availability of production expertise

Other aspects of the model

Each of the categories discussed will have a degree of importance to the firm, and each will have a probability of occurrence; there will be obtained from the model a series of indexes for each category. These can be compared with scores for other products within the same company to enable management to obtain a more objective assessment of the project viability, and how it fits into the strategic/long-term view of the company development.

Having developed the value of the new product within this framework one can come to a reasonably clear view as to the likely commercial acceptability of the project.

This factor can then be used to evaluate the short-term profitability of the given product, to produce a form of pay-back index.

A series of other subjective assessments will need to be made to complete this equation:

1 Likely first year sales levels (in units), derived from the company's forecasting system.

2 Estimated selling price per unit (taking account of the market price elasticities).

3 Estimated cost of production (best estimate using various levels of overhead recovery).

4 Launch costs For an accurate reflection of the true cost to the company launch costs should include all the time spent by management and sales forces, together with some measure of the lost opportunity cost involved, that is the value of the time spent if it had been on some other project.

5 Capital expenditure This should include all extra expenditure the company is required to make – extra office space/production plant, and other equipment.

6 Working capital levels The introduction of a new product will obviously mean increased inventory expenditure, but may also mean changes in the levels of trade debtors.

7 Period without major competition (in years). The longer the product has an undisputed lead in the market place the more profitable it will be.

8 Index value of the new product evaluation This will be obtained from the initial product evaluation.

From this calculation an estimate of the value of the product can be obtained in comparison with other items in the range.

A similar exercise can be carried out for long-term profitability, by combining an estimate of the sales with a likely probability of achieving a certain gross margin level, and from that subtracting the investment needed to maintain the product (advertising/sales). Obviously in addition to this fairly crude approach there are a number of extremely sophisticated financial models using discounted cash flow techniques which can be used, but a rapid calculation can yield some valuable insight into the likely progress of the product in the market.

Using the product diversification model

The *Go To* column in Listing 9.1 tells you the cell number and the cursor position.

The next column specifies the spreadsheet option (LO = Label Option; VO = Value Option). The *Type In* column gives you instructions within the inverted commas which you must type in or asks you to supply the necessary data. These commas are not part of the instructions supplied here and should not be typed in. Beware however that some spreadsheets, the *Lotus 1-2-3*, for example, enter the Label Option by using the inverted-comma key. Under the *Type In* column the symbols * = multiply and / = divide. R in the *Return* column instructs you to commit the information to memory by pressing the Return key.
Remember: When you have finished, save your model.

Listing 9.1 Product diversification model

Go To		Type In	Return
C2	LO	"Product"	R
D2	LO	"Divers" for Diversification	R
E2	LO	"Analysis"	R
F4/	LO	"PROBABILITY"	R
G4			R
A5	LO	"FACTOR"	R
C5	LO	"Weight" for Weighting	R

The sum of the weighting values allocated in each section of the model – Market Dynamics, Product Position, Long Term, Management, and Production must add up to 10 and the formula for cells C16, C29, C38, C45, and C54 are designed to ensure this. The model is working to a probability of one that a particular event will take place. If you consider that a particular event is very likely to occur assign a high value to 'Very Good Probability' or 'Good Probability' cells – likely to be between .5 and .7. The split between the range Very Good to Very Poor must add up to one.

Go To		Type In	Return
D5	LO	"V.Good" for Very Good	R
E5	LO	"Good"	R

Go To		Type In	Return
F5	LO	"Average"	R
G5	LO	"Poor"	R
H5	LO	"V.Poor" for Very Poor	R
J5	LO	"Index"	R
A7/	LO	"MARKET	R
B7		DYNAMICS"	R
A9	LO	"Con. Pres" for Consumer Presence	R
C9	VO	Enter weighting value for Consumer Presence	R
D9 to H9	VO	Enter probability value for Consumer Presence. The split must add up to one	R
I9	VO	"IFSUM(D9:H9)=1 THEN1ELSE0"	R
D10	VO	"C9*D9*1"	R
E10	VO	"C9*E9*0.8"	R
F10	VO	"C9*F9*0.6"	R
G10	VO	"C9*G9*0.4"	R
H10	VO	"C9*H9*0.2"	R
J10	VO	"SUM(C10:H10)/I9"	R
A11	LO	"Unique" for Uniqueness	R
C11	VO	Enter weighting value for Uniqueness	R

Listing 9.1 *(continued)*

Go To		Type In	Return	Go To		Type In	Return
D11 to H11	VO	Insert probability values for uniqueness. The split must add up to one	R	I15	VO	"IFSUM(D15:H15)=1 THEN1ELSE0"	R
I11	VO	"IFSUM(D11:H11)=1 THEN1ELSE0"	R	C16	VO	"IFSUM(C9:C15)=10 THEN10ELSE0"	R
D12	VO	"C11*D11*1"	R	D16	VO	"C15*D15*1"	R
E12	VO	"C11*E11*0.8"	R	E16	VO	"C15*E15*0.8"	R
F12	VO	"C11*F11*0.6"	R	F16	VO	"C15*F15*0.6"	R
G12	VO	"C11*G11*0.4"	R	G16	VO	"C15*G15*0.4"	R
H12	VO	"C11*H11*0.2"	R	H16	VO	"C15*H15*0.2"	R
J12	VO	"SUM(C12:H12)/I11"	R	J16	VO	"SUM(D16:H16)/I15"	R
A13	LO	"Fashion" for fashionability	R	J17	VO	"SUM(J10:J16)"	R
C13	VO	Enter weighting value for Fashionability	R	A18/ B18	LO	"PRODUCT POSITION"	R R
D13 to H13	VO	Insert probability values for Fashionability. The split must add up to one	R	A20	LO	"Interact" for Interaction	R
I13	VO	"IFSUM(D13:H13)=1 THEN1ELSE0	R	C20	VO	Insert Weighting values for Interaction	R
D14	VO	"C13*D13*1"	R	D20 to H20	VO	Insert probability values for Interaction The split must add up to one	R
E14	VO	"C13*E13*0.8"	R	I20	VO	"IFSUM(D20:H20)=1 THEN1ELSE0"	R
F14	VO	"C13*F13*0.6"	R	D21	VO	"C20*D20*1"	R
G14	VO	"C13*G13*0.4"	R	E21	VO	"C20*E20*0.8"	R
H14	VO	"C13*H13*0.2"	R	F21	VO	"C20*F20*0.6"	R
J14	VO	"SUM(D14:H14)/I13"	R	G21	VO	"C20*G20*0.4"	R
A15	LO	"Profit"	R	H21	VO	"C20*H20*0.2"	R
C15	VO	Enter weighting value for Profitability	R	J21	VO	"SUM(D21:H21)/I20"	R
D15 to H15	VO	Insert probability values for Profitability. The split must add up to one	R	A22	LO	"Sizes/gr"	R
				C22	VO	Insert Weighting value for Sizes	R
				D22 to H22	VO	Insert probability values for Size. The split must add up to one	R

Listing 9.1 *(continued)*

Go To		Type In	Return
I22	VO	"IFSUM(D22:H22)=1 THEN1ELSE0"	R
D23	VO	"C22*D22*1"	R
E23	VO	"C22*E22*0.8"	R
F23	VO	"C22*F22*0.6"	R
G23	VO	"C22*G22*0.4"	R
H23	VO	"C22*H22*0.2"	R
J23	VO	"SUM(D23:H23)/I22"	R
A24	LO	"Packagin" for Packaging	R
C24	VO	Insert weighting values for Packaging	R
D24 to H24	VO	Insert probability values for Packaging. The split must add up to one	R
I24	VO	"IFSUM(D24:H24)=1 THEN1ELSE0"	R
D25	VO	"C24*D24*1"	R
E25	VO	"C24*E24*0.8"	R
F25	VO	"C24*F24*0.6"	R
G25	VO	"C24*G24*0.4"	R
H25	VO	"C24*H24*0.2"	R
J25	VO	"SUM(D25:H25)/I24"	R
A26	LO	"Qual/prc" for Quality/pricing	R
C26	VO	Insert Weighting value for Quality and pricing	R
D26 to H26	VO	Insert probability values for Quality and pricing. The split must add up to one	R
I26	VO	"IFSUM(D26:H26)=1 THEN1ELSE0	R
D27	VO	"C26*D26*1"	R
E27	VO	"C26*E26*0.8"	R
F27	VO	"C26*F26*0.6"	R
G27	VO	"C26*G26*0.4"	R
H27	VO	"C26*H26*0.2"	R
J27	VO	"SUM(D27:H27)/I26"	R
A28	LO	"Distrib" for Distribution	R
C28	VO	Insert weighting value for Distribution	R
D28 to H28	VO	Insert probability values for Distribution. The split must add up to one	R
I28	VO	"IFSUM(D28:H28)=1 THEN1ELSE0"	R
C29	VO	"IFSUM(C20:C28)=10 THEN10ELSE0"	R
D29	VO	"C28*D28*1"	R
E29	VO	"C28*E28*0.8"	R
F29	VO	"C28*F28*0.6"	R
G29	VO	"C28*G28*0.4"	R
H29	VO	"C28*H28*0.2"	R
J29	VO	"SUM(D29:H29)/I28"	R
J30	VO	"SUM(J21:J29)"	R
A31/ B31	LO	"LONG TERM"	R R
A33	LO	"Fluctuat" for Fluctuation	R
C33	VO	Insert weighting value	R
D33 to H33	VO	Insert probability values for Fluctuation. The split must add up to one	R
I33	VO	"IFSUM(D33:H33)=1 THEN1ELSE0"	R

Listing 9.1 *(continued)*

Go To		Type In	Return	Go To		Type In	Return
D34	VO	"C33*D33*1"	R	G38	VO	"C37*G37*0.4"	R
E34	VO	"C33*E33*0.8"	R	H38	VO	"C37*H37*0.2"	R
F34	VO	"C33*F33*0.6"	R	J38	VO	"SUM(D38:H38)/I37"	R
G34	VO	"C33*G33*0.4"	R	J39	VO	"SUM(J34:J38)"	R
H34	VO	"C33*H33*0.2"	R	A40/	LO	"MANAGEMENT"	R
J34	VO	"SUM(D34:H34)/I33"	R	B40			R
A35	LO	"Niche"	R	A42/	LO	"Personnel"	R
C35	VO	Insert weighting value for Niche	R	B42			R
D35 to H35	VO	Insert probability values for Niche. The split must add up to one	R	C42	VO	Insert weighting value for Personnel	R
I35	VO	"IFSUM(D35:H35)=1 THEN1ELSE0"	R	D42 to H42	VO	Insert probability values for Personnel. The split must add up to one	R
D36	VO	"C35*D35*1"	R	I42	VO	"IFSUM(D42:H42)=1 THEN1ELSE0"	R
E36	VO	"C35*E35*0.8"	R	D43	VO	"C42*D42*1"	R
F36	VO	"C35*F35*0.6"	R	E43	VO	"C42*E42*0.8"	R
G36	VO	"C35*G35*0.4"	R	F43	VO	"C42*F42*0.6"	R
H36	VO	"C35*H35*0.2"	R	G43	VO	"C42*G42*0.4"	R
J36	VO	"SUM(D36:H36)/I35"	R	H43	VO	"C42*H42*0.2"	R
A37	LO	"Patent"	R	J43	VO	"SUM(D43:H43)/I42"	R
C37	VO	Insert weighting value for Patent	R	A44	LO	"Skills"	R
D37 to H37	VO	Insert probability values for Patent. The split must add up to one	R	C44	VO	Insert weighting value for Skills	R
I37	VO	"IFSUM(D37:H37)=1 THEN1ELSE0"	R	D44 to H44	VO	Insert probability values for Skills. The split must add up to one	R
C38	VO	"IFSUM(C33:C37)=10 THEN10ELSE0"	R	I44	VO	"IFSUM(D44:H44)=1 THEN1ELSE0"	R
D38	VO	"C37*D37*1"	R	C45	VO	"IFSUM(C42:C44)=10 THEN10ELSE0"	R
E38	VO	"C37*E37*0.8"	R	D45	VO	"C44*D44*1"	R
F38	VO	"C37*F37*0.6"	R	E45	VO	"C44*E44*0.8"	R

Listing 9.1 *(continued)*

Go To		Type In	Return	Go To		Type In	Return
F45	VO	"C44*F44*0.6"	R	E52	VO	"C51*E51*0.8"	R
G45	VO	"C44*G44*0.4"	R	F52	VO	"C51*F51*0.6"	R
H45	VO	"C44*H44*0.2"	R	G52	VO	"C51*G51*0.4"	R
J45	VO	"SUM(D45:H45)/I44"	R	H52	VO	"C51*H51*0.2"	R
J46	VO	"SUM(J43:J46)"	R	J52	VO	"SUM(D52:H52)/I51"	R
A47/	LO	"PRODUCTION"	R	A53/	LO	"Expertise"	R
B47			R	B53			R
A49/	LO	"Equipment"	R	C53	VO	Insert weighting value for Expertise	R
B49			R				
C49	VO	Insert weighting value for Equipment	R	D53 to H53	VO	Insert probability values for Expertise. The split must add up to one	R
D49 to H49	VO	Insert probability values for Equipment. The split must add up to one	R	I53	VO	"IFSUM(D51:H51)=1 THEN1ELSE0"	R
I49	VO	"IFSUM(D49:H49)=1 THEN1ELSE0"	R	C54	VO	"IFSUM(C49:C53)=10 THEN10ELSE0"	R
D50	VO	"C49*D49*1"	R	D54	VO	"C53*D53*1"	R
E50	VO	"C49*E49*0.8"	R	E54	VO	"C53*E53*0.8"	R
F50	VO	"C49*F49*0.6"	R	F54	VO	"C53*F53*0.6"	R
G50	VO	"C49*G49*0.4"	R	G54	VO	"C53*G53*0.4"	R
H50	VO	"C49*H49*0.2"	R	H54	VO	"C53*H53*0.2"	R
J50	VO	"SUM(D50:H50)/I49"	R	J54	VO	"SUM(D54:H54)/I53"	R
A51/	LO	"Components"	R	J55	VO	"SUM(J50:J54)"	R
B51			R	A56/	LO	"FACTOR	R
C51	VO	Insert weighting value for Components	R	B56		INDEX"	R
				A58/	LO	"Market	R
D51 to H51	VO	Insert probability values for Components. The split must add up to one	R	B58		dynamics"	R
				C58	VO	"J17/C16*10"	R
I51	VO	"IFSUM(D51:H51)=1 THEN1ELSE0"	R	A60/	LO	"Product	R
				B60		position"	R
D52	VO	"C51*D51*1"	R	C60	VO	"J30/C29*10"	R
				A62/	LO	"Long term	R

Listing 9.1 *(continued)*

Go To		Type In	Return
B62		factor"	R
C62	VO	"J39/C38*10"	R
A64/	LO	"Management"	R
B64			R
C64	VO	"J46/C45*10"	R
A66/	LO	"Production"	R
B66			R
C66	VO	"J55/C54*10"	R
A68/	LO	"PROD.DIV.	
B68		INDEX" for product diversification index	R

Note: This is the total weighting of all the factors entered in the model.

Go To		Type In	Return
C68	VO	"SUM(C58:C66)"	R
A71/	LO	"Short run	R
B71		profit"	R
A73/	LO	"Ex. sales	R
B73		level" for expected sales level	R
C73	VO	Insert expected total sales value $	R
A75/	LO	"Ex. sale	R
B75		price" for expected sale price	R
C75	VO	Insert expected sales unit price value $	R
A77/	LO	"Ex.prod.	R
B77		cost" for expected production cost	R
C77	VO	Insert value for expected unit production cost $	R
A79/	LO	"Launch	R
B79		costs"	R

Go To		Type In	Return
C79	VO	Insert value for total Launch costs $	R
A81/	LO	"Cap.	R
B81		expend." for capital expenditure	R
C81	VO	Insert capital expenditure $	R
A83/	LO	"Add. wk.	R
B83		cap." for additional working capital	R
C83	VO	Insert additional working capital $	R
A85/	LO	"Comp. free	R
B85		time"	R
C85	VO	Insert value for free time in years	R
A87/	LO	"Prod. div.	R
B87		index" for product diversification index	R
C87	VO	"C68*0.02"	R
C90	VO	"C87*C73*(C75−C77)* (1+C85)"	R
A91/	LO	"Short	R
B91		term"	R
C91	VO	"C90/(C81+C83+C79)"	R
A92	LO	" index"	R
A93/	LO	"Long	R
B93		term"	R
A95/	LO	"Quick	R
B95		analysis"	R
A96/	LO	"Total	R
B96		sales"	R
C96	VO	Enter value for eventual level of expected sales	R

Listing 9.1 *(concluded)*

Go To		Type In	Return	Go To		Type In	Return
A98/	LO	"Exp.	R	B103	LO	"30%"	R
B98		profits"	R	C103	VO	Insert probability values of achieving 30% profit level	R
B99	LO	"10%"	R				
C99	VO	Insert probability values of achieving 10% profit level	R	D103	VO	"C103*0.3*C96"	R
				B104	LO	"35%"	R
D99	VO	"C99*0.1*C96"	R	C104	VO	Insert probability values of achieving 35% profit level	R
B100	LO	"15%"	R				
C100	VO	Insert probability values of achieving 15% profit level	R	D104	VO	"C104*0.35*C96"	R
				A106/	LO	"Maintenance	R
D100	VO	"C100*0.15*C96"	R	B106		adv." for mainte-nance advertising	R
B101	LO	"20%"	R				
C101	VO	Insert probability values of achieving 20% profit level	R	C106	VO	Insert value of mainte-nance advertising	R
				A108	LO	"Net profit"	R
D101	VO	"C101*0.2*C96"	R	C108	VO	"SUM(D99:D104)−C106"	R
B102	LO	"25%"	R				
C102	VO	Insert probability values of achieving 25% profit level	R	A110	LO	"ROI" for Return On Investment	R
				C111	VO	"C108/(C83+C81)−1"	R
D102	VO	"C102*0.25*C96"	R				

Product diversification commentary

The examples given (Examples 9.1.1 and 9.1.2) show how the model could be used in two instances, the launch of a biological washing powder in the United Kingdom and the evaluation of the takeover by Nestle of Carnation Foods.

Example 9.1.1, that of Ariel Automatic, shows what values the marketing manager might put on certain elements of the market, the product's position, long-term factors, management and production considerations.

He would consider that the availability of consumers for the product would be very important, together with its profitability and whether it is meeting current consumer trends or not. The fact that it should be unique is not considered particularly crucial especially as there are a number of biological powders already in the market.

When the probability of these events occurring is considered, the marketing manager would be aware that the level of garment soiling is steadily decreasing

Proforma 9.1 Product diversification model

A/B/	C	D	E	F
2	Product	Divers.	Analysis	
4				PROBABILITY
5 FACTOR	Weight	V.Good	Good	Average
7 MARKET DYNAMICS				
9 Cons. Pres	5	0	0.2	0.3
10		C9*D9*1	C9*E9*0.8	C9*F9*0.6
11 Unique	1	0	0.2	0.3
12		C11*D11*1	C11*E11*0.8	C11*F11*0.6
13 Fashion	2	0.5	0.2	0.3
14		C13*D13*1	C13*E13*0.8	C13*F13*0.6
15 Profit	2	0	0	0.7
16	IFSUM(C9:C15)=10THEN10ELSE0	C15*D15*1	C15*E15*0.8	C15*F15*0.6
17				
18PRODUCT POSITION				
20 Interact	2	0.6	0.4	0
21		C20*D20*1	C20*E20*0.8	C20*F20*0.6
22 Sizes/gr	2	1	0	0
23		C22*D22*1	C22*E22*0.8	C22*F22*0.6
24 Packagin	2	0.2	0.2	0.2
25		C24*D24*1	C24*E24*0.8	C24*F24*0.6
26 Qual/prc	2	0.5	0.3	0.2
27		C26*D26*1	C26*E26*0.8	C26*F26*0.6
28 Distrib	2	0.6	0.4	0
29	IFSUM(C20:C28)=10THEN10ELSE0	C28*D28*1	C28*E28*0.8	C28*F28*0.6
30				
31 LONG TERM				
33 Fluctuat	5	0.2	0.4	0.3
34		C33*D33*1	C33*E33*0.8	C33*F33*0.6

Proforma 9.1 *(continued)*

	G	H	I	J	
2					□■
					□□
4					□
5	Poor	V,Poor		Index	
7					
9	0,5	0	IFSUM(D9;H9)=1THEN1ELSE0		
10	C9*G9*0,4	C9*H9*0,2		SUM(C10;H10)/I9	
11	0,5	0	IFSUM(D11;H11)=1THEN1ELSE0		
12	C11*G11*0,4	C11*H11*0,2		SUM(C12;H12)/I11	
13	0	0	IFSUM(D13;H13)=1THEN1ELSE0		
14	C13*G13*0,4	C13*H13*0,2		SUM(D14;H14)/I13	
15	0,3	0	IFSUM(D15;H15)=1THEN1ELSE0		
16	C15*G15*0,4	C15*H15*0,2		SUM(D16;H16)/I15	
17				SUM(J10;J16)	
18					
20	0	0	IFSUM(D20;H20)=1THEN1ELSE0		
21	C20*G20*0,4	C20*H20*0,2		SUM(D21;H21)/I20	
22	0	0	IFSUM(D22;H22)=1THEN1ELSE0		
23	C22*G22*0,4	C22*H22*0,2		SUM(D23;H23)/I22	
24	0,2	0,2	IFSUM(D24;H24)=1THEN1ELSE0		
25	C24*G24*0,4	C24*H24*0,2		SUM(D25;H25)/I24	
26	0	0	IFSUM(D26;H26)=1THEN1ELSE0		
27	C26*G26*0,4	C26*H26*0,2		SUM(D27;H27)/I26	
28	0	0	IFSUM(D28;H28)=1THEN1ELSE0		
29	C28*G28*0,4	C28*H28*0,2		SUM(D29;H29)I28	
30				SUM(J21;J29)	
31					
33	0,1	0	IFSUM(D33;H33)=1THEN1ELSE0		
34	C33*G33*0,4	C33*H33*0,2		SUM(D34;H34)/I33	

Proforma 9.1 *(continued)*

A/B/	C	D	E	F
35 Niche	3	0	0	0,5
36		C35*D35*1	C35*E35*0,8	C35*F35*0,6
37 Patent	2	0	0	0
38	IFSUM(C33;C37)=10THEN10ELSE0	C37*D37*1	C37*E37*0,8	C37*F37*0,6
39				
40 MANAGEMENT				
42 Personnel	2	0,7	0,3	0
43		C42*D42*1	C42*E42*0,8	C42*F42*0,6
44 Skills	8	0,5	0,5	0
45	IFSUM(C42;C44)=10THEN10ELSE0	C44*D44*1	C44*E44*0,8	C44*F44*0,6
46				
47 PRODUCTION				
49 Equipment	6	0,8	0,2	0
50		C49*D49*1	C49*E49*0,8	C49*F48*0,6
51 Components	3	0,6	0,3	0,1
52		C51*D51*1	C51*E51*0,8	C51*F51*0,6
53 Expertise	1	0,4	0,2	0,4
54	IFSUM(C49;C53)=10THEN10ELSE0	C53*D53*1	C53*E53*0,8	C53*F53*0,6
55				
56 FACTOR INDEX				
58 Market dynamics	J17/C16*10			
60 Product position	J30/C29*10			
62 Long term factor	J39/C38*10			
64 Management	J46/C45*10			
66 Production	J55/C54*10			
68 PROD,DIV,INDEX	SUM(C58;C66)			
71 Short run profit				
73 Ex, sales level	5000000			
75 Ex, sale price$	3,5			
77 Ex,prod,cost $	3			

Proforma 9.1 *(continued)*

	G	H	I	J
35	0,5	0	IFSUM(D35;H35)=1THEN1ELSE0	
36	C35*G35*0,4	C35*H35*0,2		SUM(D36;H36)/I35
37	0	1	IFSUM(D37;H37)=1THEN1ELSE0	
38	C37*G37*0,4	C37*H37*0,2		SUM(D38;H38)/I37
39				SUM(J34;J38)
40				
42	0	0	IFSUM(D42;H42)=1THEN1ELSE0	
43	C42*G42*0,4	C42*H42*0,2		SUM(D43;H43)/I42
44	0	0	IFSUM(D44;H44)=1THEN1ELSE0	
45	C44*G44*0,4	C44*H44*0,2		SUM(D45;H45)/I44
46				SUM(J43;J46)
47				
49	0	0	IFSUM(D49;H49)=1THEN1ELSE0	
50	C49*G49*0,4	C49*H49*0,2		SUM(D50;H50)/I49
51	0	0	IFSUM(D51;H51)=1THEN1ELSE0	
52	C51*G51*0,4	C51*H51*0,2		SUM(D52;H42)/I51
53	0	0	IFSUM(D51;H51)=1THEN1ELSE0	
54	C53*G53*0,4	C53*H53*0,2		SUM(D54;H54)/I53
55				SUM(J50;J54)

Proforma 9.1   *(concluded)*

A/B/	C	D	E	F
79 Launch costs$	8000000			
81 Cap.expend.$	500000			
83 Add.wk.capital$	300000			
85 Comp.free time	0			
87 Prod. div.index	C68*0.02			
90	C87*C73*(C75-C77)*(1+C85)			
91 Short term	C90/(C81+C83+C79)			
92 index				
93 Long term				
95 Quick analysis				
96 Total sales$	2.E7			
98 Exp. profits				
99 10%	0	C99*0.1*C96		
100 15%	0	C100*0.15*C96		
101 20%	0.2	C101*0.20*C96		
102 25%	0.4	C102*0.25*C96		
103 30%	0.3	C103*0.3*C96		
104 35%	0.1	C104*0.35*C96		
106Maintenance adv.3500000				
108Net profit	SUM(D99:D104)-C106			
110 ROI				
111	C108/(C83+C81)-1			

and the number of consumers available in the market place is likely to be small. This will be a particular problem in the long term for the product to withstand changes in the market environment. Both factors are therefore assigned a relatively low probability of occurrence; similarly faced with these changes it may find difficulty in establishing a niche in the market place.

Other elements receive much higher scores – the product will interact well with other products, fit into the distribution path, and probably be able to command a premium. The company has the management available to handle the product, and production will pose no major problem.

In consequence the market position and long-term strength of the product in the market would tend to raise issues requiring further consideration, whereas production, management and interaction would be very positive features of the new brand.

When the short-run aspects of the brand are considered further worrying aspects would be revealed. First that there is a need for a very high initial advertising campaign which combined with the lack of a competitive free period produces a very low short-term index, indicating that the product is not initially profitable, and indeed will cause a substantial loss even in the medium term.

Evaluation of the long-run profit suggests that the brand may be more viable eventually even though maintenance advertising will continue to be considerable.

The conclusion that could be arrived at by a casual use of this model is that the likely success of Ariel Automatic would be limited and the company would be better advised to try another approach to the market place.

The analysis of the Carnation takeover (Example 9.1.2) by Nestle would yield a different set of criteria and probability of occurrence. For the Nestle organisation the availability of consumers both in the short and long term would be very important. The chances of this occurring could be considered excellent – there will always be demand for Carnation products in the foreseeable future. In consequence, the score that this analysis obtains is much higher than that of the washing powder. Management, production skills and the position of the product in the overall company structure are also positive.

Nestle could also consider the question of short- and long-run profitability using likely sales levels costs and prices. Due to relatively high profitability and well established position in the market requiring little major additional investment, the short-term index generated would be much higher as would the return on capital employed in the long term.

References

1   E. Pesseimer, *New Product Decisions – An Analytical Approach*, McGraw Hill, 1968.

2   R. Leduc, *How to Launch a New Product*, Crosby Lockwood, 1966.

3   See, for example, Financial Times 11 Jan. 1985.

4   H.H. Harman, *Modern Factor Analysis*, University of Chicago, 1960.

5   J. Arndt, (ed), *Insights into Consumer Behaviour*, Alleyn and Bacon, 1968.

Example 9.1.1 Product diversification model

A/B/	C Product	D Divers.	E Analysis	F PROBABILITY	G	H	I	J
2	Product	Divers.	Analysis	PROBABILITY				Index
4								
5 FACTOR	Weight	V.Good	Good	Average	Poor	V.Poor		Index
7 MARKET DYNAMICS								
9 Cons. Pres	5	0	0.2	0.3	0.5	0	1	
10		0	0.8	0.9	1	0		2.7
11 Unique	1	0	0	0	0.3	0.7	1	
12		0	0	0	0.12	0.14		0.26
13 Fashion	2	0.5	0.2	0.3	0	0	1	
14		1	0.32	0.36	0	0		1.68
15 Profit	2	0	0	0.7	0.3	0	1	
16	10	0	0	0.84	0.24	0		1.08
17								5.72
18 PRODUCT POSITION								
20 Interact	2	0.6	0.4	0	0	0	1	
21		1.2	0.64	0	0	0		1.84
22 Sizes/gr	2	1	0	0	0	0	1	
23		2	0	0	0	0		2

A/B/	C	D	E	F	G	H	I	J
24 Packagin	2	0.2	0.2	0.2	0.2	0.2	1	
25		0.4	0.32	0.24	0.16	0.08		1.2
26 Qual/prc	2	0.5	0.3	0.2	0	0	1	
27		1	0.48	0.24	0	0		1.72
28 Distrib	2	0.6	0.4	0	0	0	1	
29		1.2	0.64	0	0	0		1.84
30	10							8.6
31 LONG TERM								
33 Fluctuat	5	0.2	0.4	0.3	0.1	0	1	
34		1	1.6	0.9	0.2	0		3.7
35 Niche	3			0.5	0.5	0	1	
36				0.9	0.6	0		1.5
37 Patent	2			0	0	1	1	
38				0	0	0.4		0.4
39	10							5.6
40 MANAGEMENT								
42 Personnel	2	0.7	0.3	0	0	0	1	
43		1.4	0.48	0	0	0		1.88
44 Skills	8	0.5	0.5	0	0	0	1	
45		4	3.2	0	0	0		7.2
46	10							9.08

□ ■ □ □

Example 9.1.1 *(concluded)*

A/B/	C	D	E	F	G	H	I	J
47 PRODUCTION								
49 Equipment	6	0.8	0.2	0	0	0	1	
50		4.8	0.96	0	0	0		5.76
51 Components	3	0.6	0.3	0.1	0	0	1	
52		1.8	0.72	0.18	0	0		2.7
53 Expertise	1	0.4	0.2	0.4	0	0	1	
54	10	0.4	0.16	0.24	0	0		0.8
55								9.26
56 FACTOR INDEX								
58 Market dynamics	5.72							
60 Product position	8.64							
62 Long term factor	5.6							
64 Management	9.08							
66 Production	9.26							
68 PROD DIV INDEX	38.26							
71 Short run profit								
73 Ex sales level	5000000							
75 Ex sale price$	3.5							
77 Ex prod cost $	3							
79 Launch costs$	8000000							

□□■□

A/B/	C	D	E	F	G	H	I	J
81 Cap expend $	500000							
83 Add wk capital$	300000							
85 Comp free time	0							
87 Prod div index	0.7636							
90	1909000							
91 Short term	0.21693							
92 index								
93 Long term								
95 Quick analysis								
96 Total sales$	2.E7							
98 Exp. profits								
99 10%	0	0						
100 15%	0	0						
101 20%	0.2	80000						
102 25%	0.4	200000						
103 30%	0.3	1800000						
104 35%	0.1	70000						
106Maintenance adv.3500000								
108Net profit	1800000							
110 ROI								
111	1.25							

Example 9.1.2 Product diversification model

A/B/	C	D	E	F	G	H	I	J
2	Product	Divers.	Analysis					
4				PROBABILITY				
5 FACTOR	Weight	V.Good	Good	Average	Poor	V.Poor		Index
7 MARKET DYNAMICS								
9 Cons. Pres	5	0.6	0.2	0.2	0	0	1	
10	3	3	0.8	0.6	0	0	1	4.4
11 Unique	1	0	0	0	0.3	0.7	1	
12		0	0	0	0.12	0.14		0.26
13 Fashion	0	0.5	0.2	0.3	0	0	1	
14		0	0	0	0	0		0
15 Profit	4	0.5	0.2	0.3	0	0	1	
16	10	2	0.64	0.72	0	0		3.36
17								8.02
18 PRODUCT POSITION								
20 Interact	4	0.6	0.4	0	0	0	1	
21		2.4	1.28	0	0	0		3.68
22 Sizes/gr	1	1	0	0	0	0	1	
23		1	0	0	0	0		1

A/B/	C	D	E	F	G	H	I	J
24 Packagin	1	0.2	0.2	0.2	0.2	0.2	1	
25		0.2	0.16	0.12	0.08	0.04		0.6
26 Qual/prc	2	0.5	0.3	0.2		0	1	
27		1	0.48	0.24		0		1.72
28 Distrib	2	0.6	0.4	0		0	1	
29		1.2	0.64	0		0		1.84
30	10							8.84
31 LONG TERM								
33 Fluctuat	5	0.2	0.4	0.3	0.1	0	1	
34		1	1.6	0.9	0.2	0		3.7
35 Niche	5	0.7	0.2	0	0	0	1	
36		3.5	0.8	0	0	0		4.3
37 Patent	0	0	0	0	0	1	1	
38		0	0	0	0	0		0
39	10							8
40 **MANAGEMENT**								
42 Personnel	2	0.7	0.3	0	0	0	1	
43		1.4	0.48	0	0	0		1.88
44 Skills	8	0.5	0.5	0	0	0	1	
45		4	3.2	0	0	0		7.2
46	10							9.08

Example 9.1.2 *(concluded)*

A/B/	C	D	E	F	G	H	I	J
47 PRODUCTION								
49 Equipment	5	0.8	0.2	0	0	0	1	
50		4	0.8	0	0	0		4.8
51 Components	1	0.6	0.3	0.1	0	0	1	
52		0.6	0.24	0.06	0	0		0.9
53 Expertise	4	0.4	0.2	0.4	0	0	1	
54	10	1.6	0.64	0.96	0	0		3.2
55								8.9
56 FACTOR INDEX								
58 Market dynamics	8.02							
60 Product position	8.84							
62 Long term factor	8							
64 Management	9.08							
66 Production	8.9							
68 PROD DIV INDEX	42.84							
71 Short run profit								
73 Ex sales level	8.E9							
75 Ex sale price$	0.6							
77 Ex prod cost $	0.45							
79 Launch costs$	0							

A/B/	C	D	E	F	G	H	I	J
81 Cap expend $	5.E7							
83 Add wk capital$	3000000							
85 Comp free time	0							
87 Prod div index	0.8568							
90	1.028E9							
91 Short term	19.3992							
92 index								
93 Long term								
95 Quick analysis								
96 Total sales$	8.E9							
98 Exp. profits								
99	10%	0	0					
100	15%	0.3	3.6E8					
101	20%	0.2	3.2E8					
102	25%	0.4	8.E8					
103	30%	0.1	2.4E8					
104	35%	0	0					
106Maintenance adv.5600000								
108Net profit	1.714E9							
110 ROI								
111	31.3472							

10 Forecasting

Notice in community hall:

> 'The meeting of the clairvoyance society is cancelled due to unforeseen circumstances.'

Gypsies make a good living out of their ability to create a convincing story out of the lines on people's hands, the way in which tea leaves come to lie in the cup or how the light permeates through a misty crystal (probably plastic) ball. It is one of the misfortunes of business managers' lives that they are required to be more accurate and generally more objective about the future faced by their companies. Promises of health, wealth and unspecified happiness will not satisfy the firm wanting precise forecasts of the likely sales of machinery, durables, or consumer goods in the forthcoming years.

The development of forecasts is rightly regarded as one of the most important, though difficult aspects of the business manager's job, particularly in a rapidly changing environment. In the hypothetical circumstances of a particular company selling to one end-user one product, with no competition or other variation in the environment, the need for a sophisticated, accurate forecasting system is minimal. At the other hypothetical extreme exists the situation where rapidly changing political conditions coincide with continual changes in technology. Consider the problems faced by a firm in the electronics sector receiving large infrequent orders in a country with high inflation, and low political stability, which had been protected for many years by tariff barriers. The chances are small that this company would be able to accurately predict likely changes with such areas of the business environment as pricing, product development, cash flow and the like being beyond its control.

Some essential first steps

In common with many other activities the use of a structured approach to

178

forecasting will ensure that where gaps exist, they will at least be identified and the shortfalls of the process realised and allowed for. The following steps will need to be considered in any forecasting process:

1 Identifying the forecasting problem A crucial question is how important the forecast is to the organisation's priorities and how many resources are involved in it. An evaluation can then be derived of the cost/benefit of various approaches including the problems of data collection. Obviously a simple environment will not require complex forecasting tools.

2 Determining the forecast structure This will show how various elements of the forecasting system interact and will also identify the data needed to fill gaps; the commissioning of market research would be an example. Another important decision will be the cost of the forecasting technique necessary to produce accurate results balanced against the level of investment hanging on the decision. This can be summarised in table form (Figure 10.1).

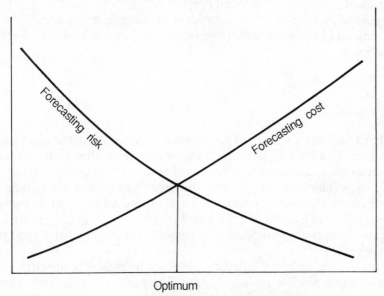

Figure 10.1 **Forecasting risk *versus* cost: defining the optimum**

3 Collecting the data for the forecast A further check as to whether the structure of the forecasting system is consistent with the problem will occur at this stage.

4 Constructing the forecasting model and carrying out the analysis The main factor in any data evaluation is that a pre-determined hypothesis should be tested against the available data, and not that the data is tested for possible correlations, as this will tend to produce numerous spurious interrelationships.

5 Preparing the forecast The assumptions underlying the forecast can now be checked against a 'reasonableness' test – whether the data is within the bounds expected.

6   *Evaluation of the forecast*   To maintain accuracy the forecast will need to be regularly updated and should the estimates differ significantly from the actual, the forecasting system should be re-evaluated.

Though the majority of forecasting exercises will be difficult, the more accurate the picture that is obtained, the smaller the area of uncertainty the business will face. The aim is to reduce the risk element through a system bounded by knowledge controlling success and failure as much as possible.

The broader problems of forecasting

The broad areas which can affect a company's prosperity are quite often those over which it has no control and in consequence has not developed sufficient expertise to evaluate. These problems will include the political, economic and technological factors earlier touched upon.

These general issues need to be considered before detailed 'number crunching' – the building up of the page after page of numbers that the modern large business requires – begins.

Political

Even within a particular system of government, the nature of the political problem will vary from company to company. For example, to the firm engaged in the aerospace business, the nature of the conflict between East and West will be of overriding importance in determining the growth in demand. It would be of far less relevance in the more mundane case of the vehicle body manufacturer producing specialised buses for the handicapped which could either benefit or suffer greatly from changes in local government attitude towards the community's underprivileged.

The nature of the political equation becomes increasingly important when the company ventures outside its home base. The problems that firms can face are only too obvious in a number of countries ranging from straightforward sequestration of assets to the restricted ability to expand or remit profits abroad.

Macro-economic

The basic economic difficulties that the firm faces will also differ. Where an organisation is actively involved in overseas trade the movement of the exchange rates over time will be vital, especially where the ability to raise prices is limited. The rate of inflation is of general importance to all firms but especially those allowed only one or two price rises in the year. Interest rates will have major implications not only because of their potential effects on demand but also for their possible impact on the firm's finances, so that forecasting changes in this area can have vital connotations in two spheres of company activity.

These major or macro-economic trends have proved practically impossible for governments let alone small to medium-sized firms to determine. There have always been and doubtless will continue to be disputes about future levels of inflation even when hundreds of governmental economists have studied the problem. This lack of any accurate prediction extends to other factors such as economic growth, and the exact interaction of the amount of money in circulation and the level of price rises.

Socio-economic

Changes in population structures can cause significant changes in the environment with which the company is required to cope. Generally, these trends are slower to emerge than others, but still can pose serious problems in many areas. The dramatic increase in the consumption of real ale and the demise of the pressurised keg beers is one example of such a rapid change altering the way in which breweries analysed their investments in plant and equipment.

Technology

The impact of technology is another area that historically has proved difficult to predict. There are several examples of conferences of 'futurist experts' coming up with a practically blank sheet of success, predicting the arrival of the currently impossible (anti-gravity, commercial nuclear fusion) while omitting the attainable (hovercraft, lasers). In common with major political and economic factors all the overall consideration of the likely effect of major technological change can do is to set a series of broad limits to any forecast.

The degree of uncertainty will widen as the time horizon lengthens. Thus the impact of the 256k silicon chip on the computer industry can perhaps be predicted with some degree of accuracy. Looking forward two or three years the advent of the 1 megabyte chip will surely introduce entirely new problems and opportunities each with their influences on demand.

Forecasting techniques

One can develop a series of ground rules for the credibility that can be placed on the forecasting of any eventual trend: from the most simple to the most complex. The key is in the simplicity of the information and the degree to which the data bears a steady relationship to other factors. Returning to our initial hypothetical example of the single product sold to a single end-user, the buyer will obviously be the best source of information on the likely demand for the product in the forthcoming period. Where a limited number of outlets is involved this method is easily achievable and produces the best estimates for future demand. The sales force could also be used to develop estimates from their contact with the buyers, a particularly appropriate method when the number of end-users remains small and the product faces considerable competition with a high technical content.

Once this simple level of product and market interaction is passed the problems of forecasting become more acute and a variety of techniques are brought into play each of which has advantages and disadvantages.

1   Historical analysis

This system entails the comparison of records of similar products both within and outside the company. The data required is several years' sales records of one or more competitive products in their respective markets.

The value of the use of historical analyses is largely in the forecasting of margins and perhaps new product sales. It generally fails to identify short-term and very long-term trends, with its greatest accuracy on the medium-term horizon – 3 months to 2 years.

The main shortcoming is that it does not identify likely changes in product usage, the turning point, should this be likely to occur. Take, for example, the case of the skateboard manufacturer and the importance of determining when the popularity of the item would start to decline. Most failed to do so and collapsed with the declining market. Straightforward historical projections will also run into problems when there is a high degree of seasonality, requiring the use of smoothing techniques.

2   Visionary statement

Occasionally these can be extremely successful forecasting techniques, consisting as they do of a leap in the dark, usually by the chief executive. In general terms, however, the visionary statement can be regarded as suspect, failing to predict problems accurately, in the short, medium and long term.

3   Panel consensus

This system – in operation, for example, at the Lockheed Corporation – works on the assumption that the combination of a team of experts will produce a more sophisticated and reliable forecast than one produced by an individual (1). Psychological studies would suggest that the group will be heavily influenced by generally one, or occasionally two individuals (2). The data required is similar to that needed for the historical analysis. The accuracy of the information can, because of the nature of the group decision, be regarded as suspect for all time periods.

4   Delphi method

This system attempts to remove the dominant personality effects seen in the panel consensus. It involves the development of questionnaires to be answered by the relevant individuals in isolation to others. The process is time consuming requiring a whole series of questionnaires and therefore has relevance only to the medium- and long-term problems that the firm may be encountering such as technological changes. In the development of trends it tends to accurately identify particular worries though there may be difficulties in isolating the turning points in the product sales.

5 Cross-impact analysis

With the use of large-scale technical assistance it is possible to assign values to the interaction of each major factor on another and then to determine the probability of it occurring. The data required for this analysis is extensive and time-consuming, though the results are able to provide information on the likely decline of the product range in the medium to long term. One of the main drawbacks of this method is that it often needs extensive market research to establish the underlying interrelationships, which often have to use regression techniques (see below) for correct evaluation. As a result of this, the method is largely irrelevant once the underlying interactions have been exposed by regression calculation.

These qualitative methods suffer from the fact that they largely do not sufficiently analyse the past data nor do they identify effectively the causal relationships inherent in any changing business environment. The analysis of the changes that occur over time are particularly important when in addition to seasonal changes there may be significant changes in long-term demand.

6 Moving annual totals

The combination of annual or bi-annual totals on a month by month or quarter by quarter basis can provide valuable trend information for forecasting purposes, using small quantities of data and removing the main problems associated with seasonal variations. However the data may contain variation other than that of seasonality and the moving average method will not identify these sufficiently. Secondly, more recent sales data will tend to be a better reflection of the trends in the market place than data from two or three years ago.

7 Exponential smoothing

This technique develops a moving annual or bi-annual total which is then weighted to give more credence to the more recent elements of the record. It has the advantages of speed and data collection but in common with the qualitative methods the long-term value of the predictions will tend to be small. There are a number of ways to minimise the problems associated with the effects of the combination of trends and seasonality (3).

8 Box-Jenkins

A development of exponential smoothing, this technique involves the development of a mathematical model which accurately describes the past history of the data, enabling data such as price changes, and distribution effects to be included as explanatory factors of sales trends. The value of this system is particularly strong in the short term, enabling accurate definition of problems such as inventory control and production planning. It does, however, require more detailed mathematical analysis than the majority of forecasting models (4).

9   X-11

A further development of the exponential smoothing system, it consists of the division of historical data into a series of sub-components (5). It removes all seasonal fluctuation to short-term data and can, in consequence, produce accurate short- to medium-term forecasting showing whether growth trends are in reality declining or reversing. The data required for the evaluation is more than three years' sales history and in consequence its main application is in the areas of forecasting sales in the short term and evaluating budgets (6).

10   Boston Consulting Group

The effects of the learning or experience curve can be expanded to deal with considerable elements of companies' sales performance including such elements as sales and distribution costs, provided that several years' history is available for all the relevant products.

The problem remains with all such trend analyses that the change in the sales level over a period of time may be heavily dependent on a particular factor which if it changes significantly will lead to considerable changes in sales levels and be unpredictable by any smoothing or extrapolation system.

In consequence, causal forecasting systems are regarded as the most valuable method of developing an understanding of the business environment. They all attempt to derive an interrelationship between a company factor (such as sales) with an independent data element in the external environment (per capita income).

11   Index systems

With these a 'basket' of economic or social indicators is developed which allows an index to be produced from which the sales performance or other company data can be derived. These indexes suffer from the fact that the real underlying causes of company performance are not identified making long-term projections highly questionable.

12   Life cycle analysis

There are many companies that use the concept of product life cycle to derive forecasts of new introductions, separating the socio-economic divisions of innovators, early acceptors, and so on to derive the overall progress of the particular item. The concept of the product life cycle does however yield little of predictive value in many instances (see Chapter 1 on product viability).

13   Econometric analysis

The development of an econometric model is an attempt to develop a predictive system for one or more economic variables which affect the particular business. Thus relationships have been defined for various industries:

Automobiles: disposable income, relative price, unemployment, credit
Services: disposable income, consumption of non-durables in previous time periods

The further development of econometric models enables simulations to be developed through which 'what-if' problems can be evaluated, eventually producing extremely complicated management control systems costing hundreds of thousands of dollars.

The problem with econometric analysis as with all complex mathematics, is that it becomes divorced from the management responsible for the implementation of the results flowing from the analyses, and because the relationship is statistical in nature the results will often be viewed with scepticism. The use of such systems will also mean that power conflicts will develop within the organisation – the forecasts developed by the data processing division may be forced onto the marketing and commercial departments as being the 'correct' decisions.

14   Regression analysis

The use of a regression analysis technique appears to offer the line manager the best practical causal forecasting system available, as it provides functional analysis of the underlying variable interactions, by the use of statistical techniques which can best be calculated using computer methods. The relationships obtained provide accurate indications of short- and medium-term trends within the business environment, and are also easy to use and apply in contrast to the more complicated causal relationship techniques, providing the problems that exist with the use of any causal analysis technique are sufficiently understood.

Two forecasting models

Of the two models provided, one gives a simple approach to the use of moving annual totals, discussed in the section on forecasting techniques, and various smoothing parameters; the other uses regression techniques which enable the manager to determine the interaction of one variable on another and from that to predict the future behaviour of those criteria for forecasting purposes. The use of a moving annual total system will supply information on gross movements in any particular factor. It may hide important seasonal and non-seasonal trend data. The model allows the manager to introduce a weighting factor into the analysis to make the recent data more important in the trend calculation.

Regression analysis demands that the variables chosen do, in fact bear some relation to each other: otherwise the result may produce a correlation which does not, in fact, exist. Thus there may be a surface correlation between the number of red-headed children and the number of computers sold during the Christmas period. Nevertheless it would be an unwise firm that based future sales on the production of red-headed children! Often such a correlation will arrive from the lack of data that is correlated, as spurious results will be more likely to appear from small data sets.

Other problems can occur in other areas. When the two factors are interactive the results cannot be trusted as the result of one set of data is dependent on another creating a loop which needs to be broken before reliable output can be achieved. This is also true when the factors are practically identical. The number of cars on the roads and the number of car registrations would be an example in point. To enable the procedure to be most effective a number of precautionary preliminary steps need to be taken with the data:

1 Identify and smooth out any major seasonal trend in the data.
2 Identify the logical variables for analysis and then initially graph the relationships to ensure that the variables are independent (disposable income and car ownership would in this context be classified as independent variables, car ownership and car registration would not).
3 Convert variables into their necessary form, and perform the regression equations.
4 Test for predictability.

The model deals with the case where one data set is additional to another in a relationship such as:

$$X = y1 + y2 + y3$$

X could be a factor such as sales or demand, y1 would be the base level of demand without the existence of y2 and y3 which could be per capita income factors or ownership of video recorders. It can be seen that what the model is attempting to do is to explain a particular factor in respect of the underlying variables that are responsible for the change that is observable over time.

What is derived from the use of regression equations is the identification of possible factors that explain the variation over time of the main variable such as sales that the organisation wishes to identify. The nature of the information provided can be used to determine whether these relationships are significant or not. From that the model can be used to investigate factors which have a greater level of significance or to use the system to predict values in 'what-if' simulations.

The data sources for use in the model remain an important problem area that the majority of firms need to overcome so that the underlying causal relationships can be fully explored. Such considerations again underlie the value of the model in the development of control systems within the firm to collect and analyse relevant data.

Using the two forecasting models

The *Go To* column in Listings 10.1 and 10.2 tells you the cell number and the cursor position. The next column specifies the spreadsheet option (LO = Label Option; VO = Value Option). The *Type In* column gives you instructions within the inverted commas which you must type in or asks you to supply the necessary data. These commas are not part of the instructions supplied here and should not be typed in. Beware however that some spreadsheets, the *Lotus 1-2-3* for example, enter the Label Option by using the inverted-comma key. Under the *Type In* column the symbols * = multiply and / = divide. R in the *Return* column instructs you to commit the information to memory by pressing the Return key.

Remember: When you have finished, save your model.

Model 1   Moving annual total analysis

Note: Unlike the majority of other models listed in this book, Listing 10.1 is not presented on a line by line basis. Because you will be entering sets of monthly figures over a twelve-month period the listing by alphabetical column will help you to avoid confusing the data.

Listing 10.1   Moving annual total analysis model

Go To		Type In	Return	Go To		Type In	Return
A2/	LO	"MAT	R	A6	LO	"2"	R
B2		ANALYSIS"	R	A7	LO	"3"	R
B4	LO	"Month 0"	R	A8	LO	"4"	R
				A9	LO	"5"	R
Month 0 is the base figure.				A10	LO	"6"	R
C4	LO	"Month 1"	R	A11	LO	"7"	R
D4	LO	"Month 2"	R	A12	LO	"8"	R
E4	LO	"Month 3"	R	A13	LO	"9"	R
F4	LO	"Month 4"	R	A14	LO	"10"	R
G4	LO	"Month 5"	R	A15	LO	"11"	R
H4	LO	"Month 6"	R	A16	LO	"12"	R
I4	LO	"Month 7"	R	B5	VO	Enter sales figures for	
J4	LO	"Month 8"	R	to		months 1–12 for pre-	
K4	LO	"Month 9"	R	B16		vious twelvemonth	R
L4	LO	"Month 10"	R				
M4	LO	"Month 11"	R	Note: These figures represent the Moving Annual Totals of sales for the previous twelvemonth.			
N4	LO	"Month 12"	R				
A5	LO	"1"	R	B17	VO	"SUM(B5:B16)"	R

Listing 10.1 *(continued)*

Go To		Type In	Return	Go To		Type In	Return
C5 to C16	VO	Enter sales figures for months 1–12 for previous twelvemonth for Month 1	R	K5 to K16	VO	Enter sales figures for months 1–12 for previous twelvemonth for Month 9	R
C17	VO	"SUM(C5:C16)"	R	K17	VO	"SUM(K5:K16)"	R
D5 to D16	VO	Enter sales figures for months 1–12 for previous twelvemonth for Month 2	R	L5 to L16	VO	Enter sales figures for months 1–12 for previous twelvemonth for Month 10	R
D17	VO	"SUM(D5:D16)"	R	L17	VO	"SUM(L5:L16)"	R
E5 to E16	VO	Enter sales figures for months 1–12 for previous twelvemonth for Month 3	R	M5 to M16	VO	Enter sales figures for months 1–12 for previous twelvemonth for Month 11	R
E17	VO	"SUM(E5:E16)"	R	M17	VO	"SUM(M5:M16)"	R
F5 to F16	VO	Enter sales figures for months 1–12 for previous twelvemonth for Month 4	R	N5 to N16	VO	Enter sales figures for months 1–12 for previous twelvemonth for Month 12	R
F17	VO	"SUM(F5:F16)"	R	N17	VO	"SUM(N5:N16)"	R
G5 to G16	VO	Enter sales figures for months 1–12 for previous twelvemonth for Month 5	R	A19	LO	"Growth"	R
				A20	LO	"Factor"	R
G17	VO	"SUM(G5:G16)"	R	B20	VO	Enter value for growth or decline. A minus value should be entered if you are concerned with sales decline	R
H5 to H16	VO	Enter sales figures for months 1–12 for previous twelvemonth for Month 6	R				
H17	VO	"SUM(H5:H16)"	R				
I5 to I16	VO	Enter sales figures for months 1–12 for previous twelvemonth for Month 7	R				
I17	VO	"SUM(I5:I16)"	R				
J5 to J16	VO	Enter sales figures for months 1–12 for previous twelvemonth for Month 8	R				
J17	VO	"SUM(J5:J16)"	R				

By entering a growth factor in B20 you can compare Moving Annual Totals on a month by month basis with that particular growth factor and graph the results of the actual sales of the last 12 months against the sales predicted. The factor entered in B20 will determine the 12 month projection appearing in line 21. By matching the totals along line 17 you will have an evaluation of the best fit growth or decline in the market.

Listing 10.1   *(concluded)*

Go To		Type In	Return	Go To		Type In	Return
C21	VO	"B17*(1+B20)"	R	A26	LO	"Revised"	R
D21	VO	"C21*(1+B20)"	R	B26	VO	Enter value of revised factor	R
E21	VO	"D21*(1+B20)"	R	A27	LO	"Factor"	R
F21	VO	"E21*(1+B20)"	R	C27	VO	"B17*B24*(1+B26)"	R
G21	VO	"F21*(1+B20)"	R	D27	VO	"C27*C24*(1+B26)"	R
H21	VO	"G21*(1+B20)"	R	E27	VO	"D27*D24*(1+B26)"	R
I21	VO	"H21*(1+B20)"	R	F27	VO	"E27*E24*(1+B26)"	R
J21	VO	"I21*(1+B20)"	R	G27	VO	"F27*F24*(1+B26)"	R
K21	VO	"J21*(1+B20)"	R	H27	VO	"G27*G24*(1+B26)"	R
L21	VO	"K21*(1+B20)"	R	I27	VO	"H27*H24*(1+B26)"	R
M21	VO	"L21*(1+B20)"	R	J27	VO	"I27*I24*(1+B26)"	R
N21	VO	"M21*(1+B20)"	R	K27	VO	"J27*J24*(1+B26)"	R
A23/	LO	"Smoothing"	R	L27	VO	"K27*K24*(1+B26)"	R
B23			R	M27	VO	"L27*L24*(1+B26)"	R
A24	LO	"Factor"	R	N27	VO	"M27*M24*(1+B26)"	R
B24 to M24	VO	Enter Smoothing Factors to value old data with recent data	R				

Forecasting commentary

The moving annual total model (Example 10.1) shows the effects of changing monthly sales on an underlying trend which is shown graphically in Figure 10.2. The model can also be used to examine the effects of various weighting factors on monthly totals to value the more recent sales data more highly than old data, by introducing a series of monthly weighting factors and then a revised growth factor to recalculate the month by month movement in sales. Correlation between the uncorrected moving totals and the weighted totals may provide a further backcheck as to the likely sales progression.

In the Example 10.1, lines C17 to N17 show the moving annual total for twelve months for a particular product, the underlying trend moving from 54090 to 60200. The movement in these sales volumes or values can then be correlated with a standard growth (or decline) factor in B20 which will produce a new line of figures from C21 to N21. The manager can then introduce a series of smoothing factors from B24 to M24 and a revised growth factor to recalculate the volume changes.

Proforma 10.1 Moving annual total analysis model

	A	B	C	D	E	F	G	H
		MONTH 0	MONTH 1	MONTH 2	MONTH 3	MONTH 4	MONTH 5	MONTH 6
2	MAT ANALYSIS							
4		MONTH 0	MONTH 1	MONTH 2	MONTH 3	MONTH 4	MONTH 5	MONTH 6
5	1	5000	5500	5500	5500	5500	5500	5500
6	2	2400	2400	3200	3200	3200	3200	3200
7	3	3400	3400	3400	3700	3700	3700	3700
8	4	4000	4000	4000	4000	4500	4500	4500
9	5	5000	5000	5000	5000	5000	6000	6000
10	6	4500	4500	4500	4500	4500	4500	5500
11	7	4790	4790	4790	4790	4790	4790	4790
12	8	4500	4500	4500	4500	4500	4500	4500
13	9	6000	6000	6000	6000	6000	6000	6000
14	10	7000	7000	7000	7000	7000	7000	7000
15	11	4000	4000	4000	4000	4000	4000	4000
16	12	3000	3000	3000	3000	3000	3000	3000
17		SUM(B5:B16)	SUM(C5:C16)	SUM(D5:D16)	SUM(E5:E16)	SUM(F5:F16)	SUM(G5:G16)	SUM(H5:H16)
19	Growth							
20	factor	0.02						
21			B17*(1+B20)	C21*(1+B20)	D21*(1+B20)	E21*(1+B20)	F21*(1+B20)	G21*(1+B20)
23	Smoothing							
24	Factor	0.083	0.166	0.25	0.33	0.417	0.5	0.583
26	Revised	1.3						
27	Factor		B17*C24*(1+B26)	C27*C24*(1+B26)	D27*D24*(1+B26)	E27*E24*(1+B26)	F27*F24*(1+B26)	G27*G24*(1+B26)

190

Proforma 10.1 *(concluded)*

	I	J	K	L	M	N
2						
4	MONTH7	MONTH8	MONTH9	MONTH10	MONTH11	MONTH12
5	5500	5500	5500	5500	5500	5500
6	3200	3200	3200	3200	3200	3200
7	3700	3700	3700	3700	3700	3700
8	4500	4500	4500	4500	4500	4500
9	6000	6000	6000	6000	6000	6000
10	5500	5500	5500	5500	5500	5500
11	7200	7200	7200	7200	7200	7200
12	4500	3800	3800	3800	3800	3800
13	6000	6000	4800	4800	4800	4800
14	7000	7000	7000	7500	7500	7500
15	4000	4000	4000	4000	4500	4500
16	3000	3000	3000	3000	3000	4000
17	SUM(I5:I16)	SUM(J5:J16)	SUM(K5:K16)	SUM(L5:L16)	SUM(M5:M16)	SUM(N5:N16)
19						
21	H21*(1+B20)	I21*(1+B20)	J21*(1+B20)	K21*(1+B20)	L21*(1+B20)	M21*(1+B20)
23						
24	0.666	0.75	0.84	0.91	1	-
26						
27	H27*H24*(1+B26)	I27*I24*(1+B26)	J27*J24*(1+B26)	K27*K24*(1+B26)	L27*L24*(1+B26)	M27*M24*(1+B26)

Model 2   Regression analysis

Listing 10.2   Regression analysis model

Go To		Type In	Return	Go To		Type In	Return
A2/	LO	"REGRESSION	R	D19	VO	"C19*C19"	R
B2/			R	D20	VO	"C20*C20"	R
C2	LO	ANALYSIS"	R	D21	VO	"C21*C21"	R
C6	LO	"X-data"	R	D22	VO	"C22*C22"	R

This refers to one set of data from the same data set for evaluation.

Go To		Type In	Return
E8 to E22	VO	Enter second set of values for analysis	R
F8	VO	"E8*E8"	R
F9	VO	"E9*E9"	R

Go To		Type In	Return
D6	LO	"X2" i.e. X squared	R
E6	LO	"Y-data"	R

This refers to the other set of data for evaluation.

Go To		Type In	Return
F10	VO	"E10*E10"	R
F11	VO	"E11*E11"	R
F6	LO	"Y2" i.e. Y squared	R
F12	VO	"E12*E12"	R
G6	LO	"X*Y"	R
F13	VO	"E13*E13"	R
H6	LO	"(X−Y)2" i.e. X−Y squared	R
F14	VO	"E14*E14"	R
F15	VO	"E15*E15"	R
C8 to C22	VO	Enter values for analysis	R
F16	VO	"E16*E16"	R
F17	VO	"E17*E17"	R
D8	VO	"C8*C8"	R
F18	VO	"E18*E18"	R
D9	VO	"C9*C9"	R
F19	VO	"E19*E19"	R
D10	VO	"C10*C10"	R
F20	VO	"E20*E20"	R
D11	VO	"C11*C11"	R
F21	VO	"E21*E21"	R
D12	VO	"C12*C12"	R
F22	VO	"E22*E22"	R
D13	VO	"C13*C13"	R
G8	VO	"C8*E8"	R
D14	VO	"C14*C14"	R
G9	VO	"C9*E9"	R
D15	VO	"C15*C15"	R
G10	VO	"C10*E10"	R
D16	VO	"C16*C16"	R
G11	VO	"C11*E11"	R
D17	VO	"C17*C17"	R
G12	VO	"C12*E12"	R
D18	VO	"C18*C18"	R
G13	VO	"C13*E13"	R
				G14	VO	"C14*E14"	R
				G15	VO	"C15*E15"	R

Go To		Type In	Return	Go To		Type In	Return
G16	VO	"C16*E16"	R	H20	VO	"C20−E20*(C20−E20)"	R
G17	VO	"C17*E17"	R	H21	VO	"C21−E21*(C21−E21)"	R
G18	VO	"C18*E18"	R	H22	VO	"C22−E22*(C22−E22)"	R
G19	VO	"C19*E19"	R	C24	VO	"SUM(C8:C22)"	R
G20	VO	"C20*E20"	R	D24	VO	"SUM(D8:D22)"	R
G21	VO	"C21*E21"	R	E24	VO	"SUM(E8:E22)"	R
G22	VO	"C22*E22"	R	F24	VO	"SUM(F8:F22)"	R
H8	VO	"C8−E8*(C8−E8)"	R	G24	VO	"SUM(G8:G22)"	R
H9	VO	"C9−E9*(C9−E9)"	R	H24	VO	"SUM(H8:H22)/13"	R
H10	VO	"C10−E10*(C10−E10)"	R	C26	VO	"G24−C24*E24/15"	R
H11	VO	"C11−E11*(C11−E11)"	R	D26	VO	"D24−C24*C24/15"	R
H12	VO	"C12−E12*(C12−E12)"	R	E26	VO	"C26/D26"	R
H13	VO	"C13−E13*(C13−E13)"	R	C28	VO	"H24/D26"	R
H14	VO	"C14−E14*(C14−E14)"	R	D28	VO	"SQRT(C28)"	R
H15	VO	"C15−E15*(C15−E15)"	R	E28	VO	"E26/D28"	R
H16	VO	"C16−E16*(C16−E16)"	R	A30/	LO	"CORRELATION	R
H17	VO	"C17−E17*(C17−E17)"	R	C30		FACTOR"	R
H18	VO	"C18−E18*(C18−E18)"	R	D30	VO	"E28"	R
H19	VO	"C19−E19*(C19−E19)"	R				

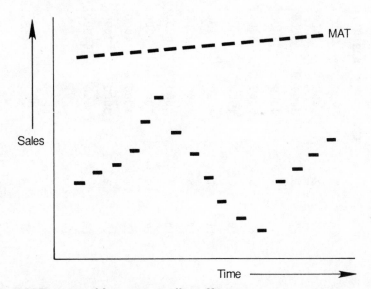

Figure 10.2   MAT: smoothing seasonality effects

Example 10.1 Moving annual total analysis model

	A	B	C	D	E	F	G	H
2	MAT ANALYSIS							
4		MONTH 0	MONTH 1	MONTH 2	MONTH 3	MONTH 4	MONTH 5	MONTH 6
5	1	5000	5500	5500	5500	5500	5500	5500
6	2	2400	2400	3200	3200	3200	3200	3200
7	3	3400	3400	3400	3700	3700	3700	3700
8	4	4000	4000	4000	4000	4500	4500	4500
9	5	5000	5000	5000	5000	5000	6000	6000
10	6	4500	4500	4500	4500	4500	4500	5500
11	7	4790	4790	4790	4790	4790	4790	4790
12	8	4500	4500	4500	4500	4500	4500	4500
13	9	6000	6000	6000	6000	6000	6000	6000
14	10	7000	7000	7000	7000	7000	7000	7000
15	11	4000	4000	4000	4000	4000	4000	4000
16	12	3000	3000	3000	3000	3000	3000	3000
17		53590	54090	54890	55190	55690	56690	57690
19	Growth							
20	factor	0.02						
21			54661.8	55755.0	56870.1	58007.5	59167.7	60351.0
23	Smoothing							
24	Factor	0.083	0.166	0.25	0.33	0.417	0.5	0.583
26	Revised	1.3						
27	Factor		10230.3	3905.94	2245.92	1704.65	1634.93	1880.17

Example 10.1 *(concluded)*

	I	J	K	L	M	N
2						
4	MONTH7	MONTH8	MONTH9	MONTH10	MONTH11	MONTH12
5	5500	5500	5500	5500	5500	5500
6	3200	3200	3200	3200	3200	3200
7	3700	3700	3700	3700	3700	3700
8	4500	4500	4500	4500	4500	4500
9	6000	6000	6000	6000	6000	6000
10	5500	5500	5500	5500	5500	5500
11	7200	7200	7200	7200	7200	7200
12	4500	3800	3800	3800	3800	3800
13	6000	6000	4800	4800	4800	4800
14	7000	7000	7000	7500	7500	7500
15	4000	4000	4000	4000	4500	4500
16	3000	3000	3000	3000	3000	4000
17	60100	59400	58200	58700	59200	60200
19						
21	61558.1	62789.2	64045.0	65325.9	66632.4	67965.1
23						
24	0.666	0.75	0.84	0.91	1	
26						
27	2521.12	3861.85	6661.69	12870.4	26937.7	61956.8

Proforma 10.2 Regression analysis model

A/B	C	D	E	F	G	H
2 Regression	Analysis					
6	X-data	X2	Y-data	Y2	X*Y	(X-Y)2
8	15	C8*C8	23	E8*E8	C8*E8	C8-E8*(C8-E8)
9	16	C9*C9	24	E9*E9	C9*E9	C9-E9*(C9-E9)
10	17	C10*C10	27	E10*E10	C10*E10	C10-E10*(C10-E10)
11	19	C11*C11	28	E11*E11	C11*E11	C11-E11*(C11-E11)
12	23	C12*C12	32	E12*E12	C12*E12	C12-E12*(C12-E12)
13	18	C13*C13	23	E13*E13	C13*E13	C13-E13*(C13-E13)
14	19	C14*C14	34	E14*E14	C14*E14	C14-E14*(C14-E14)
15	21	C15*C15	40	E15*E15	C15*E15	C15-E15*(C15-E15)
16	22	C16*C16	45	E16*E16	C16*E16	C16-E16*(C16-E16)
17	13	C17*C17	18	E17*E17	C17*E17	C17-E17*(C17-E17)
18	17	C18*C18	25	E18*E18	C18*E18	C18-E18*(C18-E18)
19	15	C19*C19	26	E19*E19	C19*E19	C19-E19*(C19-E19)
20	18	C20*C20	25	E20*E20	C20*E20	C20-E20*(C20-E20)
21	16	C21*C21	32	E21*E21	C21*E21	C21-E21*(C21-E21)
22	17	C22*C22	59	E22*E22	C22*E22	C22-E22*(C22-E22)
24	SUM(C8:C22)	SUM(D8:D22)	SUM(E8:E22)	SUM(F8:F22)	SUM(G8:G22)	SUM(H8:H22)/13
26	G24-C24*E24/15	D24-C24*C24/15	C26/D26			
28	H24/D26	SQ,RT(C28)	E26/D28			
30 Correlation Factor	E28					

196

Example 10.2 Regression analysis model

A/B	C	D	E	F	G	H
2	Regression					
	Analysis					
6	X-data	X2	Y-data	Y2	X*Y	(X-Y)2
8	15	225	23	529	345	199
9	16	256	24	576	384	208
10	17	289	27	729	459	287
11	19	361	28	784	532	271
12	23	529	32	1024	736	311
13	18	324	23	529	414	133
14	19	361	34	1156	646	529
15	21	441	40	1600	840	781
16	22	484	45	2025	990	1057
17	13	169	18	324	234	103
18	17	289	25	625	425	217
19	15	225	26	676	390	301
20	18	324	25	625	450	193
21	16	256	32	1024	512	528
22	17	289	59	3481	1003	2495
24	266	4822	461	15707	8360	585.615
26	184.933	104.933	1.76239			
28	5.58083	2.363	0.74583			
30 Correlation Factor		0.74583				

The regression analysis model (Example 10.2) considers the interrelationship between two sets of data and whether the differences between the two can be explained by chance. The correlation factor given in D30 is the degree to which the two columns differ – should the figure be zero the interrelationship will be totally random. The manager will need to check with statistical tables to find out whether the figure arrived at in D30 can be explained by chance at varying levels of statistical confidence.

References

1   G.A. Busch, 'Prudent Manager Forecasting' in E.C. Bursk, J.F. Chapman, *New Decision Making for Managers*, Mentor, 1963.

2   P.J. Harrison, 'Short Term Sales Forecasting', *Applied Statistics*, Vol. 14, No. 2/3, 1965.

3   R.G. Brown, *Statistical Forecasting for Inventory Control*, McGraw Hill, 1959.

4   G.E.P. Box, G.M. Jenkins, *Time Series Analysis, Forecasting and Control*, Holden Day Inc., 1970.

5   R.L. McLaughlin, *Time Series Forecasting*, Market Research Techniques Series No. 6, A.M.A., 1962.

6   J.C. Chambers, S.K. Mullick, D.D. Smith, *An Executive's Guide to Forecasting*, John Wiley and Sons, 1974.

11 Media investment

The investment aspect of media advertising is often overlooked by all members of a firm, with the vast sum expended every year receiving very little detailed attention. Money is spent apparently regardless of any return to the organisation. When one compares the documentation that supports the investment by an organisation in a production plant of $2 million with an advertising campaign of similar cost, the difference in length and complexity will often be ten-fold and is rarely less than five-or six-fold.

The divergence of the two approaches surely lies in the fact that the investment in plant tends to have a series of agreed and quantifiable criteria. A certain *number* of machines will need to be purchased at a certain *cost*. These machines will need a certain number of *people* to run them and will produce a certain quantity of *goods*. The latter will be costed on the basis of what the market will bear and the profit will be calculated after removing the costs of *materials* and *labour*. The reader will see that in this example all the criteria for judgement are quantifiable and are commonly agreed to have a bearing on the effectiveness of the investment. As the elements are easily identified, this common ground has also been substantially investigated by a variety of research techniques to yield a greater understanding of the best procedures that should be followed.

In the case of the $2 million advertising campaign the clarity that is apparent with the investment in plant immediately disappears. Within the majority of organisations there is considerable disagreement inside even the marketing departments on the exact role that advertising is or should be playing. One could derive a similar set of input and output criteria with the need to invest in a number of media campaigns (*machines*) and the *people* that they require. Once these are available a certain number of consumer contacts can be acquired (*labour, raw materials*). Output criteria equivalent to profit are less easy to standardise and this is the initial problem that any planner would face in attempting to transfer the operations approach to media planning. Marketing managers may for instance claim that they are attempting to affect brand awareness, others that it causes sales by some form of direct process.

The advertising mystery

Unfortunately very little research is done to identify the exact causal relationships between the expenditure of advertising money and the resulting change in market share (1).

Why this should be so, particularly in the light of the enormous sums spent by the advertising industry, is somewhat of a mystery. The problem is undeniably complex, consisting as it does of the interplay of a wide range of physical and emotional responses at various stages between the reception of the advertisement and the eventual purchase of the goods, with different criteria perhaps being important for different products, especially at different times. However true this is, the continuing shrouding in mystery of this most important area of marketing does suggest that powerful interest groups exist that consciously or unconsciously decide not to fully explore the topic. Discussion on how advertising actually works tends to be very limited even in specific studies on the advertising world and how it functions – the major chapters being concerned with the description of the advantages and disadvantages of certain advertising methods.

One can see in a cynical fashion, the rationale from the point of the advertising agency which exists on the commission that it gains from media expenditure – the larger the advertising campaign, the better. It is interesting to note in this context that the 'acceptable' level of Gross Rating Points per campaign has been steadily declining over the years, in line with increased media costs. The motives underlying companies' unwillingness to pursue advertising research are less obvious but often no less compelling. First, there is the factor that research of this nature tends to be long-term, is often very expensive, and the results may not necessarily be useful.

The reliable media experiment will demand rigid control areas, accurate design – including an understanding of the price, distribution and economic differences between the regions – and a long time period to ensure that the differences seen between the two areas could not simply have been explained by chance (see Chapter 12 on test markets and the statistical design of test areas). Secondly, the results are often highly statistical in nature, a feature that tends to appeal only to academics and not the practical businessman. Finally, the 'special case' argument is especially potent in this area. This would hold that the specific problems of the shampoo market say, would make research information gained in the tobacco industry inapplicable. Certain gross changes in the environment can however indicate important lessons – a television strike may, for example, show that the lack of advertising appears to cause a decline in sales, a fact that could not be explained in terms of any other variable (2). Similarly, studies of direct mail can also show the immediate effects of advertising and changes in size of advertisement, the inclusion of coupons, the use of colour and so on.

The lack of research does however magnify the need for a model of advertising effects on the consumer to minimise the fog of inconsistencies that surrounds the concept. A model can isolate the most important criteria that should be used to judge the design and control of advertising expenditure.

Factors in the puzzle

Most of the literature in the field identifies a number of crucial factors in the media/consumer equation:

1 Frequency distribution

All research into advertising expenditure shows that some recipients receive far more messages than might be expected by chance and many individuals see the advertisement only once or twice. This is the often reported division into heavy users and light users of the medium that is chosen. The bored student who sits glued to the television screen will receive the highest number of opportunities to see – often over a thousand a week; the busy executive, the lowest.

This phenomenon, which appears to exist in all media, has an important effect on the design and control of advertising expenditure. In other words, a considerable element of advertising will be lost on the heavy viewer, which will be an especially important feature of heavy concentrations of advertising – the 'burst'. The relationship between levels of expenditure and the percentage of the population being reached by the advertising is also not linear: from quite low levels of expenditure there is a period of rapid increase in the numbers of the viewing population who have seen the commercial, followed by a slow incremental gain as additional money is spent. To ensure that 90 per cent or more of the population has seen any particular advertisement over a short time period will therefore mean that considerable amounts of money will have to be spent. A large proportion of this spending will provide the viewing population with a chance to see the commercial six or more times. This may be regarded as counter-productive and has led to a series of discussions on the nature of the response curve, how the population reacts to increasing levels of advertising expenditure. The current consensus appears to be that convex response is the most likely phenomenon with diminishing returns always being present (Figure 11.1).

2 Media effectiveness

There is an enormous literature on the psychology and physiology of perception and how it operates (3). The general conclusions as they relate to advertising and media choice are in the broadest of generalities fairly straightforward before all the warnings and caveats such as cost, legal constraints and the like are added. First, the majority of information that we receive about the world around us comes through the eyes, indicating that visual acuity is greatest where there is both movement and colour. Size is also an important criterion and one firm has shown that the response to direct mail advertising increases as a square root of the advert size – double the size and you increase response by 1.4 (4). More complex is the fact that people will vary considerably as to the way that they receive their information – individuals by choice may prefer to listen to the radio rather than watch the television. One can separate this question of media effectiveness from the purely physiological to determine the role of multi-media campaigns.

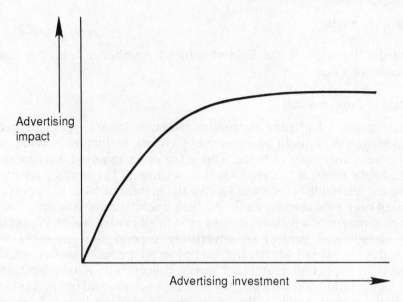

Figure 11.1   Advertising response curve

How effectiveness of different media can be compared will however remain an important problem. Classical media descriptions include the concept of the OTS or 'Opportunity To See' in relation to television commercials. Even here the terminology is imprecise. Does a ten-second commercial provide an equal OTS to that of a thirty-second for example? How many times must an individual see a poster to equal the message impact of a television commercial? Research in the first area would suggest that the relationship between the first two is not linear, and research in France proposes that the average equivalence is thirty-three exposures to a poster equalling one standard OTS (5).

One can, for the purposes of model building, follow the commonly held view that the expenditure of money on television is the most sales effective method, followed by other media in descending order. Published research in this area is also scanty and will to an extent vary from country to country. Posters appear always to be the least sales effective with radio, press and colour magazines occupying intermediate positions (6).

3   Advertising decay

There have been several studies that support the commonsense view that advertising (in common with books, films, and even wives'/husbands' complaints) is forgotten over time. The majority of research tends to suggest that for the normal range of household goods an average figure of around 30 per cent is normal, though with new brand introductions this can be considerably higher: well over 60 per cent is common. This indicates that the carry-over effect of advertising will be quite substantial. Readers with a pocket calculator will easily work out, for example, that 8 per cent of the original advertising will still be remembered after seven months. In consequence, advertising will be cumulative if it occurs on a regular basis. This is one of the strongest arguments for continuous or 'flighted' advertising.

4   Purchase threshold

There is a large body of psychological evidence that the ability of the human brain to cope with the large quantities of information that flow into it can only be achieved by rigid control and elimination of unnecessary data. This concept of information redundancy has been extended to the commercial indicating that something like the following process is taking place (7):

> *First exposure*: What is this? I have not seen this advert before.
> *Second exposure*: Yes I have seen this ad before, but there are still some elements that I do not understand.
> *Third exposure*: I have seen this commercial before, and I will now make the coffee/tea or go and get a drink.

This generalised approach does however have to take account of the fact that the brain will be forgetting the contents of the commercial quite rapidly, and well spaced advertisements may always appear as a repeat 'second exposure'.

Approaches such as these to the advertising problem imply that advertising response on an individual basis may level off very quickly after the first two or three exposures and that little additional benefit will be achieved by greater exposure. In other words a plateau is rapidly attained above which there will be no further advertising effect (8). This tends to accord with certain studies suggesting that there are no discernible economies of scale in advertising, that is, that there is a rapid tail off in return of advertising expenditure, and that the population response to advertising tends to be convex (9).

The majority of this research tends to be concerned with fast moving consumer goods where the amount of information the consumer requires to make a purchase decision is relatively small and the risks inherent in the purchase are minimal. Where consumer durables are concerned the information-gathering phase will tend to be considerably longer and the number of advertisements required to initiate a purchase will be correspondingly greater. The plateau in these occasions will be reached after a larger number of exposures.

5   Share of voice

One of the important criteria that drive many companies to advertise during the same period is the share of voice notion which states that the greater the share of total category advertising that the company can achieve during the particular advertising period, the better the sales effectiveness will be. Work on cable television systems in the United States tends to support this view showing that share of exposure does affect probability of purchase, but that the drop bears no linear relationship to the decline in share of voice. Decreasing advertising expenditure to 10 per cent of original levels only drops the propensity to purchase by 15 per cent. Other research on the level of advertising and long-term brand performance also inclines towards the case that the percentage of expenditure may have a contributory role in brand leadership with brand leaders spending more than the average on media expenditure (10). The share of voice argument supports the 'burst' or concentration of advertising in a particular time period.

6 Advertising sales rate

Should advertising produce sales, which is the commonly held view, the level of investment will change the demand curve. In other words there will be, in addition to a promotional and pricing elasticity, an advertising elasticity operating within the market. The exact relationship will never be easily described due to constraints both at the lower level of expenditure and then once saturation is achieved: very low levels of advertising expenditure may not achieve even minimal levels of consumer demand; whereas high levels of outlay will tend to mean that a significant percentage of the advertising outlay will be wasted and not generate advertising sales. A typical advertising elasticity of 1/12 may not in consequence operate throughout all the ranges of expenditure. A further complication will obviously occur with highly seasonal products as the generation of sales by advertising will be proportionate to the actual rate of product sale at the period of advertising. Advertising at the period of peak sales will naturally, in these particular fields, be more effective than would otherwise be the case. For example, promoting ski clothes in the middle of summer would not seem to be a particularly sensible proposition as the market of people intending to buy ski wear at that period would be very small.

7 Advertising cost

Relevant to most of these issues is the problem of advertising cost not only in relation to the media chosen but also to the timing of the campaign. The cost of the time period needs to be interrelated to the sales pattern to gain the most effective period for advertising to take place. For example, a product with two seasonal peaks may have one that coincides with a period of low advertising cost (mid-summer). The advertising sales/cost equation would suggest that more expenditure should be placed at this period rather than at the other sales peak which might be happening over the Christmas period when advertising is very expensive.

   The interrelationships of these factors can have very important implications for the design of any media campaign. The use of a model can do much to overcome the standard criteria used for evaluation; that one hundred 'Opportunities To See' (OTS) in a month is the *absolute minimum* necessary for an effective campaign.

The marketing investment model

Any model analysing the structural implications of advertising expenditure must rely on the calculation of the frequency distribution relating to the particular region and the nature of the target audience. The model, therefore, contains a frequency distribution table which can be changed to take account of particular company criteria. The frequency distribution table provides the data relating to the interaction of expenditure and the distribution of opportunities to see within the target group. As expenditure increases, the numbers receiving the advertisement a number of times (or 'cover') will increase. The increase will tend to be more marked in those receiving the advertisement once or twice but there will be a steady increase in the numbers of individuals seeing the advertisement five or six times.

Consideration of this pattern will provide the advertising structure for any single month. The change in advertising over time will be affected by advertising in previous time periods and the decay or forgetting rate in operation for the particular product, ranging from the normal 30 per cent to a higher figure.

The level of opportunity to see will naturally be determined by the total level of media expenditure in any time period. The amount available will be influenced by the cost of advertising. Advertising over Christmas is always more expensive than mid-summer and therefore the expenditure of the same amount of money at Christmas will inevitably mean less media coverage than during the summer. The model takes this into account by introducing an index factor for media cost; a monthly average of 1.00 will mean that certain periods are more expensive (say, 1.6) and some are less expensive (say, 0.2).

Similarly the level of advertising sales achieved will be greater in those periods of high sales and the model will again consider this effect to provide a combined cost and seasonality of sales index.

The effectiveness of the media can also be allowed for in an index figure, placing television at 1 and colour magazines at 0.8, radio at 0.6, and posters at 0.25 for example. The user of the model can make a judgement in this area as to the comparative effectiveness of the media used to evaluate different media strategies.

The model will provide an analysis on these assumptions of the opportunities to see on a month by month basis. It enables the user to choose the criteria for evaluating the structure of a media campaign, whether it be one, two, three, four, five or six cover or some other feature.

Using the marketing investment model

The *Go To* column in Listing 11.1 tells you the cell number and the cursor position. The next column specifies the spreadsheet option (LO = Label Option; VO = Value Option). The *Type In* column gives you instructions within the inverted commas which you must type in or asks you to supply the necessary data. These commas are not part of the instructions supplied here and should not be typed in. Beware however that some spreadsheets, the *Lotus 1-2-3*, for example, enter the Label Option by using the inverted-comma key. Under the *Type In* column the symbols * = multiply and / = divide. R in the *Return* column instructs you to commit the information to memory by pressing the Return key.
Remember: When you have finished, save your model.

Listing 11.1 Marketing investment model

A large number of cells in this spreadsheet contain very similar formulae. Rather than detailing them all, this listing contains instructions on how to produce them from a selection. Proforma 11.1 contains every cell.

Go To		Type In	Return
B4/	LO	"MARKETING	R
D4		INVESTMENT"	R
A6	LO	"BUDGET"	R
B6	VO	Enter Budget figure in $	R
A8	LO	"MEDIA"	R
A9	LO	" EFFECT %"	R
B9	VO	Enter % value for media effectiveness. See description of model in this chapter	R
A12	LO	"BUDGET"	R
B12	VO	"B6*B9/100"	R
A14	LO	"GRP/$000" for Gross Rating Points per '000 $	R
B14	VO	Enter number of GRP's per '000 $	R
A15	LO	"GRP TOT." for total GRP	R
B15	VO	"B12/(B14*1000)"	R
A17	LO	"CAMPAIGN"	R
B17	LO	"MONTH"	R
C17	LO	"% TOTAL"	R
A18	LO	"STRUCT" for Structure	R
B18 to B29	LO	Type in numbers "1" to "12" as Label Options	R
C18 to C29	VO	Enter % of annual expenditure in each month. These figures must add up to 100	R
A30	LO	"TOTAL"	R

Go To		Type In	Return
C30	VO	"IFSUM(C18:C29)=100 THEN100ELSE0"	R
D17	LO	"% SALES"	R
D18 to D29	VO	Enter % of annual sales by month. These figures must add up to 100	R
D30	VO	"IFSUM(D18:D29)=100 THEN100ELSE0"	R
E17	LO	"AD.COST"	R
E18 to E29	VO	Enter value of advertising cost by month	R

The value of advertising cost is an index of the average cost across the year. There is an average cost of advertising of unity, i.e. one, in each month; some months will be more expensive than others, and some less so. These figures must add up to 12.

Go To		Type In	Return
E30	VO	"IFSUM(E18:E29)=12 THEN12ELSE0"	R
F17	LO	"INDEX"	R
F18	VO	"D18/8.33/E18"	R
F19	VO	"D19/8.33/E19"	R
F20	VO	"D20/8.33/E20"	R
F21	VO	"D21/8.33/E21"	R
F22	VO	"D22/8.33/E22"	R
F23	VO	"D23/8.33/E23"	R
F24	VO	"D24/8.33/E24"	R
F25	VO	"D25/8.33/E25"	R
F26	VO	"D26/8.33/E26"	R
F27	VO	"D27/8.33/E27"	R

Listing 11.1 *(continued)*

Go To		Type In	Return	Go To		Type In	Return
F28	VO	"D28/8.33/E28"	R	H26	VO	"(H25+C167)*(1−B34/100)"	R
F29	VO	"D29/8.33/E29"	R	H27	VO	"(H26+C180)*(1−B34/100)"	R
G17	LO	"EFF.GRP" for Effective GRP	R	H28	VO	"(H27+C193)*(1−B34/100)"	R
G18	VO	"C18/100*F18*B15"	R	H29	VO	"(H28+C206)*(1−B34/100)"	R
G19	VO	"C19/100*F19*B15"	R				
G20	VO	"C20/100*F20*B15"	R	H30	VO	"SUM(H18:H29)"	R
G21	VO	"C21/100*F21*B15"	R	I17	LO	"2+COVER"	R
G22	VO	"C22/100*F22*B15"	R	I18	VO	"D63"	R
G23	VO	"C23/100*F23*B15"	R	I19	VO	"(I18+D76)*(1−B34/100)"	R
G24	VO	"C24/100*F24*B15"	R	I20	VO	"(I19+D89)*(1−B34/100)"	R
G25	VO	"C25/100*F25*B15"	R				
G26	VO	"C26/100*F26*B15"	R	I21	VO	"(I20+D102)*(1−B34/100)"	R
G27	VO	"C27/100*F27*B15"	R	I22	VO	"(I21+D115)*(1−B34/100)"	R
G28	VO	"C28/100*F28*B15"	R				
G29	VO	"C29/100*F29*B15"	R	I23	VO	"(I22+D128)*(1−B34/100)"	R
G30	VO	"SUM(G18:G29)"	R	I24	VO	"(I23+D141)*(1−B34/100)"	R
H17	LO	"1+COVER" explained in the section in this chapter on the model	R	I25	VO	"(I24+D154)*(1−B34/100)"	R
H18	VO	"C63"	R	I26	VO	"(I25+D167)*(1−B34/100)"	R
H19	VO	"(H18+C76)*(1−B34/100)"	R	I27	VO	"(I26+D180)*(1−B34/100)"	R
H20	VO	"(H19+C89)*(1−B34/100)"	R	I28	VO	"(I27+D193)*(1−B34/100)"	R
H21	VO	"(H20+C102)*(1−B34/100)"	R	I29	VO	"(I28+D206)*(1−B34/100)"	R
H22	VO	"(H21+C115)*(1−B34/100)"	R	I30	VO	"SUM(I18:I29)"	R
H23	VO	"(H22+C128)*(1−B34/100)"	R	J17	LO	"3+COVER"	R
H24	VO	"(H23+C141)*(1−B34/100)"	R	J18	VO	"E63"	R
H25	VO	"(H24+C154)*(1−B34/100)"	R				

Listing 11.1 *(continued)*

Go To		Type In	Return	Go To		Type In	Return
J19	VO	"(J18+E76)*(1−B34/100)"	R	K25	VO	"(K24+F154)*(1−B34/100)"	R
J20	VO	"(J19+E89)*(1−B34/100)"	R	K26	VO	"(K25+F167)*(1−B34/100)"	R
J21	VO	"(J20+E102)*(1−B34/100)"	R	K27	VO	"(K26+F180)*(1−B34/100)"	R
J22	VO	"(J21+E115)*(1−B34/100)"	R	K28	VO	"(K27+F193)*(1−B34/100)"	R
J23	VO	"(J22+E128)*(1−B34/100)"	R	K29	VO	"(K28+F206)*(1−B34/100)"	R
J24	VO	"(J23+E141)*(1−B34/100)"	R	K30	VO	"SUM(K18:K29)"	R
J25	VO	"(J24+E154)*(1−B34/100)"	R	L17	LO	"5+COVER"	R
J26	VO	"(J25+E167)*(1−B34/100)"	R	L18	VO	"G63"	R
J27	VO	"(J26+E180)*(1−B34/100)"	R	L19	VO	"(L18+G76)*(1−B34/100)"	R
J28	VO	"(J27+E193)*(1−B34/100)"	R	L20	VO	"(L19+G89)*(1−B34/100)"	R
J29	VO	"(J28+E206)*(1−B34/100)"	R	L21	VO	"(L20+G102)*(1−B34/100)"	R
J30	VO	"SUM(J18:J29)"	R	L22	VO	"(L21+G115)*(1−B34/100)"	R
K17	LO	"4+COVER"	R	L23	VO	"(L22+G128)*(1−B34/100)"	R
K18	VO	"F63"	R	L24	VO	"(L23+G141)*(1−B34/100)"	R
K19	VO	"(K18+F76)*(1−B34/100)"	R	L25	VO	"(L24+G154)*(1−B34/100)"	R
K20	VO	"(K19+F89)*(1−B34/100)"	R	L26	VO	"(L25+G167)*(1−B34/100)"	R
K21	VO	"(K20+F102)*(1−B34/100)"	R	L27	VO	"(L26+G180)*(1−B34/100)"	R
K22	VO	"(K21+F115)*(1−B34/100)"	R	L28	VO	"(L27+G193)*(1−B34/100)"	R
K23	VO	"(K22+F128)*(1−B34/100)"	R	L29	VO	"(L28+G206)*(1−B34/100)"	R
K24	VO	"(K23+F141)*(1−B34/100)"	R	L30	VO	"SUM(L18:L29)"	R

Listing 11.1   *(continued)*

Go To		Type In	Return	Go To		Type In	Return
M17	LO	"6+COVER"	R	E38	LO	"3"	R
M18	VO	"H63"	R	F38	LO	"4"	R
M19	VO	"(M18+H76)*(1−B34/ 100)"	R	G38	LO	"5"	R
				H38	LO	"6"	R
M20	VO	"(M19+H89)*(1−B34/ 100)"	R	B39	LO	"GRP"	R
M21	VO	"(M20+H102)*(1−B34/ 100)"	R	B40	LO	"10"	R
				B41	LO	"20"	R
M22	VO	"(M21+H115)*(1−B34/ 100)"	R	B42	LO	"40"	R
				B43	LO	"60"	R
M23	VO	"(M22+H128)*(1−B34/ 100)"	R	B44	LO	"80"	R
M24	VO	"(M23+H141)*(1−B34/ 100)"	R	B45	LO	"100"	R
				B46	LO	"120"	R
M25	VO	"(M24+H154)*(1−B34/ 100)"	R	B47	LO	"140"	R
				B48	LO	"160"	R
M26	VO	"(M25+H167)*(1−B34/ 100)"	R	B49	LO	"180"	R
M27	VO	"(M26+H180)*(1−B34/ 100)"	R	B50	LO	"200"	R
M28	VO	"(M27+H193)*(1−B34/ 100)"	R	C40 to H50	VO	C40 to H50 is a grid, containing information from a frequency distribution table for the respective area. In the columns C to H enter the relevant values	R
M29	VO	"(M28+H206)*(1−B34/ 100)"	R				
M30	VO	"SUM(M18:M29)"	R				
A33	LO	"MONTHLY"	R	A52	LO	"OTS.MNH1" for Opportunities to see for Month 1	R
A34	LO	"DECAY %"	R				
B34	VO	Enter value for percentage of advertising forgotten every month	R	C52	VO	"IFG18>0 ANDG18<10THENC40 ELSE0"	R
D36	LO	"COVER"	R				
A37/	LO	"FREQUENCY"	R	Replicate C52 in cells C65, C78, C91, C104, C117, C130, C143, C156, C169, C182, C195			
B37			R				
A38	LO	"DIST"	R				
C38	LO	"1"	R	D52	VO	"IFG18>0 ANDG18<10THEND40 ELSE0"	R
D38	LO	"2"	R				

Listing 11.1 *(continued)*

Go To	Type In	Return

Replicate D52 in cells D65, D78, D91, D104, D117, D130, D143, D156, D169, D182, D195

Go To	Type In	Return
E52	VO	"IFG18>0
		ANDG18<10THENE40
		ELSE0" R

Replicate E52 in cells E65, E78, E91, E104, E117, E130, E143, E156, E169, E182, E195

F52	VO	"IFG18>0
		ANDG18<10THENF40
		ELSE0" R

Replicate F52 in cells F65, F78, F91, F104, F117, F130, F143, F156, F169, F182, F195

G52	VO	"IFG18>0
		ANDG18<10THENG40
		ELSE0" R

Replicate G52 in cells G65, G78, G91, G104, G117, G130, G143, G156, G169, G182, G195

H52	VO	"IFG18>0
		ANDG18<10THENH40
		ELSE0" R

Replicate H52 in cells H65, H78, H91, H104, H117, H130, H143, H156, H169, H182, H195

C53	VO	"IFG18>=10
		ANDG18<20THENC41
		ELSE0" R

Replicate C53 in cells C66, C79, C92, C105, C118, C131, C144, C157, C170, C183, C196

D53	VO	"IFG18>=10
		ANDG18<20THEND41
		ELSE0" R

Replicate D53 in cells D66, D79, D92, D105, D118, D131, D144, D157, D170, D183, D196

E53	VO	"IFG18>=10
		ANDG18<20THENE41
		ELSE0" R

Replicate E53 in cells E66, E79, E92, E105, E118, E131, E144, E157, E170, E183, E196

F53	VO	"IFG18>=10
		ANDG18<20THENF41
		ELSE0" R

Replicate F53 in cells F66, F79, F92, F105, F118, F131, F144, F157, F170, F183, F196

G53	VO	"IFG18>=10
		ANDG18<20THENG41
		ELSE0" R

Replicate G53 in cells G66, G79, G92, G105, G118, G131, G144, G157, G170, G183, G196

H53	VO	"IFG18>=10
		ANDG18<20THENH41
		ELSE0" R

Replicate H53 in cells H66, H79, H92, H105, H118, H131, H144, H157, H170, H183, H196

Listing 11.1 *(continued)*

Go To		Type In	Return
C54	VO	"IFG18>=20.01	
		ANDG18=<40	
		THENC42ELSE0"	R

Replicate C54 in cells C67, C80, C93, C106, C119, C132, C145, C158, C171, C184, C197

Go To		Type In	Return
D54	VO	"IFG18>=20.01	
		ANDG18=<40	
		THEND42ELSE0"	R

Replicate D54 in cells D67, D80, D93, D106, D119, D132, D145, D158, D171, D184, D197

Go To		Type In	Return
E54	VO	"IFG18>=20.01	
		ANDG18=<40	
		THENE42ELSE0"	R

Replicate E54 in cells E67, E80, E93, E106, E119, E132, E145, E158, E171, E184, E197

Go To		Type In	Return
F54	VO	"IFG18>=20.01	
		ANDG18=<40	
		THENF42ELSE0"	R

Replicate F54 in cells F67, F80, F93, F106, F119, F132, F145, F158, F171, F184, F197

Go To		Type In	Return
G54	VO	"IFG18>=20.01	
		ANDG18=<40	
		THENG42ELSE0"	R

Replicate G54 in cells G67, G80, G93, G106, G119, G132, G145, G158, G171, G184, G197

Go To		Type In	Return
H54	VO	"IFG18>=20.01	
		ANDG18=<40	
		THENH42ELSE0"	R

Replicate H54 in cells H67, H80, H93, H106, H119, H132, H145, H158, H171, H184, H197

Go To		Type In	Return
C55	VO	"IFG18>=40.01	
		ANDG18=<60	
		THENC43ELSE0"	R

Replicate C55 in cells C68, C81, C94, C107, C120, C133, C146, C159, C172, C185, C198

Go To		Type In	Return
D55	VO	"IFG18>=40.01	
		ANDG18=<60	R
		THEND43ELSE0"	

Replicate D55 in cells D68, D81, D94, D107, D120, D133, D146, D159, D172, D185, D198

Go To		Type In	Return
E55	VO	"IFG18>=40.01	
		ANDG18=<60	
		THENE43ELSE0"	R

Replicate E55 in cells E68, E81, E94, E107, E120, E133, E146, E159, E172, E185, E198

Go To		Type In	Return
F55	VO	"IFG18>=40.01	
		ANDG18=<60	
		THENF43ELSE0"	R

Replicate F55 in cells F68, F81, F94, F107, F120, F133, F146, F159, F172, F185, F198

Listing 11.1   *(continued)*

Go To		Type In	Return	Go To		Type In	Return
G55	VO	"IFG18>=40.01 ANDG18=<60 THENG43ELSE0"	R	F56	VO	"IFG18>=60.01 ANDG18=<80 THENF44ELSE0"	R

Replicate G55 in cells G68, G81, G94, G107, G120, G133, G146, G159, G172, G185, G198

Replicate F56 in cells F69, F82, F95, F108, F121, F134, F147, F160, F173, F186, F199

Go To		Type In	Return	Go To		Type In	Return
H55	VO	"IFG18>=40.01 ANDG18=<60 THENH43ELSE0"	R	G56	VO	"IFG18>=60.01 ANDG18=<80 THENG44ELSE0"	R

Replicate H55 in cells H68, H81, H94, H107, H120, H133, H146, H159, H172, H185, H198

Replicate G56 in cells G69, G82, G95, G108, G121, G134, G147, G160, G173, G186, G199

Go To		Type In	Return	Go To		Type In	Return
C56	VO	"IFG18>=60.01 ANDG18=<80 THENC44ELSE0"	R	H56	VO	"IFG18>=60.01 ANDG18=<80 THENH44ELSE0"	R

Replicate C56 in cells C69, C82, C95, C108, C121, C134, C147, C160, C173, C186, C199

Replicate H56 in cells H69, H82, H95, H108, H121, H134, H147, H160, H173, H186, H199

Go To		Type In	Return	Go To		Type In	Return
D56	VO	"IFG18>=60.01 ANDG18=<80 THEND44ELSE0"	R	C57	VO	"IFG18>=80.00 ANDG18=<100 THENC45ELSE0"	R

Replicate D56 in cells D69, D82, D95, D108, D121, D134, D147, D160, D173, D186, D199

Replicate C57 in cells C70, C83, C96, C109, C122, C135, C148, C161, C174, C187, C200

Go To		Type In	Return	Go To		Type In	Return
E56	VO	"IFG18>=60.01 ANDG18=<80 THENE44ELSE0"	R	D57	VO	"IFG18>=80.00 ANDG18=<100 THEND45ELSE0"	R

Replicate E56 in cells E69, E82, E95, E108, E121, E134, E147, E160, E173, E186, E199

Replicate D57 in cells D70, D83, D96, D109, D122, D135, D148, D161, D174, D187, D200

Listing 11.1 *(continued)*

Go To		Type In	Return
E57	VO	"IFG18>=80.00 ANDG18=<100 THENE45ELSE0"	R

Replicate E57 in cells E70, E83, E96, E109, E122, E135, E148, E161, E174, E187, E200

Go To		Type In	Return
F57	VO	"IFG18>=80.00 ANDG18=<100 THENF45ELSE0"	R

Replicate F57 in cells F70, F83, F96, F109, F122, F135, F148, F161, F174, F187, F200

Go To		Type In	Return
G57	VO	"IFG18>=80.00 ANDG18=<100 THENG45ELSE0"	R

Replicate G57 in cells G70, G83, G96, G109, G122, G135, G148, G161, G174, G187, G200

Go To		Type In	Return
H57	VO	"IFG18>=80.00 ANDG18=<100 THENH45ELSE0"	R

Replicate H57 in cells H70, H83, H96, H109, H122, H135, H148, H161, H174, H187, H200

Go To		Type In	Return
C58	VO	"IFG18>=100.01 ANDG18=<120 THENC46ELSE0"	R

Replicate C58 in cells C71, C84, C97, C110, C123, C136, C149, C162, C175, C188, C201

Go To		Type In	Return
D58	VO	"IFG18>=100.01 ANDG18=<120 THEND46ELSE0"	R

Replicate D58 in cells D71, D84, D97, D110, D123, D136, D149, D162, D175, D188, D201

Go To		Type In	Return
E58	VO	"IFG18>=100.01 ANDG18=<120 THENE46ELSE0"	R

Replicate E58 in cells E71, E84, E97, E110, E123, E136, E149, E162, E175, E188, E201

Go To		Type In	Return
F58	VO	"IFG18>=100.01 ANDG18=<120 THENF46ELSE0"	R

Replicate F58 in cells F71, F84, F97, F110, F123, F136, F149, F162, F175, F188, F201

Go To		Type In	Return
G58	VO	"IFG18>=100.01 ANDG18=<120 THENG46ELSE0"	R

Replicate G58 in cells G71, G84, G97, G110, G123, G136, G149, G162, G175, G188, G201

Go To		Type In	Return
H58	VO	"IFG18>=100.01 ANDG18=<120 THENH46ELSE0"	R

Replicate H58 in cells H71, H84, H97, H110, H123, H136, H149, H162, H175, H188, H201

Listing 11.1 *(continued)*

Go To		Type In	Return	Go To		Type In	Return
C59	VO	"IFG18>=120.01 ANDG18=<140 THENC47ELSE0"	R	H59	VO	"IFG18>=120.01 ANDG18=<140 THENH47ELSE0"	R

Replicate C59 in cells C72, C85, C98, C111, C124, C137, C150, C163, C176, C189, C202

Replicate H59 in cells H72, H85, H98, H111, H124, H137, H150, H163, H176, H189, H202

| D59 | VO | "IFG18>=120.01 ANDG18=<140 THEND47ELSE0" | R | C60 | VO | "IFG18>=140.01 ANDG18=<160 THENC48ELSE0" | R |

Replicate D59 in cells D72, D85, D98, D111, D124, D137, D150, D163, D176, D189, D202

Replicate C60 in cells C73, C86, C99, C112, C125, C138, C151, C164, C177, C190, C203

| E59 | VO | "IFG18>=120.01 ANDG18=<140 THENE47ELSE0" | R | D60 | VO | "IFG18>=140.01 ANDG18=<160 THEND48ELSE0" | R |

Replicate E59 in cells E72, E85, E98, E111, E124, E137, E150, E163, E176, E189, E202

Replicate D60 in cells D73, D86, D99, D112, D125, D138, D151, D164, D177, D190, D203

| F59 | VO | "IFG18>=120.01 ANDG18=<140 THENF47ELSE0" | R | E60 | VO | "IFG18>=140.01 ANDG18=<160 THENE48ELSE0" | R |

Replicate F59 in cells F72, F85, F98, F111, F124, F137, F150, F163, F176, F189, F202

Replicate E60 in cells E73, E86, E99, E112, E125, E138, E151, E164, E177, E190, E203

| G59 | VO | "IFG18>=120.01 ANDG18=<140 THENG47ELSE0" | R | F60 | VO | "IFG18>=140.01 ANDG18=<160 THENF48ELSE0" | R |

Replicate G59 in cells G72, G85, G98, G111, G124, G137, G150, G163, G176, G189, G202

Replicate F60 in cells F73, F86, F99, F112, F125, F138, F151, F164, F177, F190, F203

Listing 11.1 *(continued)*

Go To		Type In	Return
G60	VO	"IFG18>=140.01 ANDG18=<160 THENG48ELSE0"	R

Replicate G60 in cells G73, G86, G99, G112, G125, G138, G151, G164, G177, G190, G203

Go To		Type In	Return
H60	VO	"IFG18>=140.01 ANDG18=<160 THENH48ELSE0"	R

Replicate H60 in cells H73, H86, H99, H112, H125, H138, H151, H164, H177, H190, H203

Go To		Type In	Return
C61	VO	"IFG18>=160.01 ANDG18=<180 THENC49ELSE0"	R

Replicate C61 in cells C74, C87, C100, C113, C126, C139, C152, C165, C178, C191, C204

Go To		Type In	Return
D61	VO	"IFG18>=160.01 ANDG18=<180 THEND49ELSE0"	R

Replicate D61 in cells D74, D87, D100, D113, D126, D139, D152, D165, D178, D191, D204

Go To		Type In	Return
E61	VO	"IFG18>=160.01 ANDG18=<180 THENE49ELSE0"	R

Replicate E61 in cells E74, E87, E100, E113, E126, E139, E152, E165, E178, E191, E204

Go To		Type In	Return
F61	VO	"IFG18>=160.01 ANDG18=<180 THENF49ELSE0"	R

Replicate F61 in cells F74, F87, F100, F113, F126, F139, F152, F165, F178, F191, F204

Go To		Type In	Return
G61	VO	"IFG18>=160.01 ANDG18=<180 THENG49ELSE0"	R

Replicate G61 in cells G74, G87, G100, G113, G126, G139, G152, G165, G178, G191, G204

Go To		Type In	Return
H61	VO	"IFG18>=160.01 ANDG18=<180 THENH49ELSE0"	R

Replicate H61 in cells H74, H87, H100, H113, H126, H139, H152, H165, H178, H191, H204

Go To		Type In	Return
C62	VO	"IFG18>=180.0 ANDG18=<200 THENC50ELSE0"	R

Replicate C62 in cells C75, C88, C101, C114, C127, C140, C153, C166, C179, C192, C205

Go To		Type In	Return
D62	VO	"IFG18>=180.0 ANDG18=<200 THEND50ELSE0"	R

Replicate D62 in cells D75, D88, D101, D114, D127, D140, D153, D166, D179, D192, D205

Listing 11.1 *(continued)*

Go To		Type In	Return
E62	VO	"IFG18>=180.0 ANDG18=<200 THENE50ELSE0"	R

Replicate E62 in cells E75, E88, E101, E114, E127, E140, E153, E166, E179, E192, E205

Go To		Type In	Return
F62	VO	"IFG18>=180.0 ANDG18=<200 THENF50ELSE0"	R

Replicate F62 in cells F75, F88, F101, F114, F127, F140, F153, F166, F179, F192, F205

Go To		Type In	Return
G62	VO	"IFG18>=180.0 ANDG18=<200 THENG50ELSE0"	R

Replicate G62 in cells G75, G88, G101, G114, G127, G140, G153, G166, G179, G192, G205

Go To		Type In	Return
H62	VO	"IFG18>=180.0 ANDG18=<200 THENH50ELSE0"	R

Replicate H62 in cells H75, H88, H101, H114, H127, H140, H153, H166, H179, H192, H205

Go To		Type In	Return
A63	LO	"TOTAL"	R
C63	VO	"SUM(C52:C62)"	R
D63	VO	"SUM(D52:D62)"	R
E63	VO	"SUM(E52:E62)"	R
F63	VO	"SUM(F52:F62")"	R
G63	VO	"SUM(G52:G62)"	R
H63	VO	"SUM(H52:H62)"	R

Go To		Type In	Return
A65	LO	"OTS.MNH2"	R

In lines 65 to 75: change the figure 18 to 19 in the replicated formulae

Go To		Type In	Return
A76	LO	"TOTAL"	R
C76	VO	"SUM(C65:C75)"	R
D76	VO	"SUM(D65:D75)"	R
E76	VO	"SUM(E65:E75)"	R
F76	VO	"SUM(F65:F75)"	R
G76	VO	"SUM(G65:G75)"	R
H76	VO	"SUM(H65:H75)"	R
A78	LO	"OTS.MNH3"	R

In lines 78 to 88: change the figure 18 to 20 in the replicated formulae

Go To		Type In	Return
A89	LO	"TOTAL"	R
C89	VO	"SUM(C78:C88)"	R
D89	VO	"SUM(D78:D88)"	R
E89	VO	"SUM(E78:E88)"	R
F89	VO	"SUM(F78:F88)"	R
G89	VO	"SUM(G78:G88)"	R
H89	VO	"SUM(H78:H88)"	R
A91	LO	"OTS.MNH4"	R

In lines 91 to 101: change the figure 18 to 21 in the replicated formulae

Go To		Type In	Return
A102	LO	"TOTAL"	R
C102	VO	"SUM(C91:C101)"	R
D102	VO	"SUM(D91:D101)"	R
E102	VO	"SUM(E91:E101)"	R
F102	VO	"SUM(F91:F101)"	R

Listing 11.1 *(continued)*

Go To		Type In	Return
G102	VO	"SUM(G91:G101)"	R
H102	VO	"SUM(H91:H101)"	R
A104	LO	"OTS.MNH5"	R

In lines 104 to 114: change 18 to 22 in the replicated formulae

A115	LO	"TOTAL"	R
C115	VO	"SUM(C104:C114)"	R
D115	VO	"SUM(D104:D114)"	R
E115	VO	"SUM(E104:E114)"	R
F115	VO	"SUM(F104:F114)"	R
G115	VO	"SUM(G104:G114)"	R
H115	VO	"SUM(H104:H114)"	R
A117	LO	"OTS.MNH6"	R

In lines 117 to 127: change 18 to 23 in the replicated formulae

A128	LO	"TOTAL"	R
C128	VO	"SUM(C117:C127)"	R
D128	VO	"SUM(D117:D127)"	R
E128	VO	"SUM(E117:E127)"	R
F128	VO	"SUM(F117:F127)"	R
G128	VO	"SUM(G117:G127)"	R
H128	VO	"SUM(H117:H127)"	R
A130	LO	"OTS.MNH7"	R

In lines 130 to 140 change 18 to 24 in the replicated formulae

A141	LO	"TOTAL"	R
C141	VO	"SUM(C130:C140)"	R
D141	VO	"SUM(D130:D140)"	R

Go To		Type In	Return
E141	VO	"SUM(E130:E140)"	R
F141	VO	"SUM(F130:F140)"	R
G141	VO	"SUM(G130:G140)"	R
H141	VO	"SUM(H130:H140)"	R
A143	LO	"OTS.MNH8"	R

In lines 143 to 153: change 18 to 25 in the replicated formulae

A154	LO	"TOTAL"	R
C154	VO	"SUM(C143:C153)"	R
D154	VO	"SUM(D143:D153)"	R
E154	VO	"SUM(E143:E153)"	R
F154	VO	"SUM(F143:F153)"	R
G154	VO	"SUM(G143:G153)"	R
H154	VO	"SUM(H143:H153)"	R
A156	LO	"OTS.MNH9"	R

In lines 156 to 166: change 18 to 26 in the replicated formulae

A167	LO	"TOTAL"	R
C167	VO	"SUM(C156:C166)"	R
D167	VO	"SUM(D156:D166)"	R
E167	VO	"SUM(E156:E166)"	R
F167	VO	"SUM(F156:F166)"	R
G167	VO	"SUM(G156:G166)"	R
H167	VO	"SUM(H156:H166)"	R
A169	LO	"OTS.MNH10"	R

In lines 169 to 179: change 18 to 27 in the replicated formulae

| A180 | LO | "TOTAL" | R |

218 SPREADSHEET MARKETING

Listing 11.1 *(concluded)*

Go To		Type In	Return	Go To		Type In	Return
C180	VO	"SUM(C169:C179)"	R	F193	VO	"SUM(F182:F192)"	R
D180	VO	"SUM(D169:D179)"	R	G193	VO	"SUM(G182:G192)"	R
E180	VO	"SUM(E169:E179)"	R	H193	VO	"SUM(H182:H192)"	R
F180	VO	"SUM(F169:F179)"	R	A195	LO	"OTS.MNH12"	R
G180	VO	"SUM(G169:G179)"	R				
H180	VO	"SUM(H169:H179)"	R				
A182	LO	"OTS.MNH11"	R				

In lines 182 to 192: change 18 to 28 in the replicated formulae

In lines 195 to 205: change 18 to 29 in the replicated formulae

A193	LO	"TOTAL"	R	A206	LO	"TOTAL"	R
C193	VO	"SUM(C182:C192)"	R	C206	VO	"SUM(C195:C205)"	R
D193	VO	"SUM(D182:D192)"	R	D206	VO	"SUM(D195:D205)"	R
E193	VO	"SUM(E182:E192)"	R	E206	VO	"SUM(E195:E205)"	R
				F206	VO	"SUM(F195:F205)"	R
				G206	VO	"SUM(G195:G205)"	R
				H206	VO	"SUM(H195:H205)"	R

Marketing investment commentary

First, the manager enters the frequency distribution table for his particular market, relating the number of gross rating points to exposure cover. The model (Example 11.1) contains an example of frequency distribution – it is only included to provide a rough indication as to how the model works. Frequency distribution tables will vary from country to country and media to media. The manager can then introduce the total budget under consideration and whether the media chosen requires a weighting factor to be introduced (for example, press could be weighted at 0.8, radio at 0.6, as mentioned in the section describing the model).

Enter the campaign structure percentage on a month by month basis, together with the sales seasonality and the media cost based on an average cost of 1 per month.

The manager will then enter the value for the advertising decay rate relative to the particular product field or campaign in which he is involved, or taking an industry average of 30 per cent for the purposes of analysis.

The model will then calculate the percentage of the population receiving the advertising on a month by month basis. The manager can then decide the criteria on which he wishes to judge the campaign – the level of advertising coverage required by month, the share of voice argument or the most effective spread of advertising expenditure – the continuous advertising approach.

The model does concentrate the attention on a number of particular issues. First, the nature of the decay rate is crucial to the effective investment – reduce the decay rate by making the advertising more memorable and this can improve the return dramatically. Secondly, the interaction between advertising costs and sales levels can yield valuable insights into when advertising should be commenced or ended. By concentrating on the OTS level ('Opportunities To See') on a month by month basis it leaves on one side the issue of how advertising affects sales, except for stating that the most efficient advertising structure *may* easily be the most effective in generating sales.

There is one word of warning. Using the data provided the manager can, by spending all the budget in the early part of the year, produce a position whereby more than 100 per cent of the population have seen the advertisement once!

References

1 J.W. Forrester, 'Advertising: A Problem in Industrial Dynamics', *Harvard Business Review*, No. 2, 1959.

2 T. Douglas, 'Television advertising is worth the money and here are the facts to prove it', *Marketing Week*, 22 February 1980.

3 J.E. Woolridge, *Machinery of the Brain*, McGraw Hill, 1961.

4 Great Universal Stores – personal communication.

5 E. Delaton, *Ca c'est l'affiche*, Les Presses du Temps Present, 1979.

6 Unpublished B.A. dissertation, Thames Polytechnic, London, 1982.

7 H.G. Krugman, 'What Makes Advertising Effective?', *Harvard Business Review*, No. 2, 1975.

8 M.J. Naples, *Effective Frequency: The Relationship between Frequency and Advertising Effectiveness*, Association of National Advertisers Inc., 1979.

9 S. Broadbent, B. Jacobs, *Spending Advertising Money*, Business Books, 1984.

10 S. Broadbent, 'The Struggle for Brand Leadership', *Nielsen Researcher*, No. 3, 1972.

Proforma 11.1 Marketing investment model

	A	B	C	D	E
4		MARKETING	INVESTMENT		
6	BUDGET$	230000			
8	MEDIA				
9	EFFECT%	100			
12	BUDGET	B6*B9/100			
14	GRP/$0	1			
15	GRP TOT.	B12/(B14*1000)			
17	CAMPAIGN	MONTH	%TOTAL	%SALES	AD.COST
18	STRUCT	1	30	10	1.2
19		2	15	2	0.9
20		3	10	5	0.9
21		4	5	3	1
22		5	0	10	1
23		6	0	15	1
24		7	20	5	1
25		8	20	10	1
26		9	0	10	1
27		10	0	5	1
28		11	0	15	1
29		12	0	10	1
30	TOTAL		IFSUM(C18:C29)=100THEN100ELSE0	IFSUM(D18:D29)=100THEN100ELSE0	IFSUM(E18:E29)=12THEN12ELSE0
33	MONTHLY				
34	DECAY%	30			
36				COVER	
37	FREQUENCY				
38	DIST		1	2	3
39		GRP			
40		10			
41		20			
42		40			
43		60			
44		80			

Proforma 11.1 *(continued)*

	F	G	H	I
4				
6				
8				
9				
11				
12				
14				
15				
17	INDEX	EFF,GRP	1+COVER	2+COVER
18	D18/8,33/E18	C18/100*F18*B15	C63	D63
19	D19/8,33/E19	C19/100*F19*B15	(H18+C76)*(1-B34/100)	(I18+D76)*(1-B34/100)
20	D20/8,33/E20	C20/100*F20*B15	(H19+C89)*(1-B34/100)	(I19+D89)*(1-B34/100)
21	D21/8,33/E21	C21/100*F21*B15	(H20+C102)*(1-B34/100)	(I20+D102)*(1-B34/100)
22	D22/8,33/E22	C22/100*F22*B15	(H21+C115)*(1-B34/100)	(I21+D115)*(1-B34/100)
23	D23/8,33/E23	C23/100*F23*B15	(H22+C128)*(1-B34/100)	(I22+D128)*(1-B34/100)
24	D24/8,33/E24	C24/100*F24*B15	(H23+C141)*(1-B34/100)	(I23+D141)*(1-B34/100)
25	D25/8,33/E25	C25/100*F25*B15	(H24+C154)*(1-B34/100)	(I24+D154)*(1-B34/100)
26	D26/8,33/E26	C26/100*F26*B15	(H25+C167)*(1-B34/100)	(I25+D167)8(1-B34/100)
27	D27/8,33/E27	C27/100*F27*B15	(H26+C180)*(1-B34/100)	(I26+D167)*(1-B34/100)
28	D28/8,33/E28	C28/100*F28*B15	(H27+C193)*(1-B34/100)	(I27+D193)*(1-B34/100)
29	D29/8,33/E29	C29/100*F28*B15	(H28+C206)*(1-B34/100)	(I28+D206)*(1-B34/100)
30		SUM(G18;G29)	SUM(H18;H29)	SUM(I18;I29)
33				
34				
36				
37				
38	4	5	6	
39				
40				
41				
42				
43				
44				

Proforma 11.1 (*continued***)**

	J	K	L	M
4				
6				
8				
9				
12				
14				
15				
17	3+COVER	4+COVER	5+COVER	6+COVER
18	E63	F63	G63	H63
19	(J18+E76)*(1-B34/100)	(K18+F76)*(1-B34/100)	(L18+G76)*(1-B34/100)	(M18+H76)*(1-B34/100)
20	(J19+E89)*(1-B34/100)	(K19+F89)*(1-B34/100)	(L19+G89)*(1-B34/100)	(M19+H89)*(1-B34/100)
21	(J20+E102)*(1-B34/100)	(K20+F102)*(1-B34/100)	(L20+G102)*(1-B34/100)	(M20+H102)*(1-B34/100)
22	(J21+E115)*(1-B34/100)	(K21+F115)*(1-B34/100)	(L21+G115)*(1-B34/100)	(M21+H115)*(1-B34/100)
23	(J22+E128)*(1-B34/100)	(K22+F128)*(1-B34/100)	(L22+G128)*(1-B34/100)	(M22+H128)*(1-B34/100)
24	(J23+E141)*(1-B34/100)	(K23+F141)*(1-B34/100)	(L23+G141)*(1-B34/100)	(M23+H141)*(1-B34/100)
25	(J24+E154)*(1-B34/100)	(K24+F154)*(1-B34/100)	(L24+G154)*(1-B34/100)	(M24+H154)*(1-B34/100)
26	(J25+E167)*(1-B34/100)	(K25+F167)*(1-B34/100)	(L25+G167)*(1-B34/100)	(M25+H167)*(1-B34/100)
27	(J26+E180)*(1-B34/100)	(K26+F180)*(1-B34/100)	(L26+G180)*(1-B34/100)	(M26+H180)*(1-B34/100)

Proforma 11.1 *(continued)*

A	B	C	D	E		
45	100				☐☐☐	
46	120				■	
47	140				☐☐	
48	160				☐☐	
49	180				☐☐	
50	200				☐☐	

Proforma 11.1 (*continued*)

	A	C	D	E
52	OTS MNH,1	IFG18)0ANDG18<10THENC40ELSE0	IFG18>0ANDG18<10THEND40ELSE0	IFG18>0ANDG18<10THENE40ELSE0
53		IFG18)=10ANDG18<20THENC41ELSE0	IFG18)=10ANDG18<20THEND41ELSE0	IFG18)=10ANDG18<20THENE41ELSE0
54		IFG18)=20,01ANDG18=<40THENC42ELSE0	IFG18)=20,01ANDG18=<40THEND42ELSE0	IFG18)=20,01ANDG18=<40THENE42ELSE0
55		IFG18)=40,01ANDG18=<60THENC43ELSE0	IFG18)=40,01ANDG18=<60THEND43ELSE0	IFG18)=40,01ANDG18=<60THENE43ELSE0
56		IFG18)=60,01ANDG18=<80THENC44ELSE0	IFG18)=60,01ANDG18=<80THEND44ELSE0	IFG18)=60,01ANDG18=<80THENE44ELSE0
57		IFG18)=80,00ANDG18=<100THENC45ELSE0	IFG18)=80,00ANDG18=<100THEND45ELSE0	IFG18)=80,00ANDG18=<100THENE45ELSE0
58		IFG18)=100,01ANDG18=<120THENC46ELSE0	IFG18)=100,01ANDG18=<120THEND46ELSE0	IFG18)=100,01ANDG18=<120THENE46ELSE0
59		IFG18)=120,01ANDG18=<140THENC47ELSE0	IFG18)=120,01ANDG18=<140THEND47ELSE0	IFG18)=120,01ANDG18=<140THENE47ELSE0
60		IFG18)=140,01ANDG18=<160THENC48ELSE0	IFG18)=140,01ANDG18=<160THEND48ELSE0	IFG18)=140,01ANDG18=<160THENE48ELSE0
61		IFG18)=160,01ANDG18=<180THENC49ELSE0	IFG18)=160,01ANDG18=<180THEND49ELSE0	IFG18)=160,01ANDG18=<180THENE49ELSE0
62		IFG18)=180,01ANDG18=<200THENC50ELSE0	IFG18)=180,01ANDG18=<200THEND50ELSE0	IFG18)=180,01ANDG18=<200THENE50ELSE0
63	TOTAL	SUM(C52:C62)	SUM(D52:D62)	SUM(E52:E62)
65	OTS MNH,2	IFG19>0ANDG19<10THENC40ELSE0	IFG19>0ANDG19<10THEND40ELSE0	IFG19>0ANDG19<10THENE40ELSE0
66		IFG19)=10ANDG19<20THENC41ELSE0	IFG19)=10ANDG19<20THEND41ELSE0	IFG19)=10ANDG19<20THENE41ELSE0
67		IFG19)=20,01ANDG19=<40THENC42ELSE0	IFG19)=20,01ANDG19=<40THEND42ELSE0	IFG19)=20,01ANDG19=<40THENE42ELSE0
68		IFG19)=40,01ANDG19=<60THENC43ELSE0	IFG19)=40,01ANDG19=<60THEND43ELSE0	IFG19)=40,01ANDG19=<60THENE43ELSE0
69		IFG19)=60,01ANDG19=<80THENC44ELSE0	IFG19)=60,01ANDG19=<80THEND44ELSE0	IFG19)=60,01ANDG19=<80THENE44ELSE0
70		IFG19)=80,00ANDG19=<100THENC45ELSE0	IFG19)=80,00ANDG19=<100THEND45ELSE0	IFG19)=80,00ANDG19=<100THENE45ELSE0
71		IFG19)=100,01ANDG19=<120THENC46ELSE0	IFG19)=100,01ANDG19=<120THEND46ELSE0	IFG19)=100,01ANDG19=<120THENE46ELSE0
72		IFG19)=120,01ANDG19=<140THENC47ELSE0	IFG19)=120,01ANDG19=<140THEND47ELSE0	IFG19)=120,01ANDG19=<140THENE47ELSE0
73		IFG19)=140,01ANDG19=<160THENC48ELSE0	IFG19)=140,01ANDG19=<160THEND48ELSE0	IFG19)=140,01ANDG19=<160THENE48ELSE0
74		IFG19)=160,01ANDG19=<180THENC49ELSE0	IFG19)=160,01ANDG19=<180THEND49ELSE0	IFG19)=160,01ANDG19=<180THENE49ELSE0
75		IFG19)=180,01ANDG19=<200THENC50ELSE0	IFG19)=180,01ANDG19=<200THEND50ELSE0	IFG19)=180,01ANDG19=<200THENE50ELSE0
76	TOTAL	SUM(C65:C75)	SUM(D65:D75)	SUM(E65:E75)
78	OTS MNH,3	IFG20>0ANDG20<10THENC40ELSE0	IFG20>0ANDG20<10THEND40ELSE0	IFG20>0ANDG20<10THENE40ELSE0
79		IFG20)=10ANDG20<20THENC41ELSE0	IFG20)=10ANDG20<20THEND41ELSE0	IFG20)=10ANDG20<20THENE41ELSE0
80		IFG20)=20,01ANDG20=<40THENC42ELSE0	IFG20)=20,01ANDG20=<40THEND42ELSE0	IFG20)=20,01ANDG20=<40THENE42ELSE0
81		IFG20)=40,01ANDG20=<60THENC43ELSE0	IFG20)=40,01ANDG20=<60THEND43ELSE0	IFG20)=40,01ANDG20=<60THENE43ELSE0
82		IFG20)=60,01ANDG20=<80THENC44ELSE0	IFG20)=60,01ANDG20=<80THEND44ELSE0	IFG20)=60,01ANDG20=<80THENE44ELSE0
83		IFG20)=80,00ANDG20=<100THENC45ELSE0	IFG20)=80,00ANDG20=<100THEND45ELSE0	IFG20)=80,00ANDG20=<100THENE45ELSE0
84		IFG20)=100,01ANDG20=<120THENC46ELSE0	IFG20)=100,01ANDG20=<120THEND46ELSE0	IFG20)=100,01ANDG20=<120THENE46ELSE0
85		IFG20)=120,01ANDG20=<140THENC47ELSE0	IFG20)=120,01ANDG20=<140THEND47ELSE0	IFG20)=120,01ANDG20=<140THENE47ELSE0

Proforma 11.1 *(continued)*

	F	G	H
52	IFG18>0ANDG18<10THENF40ELSE0	IFG18>0ANDG18<10THENG40ELSE0	IFG18>0ANDG18<10THENH40ELSE0
53	IFG18>=10ANDG18<20THENF41ELSE0	IFG18>=10ANDG18<20THENG41ELSE0	IFG18>=10ANDG18<20THENH41ELSE0
54	IFG18>=20,01ANDG18=<40THENF42ELSE0	IFG18>=20,01ANDG18=<40THENG42ELSE0	IFG18>=20,01ANDG18=<40THENH42ELSE0
55	IFG18>=40,01ANDG18=<60THENF43ELSE0	IFG18>=40,01ANDG18=<60THENG43ELSE0	IFG18>=40,01ANDG18=<60THENH43ELSE0
56	IFG18>=60,01ANDG18=<80THENF44ELSE0	IFG18>=60,01ANDG18=<80THENG44ELSE0	IFG18>=60,01ANDG18=<80THENH44ELSE0
57	IFG18>=80,00ANDG18=<100THENF45ELSE0	IFG18>=80,00ANDG18=<100THENG45ELSE0	IFG18>=80,00ANDG18=<100THENH45ELSE0
58	IFG18>=100,01ANDG18=<120THENF46ELSE0	IFG18>=100,01ANDG18=<120THENG46ELSE0	IFG18>=100,01ANDG18=<120THENH46ELSE0
59	IFG18>=120,01ANDG18=<140THENF47ELSE0	IFG18>=120,01ANDG18=<140THENG47ELSE0	IFG18>=120,01ANDG18=<140THENH47ELSE0
60	IFG18>=140,01ANDG18=<160THENF48ELSE0	IFG18>=140,01ANDG18=<160THENG48ELSE0	IFG18>=140,01ANDG18=<160THENH48ELSE0
61	IFG18>=160,01ANDG18=<180THENF49ELSE0	IFG18>=160,01ANDG18=<180THENG49ELSE0	IFG18>=160,01ANDG18=<180THENH49ELSE0
62	IFG18>=180,01ANDG18=<200THENF50ELSE0	IFG18>=180,01ANDG18=<200THENG50ELSE0	IFG18>=180,01ANDG18=<200THENH50ELSE0
63	SUM(F52;F62)	SUM(G52;G62)	SUM(H52;H62)
65	IFG19>0ANDG19<10THENF40ELSE0	IFG19>0ANDG19<10THENG40ELSE0	IFG19>0ANDG19<10THENH40ELSE0
66	IFG19>=10ANDG19<20THENF41ELSE0	IFG19>=10ANDG19<20THENG41ELSE0	IFG19>=10ANDG19<20THENH41ELSE0
67	IFG19>=20,01ANDG19=<40THENF42ELSE0	IFG19>=20,01ANDG19=<40THENG42ELSE0	IFG19>=20,01ANDG19=<40THENH42ELSE0
68	IFG19>=40,01ANDG19=<60THENF43ELSE0	IFG19>=40,01ANDG19=<60THENG43ELSE0	IFG19>=40,01ANDG19=<60THENH43ELSE0
69	IFG19>=60,01ANDG19=<80THENF44ELSE0	IFG19>=60,01ANDG19=<80THENG44ELSE0	IFG19>=60,01ANDG19=<80THENH44ELSE0
70	IFG19>=80,00ANDG19=<100THENF45ELSE0	IFG19>=80,00ANDG19=<100THENG45ELSE0	IFG19>=80,00ANDG19=<100THENH45ELSE0
71	IFG19>=100,01ANDG19=<120THENF46ELSE0	IFG19>=100,01ANDG19=<120THENG46ELSE0	IFG19>=100,01ANDG19=<120THENH46ELSE0
72	IFG19>=120,01ANDG19=<140THENF47ELSE0	IFG19>=120,01ANDG19=<140THENG47ELSE0	IFG19>=120,01ANDG19=<140THENH47ELSE0
73	IFG19>=140,01ANDG19=<160THENF48ELSE0	IFG19>=140,01ANDG19=<160THENG48ELSE0	IFG19>=140,01ANDG19=<160THENH48ELSE0
74	IFG19>=160,01ANDG19=<180THENF49ELSE0	IFG19>=160,01ANDG19=<180THENG49ELSE0	IFG19>=160,01ANDG19=<180THENH49ELSE0
75	IFG19>=180,01ANDG19=<200THENF50ELSE0	IFG19>=180,01ANDG19=<200THENG50ELSE0	IFG19>=180,01ANDG19=<200THENH50ELSE0
76	SUM(F65;F75)	SUM(G65;G75)	SUM(H65;H75)
78	IFG20>0ANDG20<10THENF40ELSE0	IFG20>0ANDG20<10THENG40ELSE0	IFG20>0ANDG20<10THENH40ELSE0
79	IFG20>=10ANDG20<20THENF41ELSE0	IFG20>=10ANDG20<20THENG41ELSE0	IFG20>=10ANDG20<20THENH41ELSE0
80	IFG20>=20,01ANDG20=<40THENF42ELSE0	IFG20>=20,01ANDG20=<40THENG42ELSE0	IFG20>=20,01ANDG20=<40THENH42ELSE0
81	IFG20>=40,01ANDG20=<60THENF43ELSE0	IFG20>=40,01ANDG20=<60THENG43ELSE0	IFG20>=40,01ANDG20=<60THENH43ELSE0
82	IFG20>=60,01ANDG20=<80THENF44ELSE0	IFG20>=60,01ANDG20=<80THENG44ELSE0	IFG20>=60,01ANDG20=<80THENH44ELSE0
83	IFG20>=80,00ANDG20=<100THENF45ELSE0	IFG20>=80,00ANDG20=<100THENG45ELSE0	IFG20>=80,00ANDG20=<100THENH45ELSE0
84	IFG20>=100,01ANDG20=<120THENF46ELSE0	IFG20>=100,01ANDG20=<120THENG46ELSE0	IFG20>=100,01ANDG20=<120THENH46ELSE0
85	IFG20>=120,01ANDG20=<140THENF47ELSE0	IFG20>=120,01ANDG20=<140THENG47ELSE0	IFG20>=120,01ANDG20=<140THENH47ELSE0

Proforma 11.1 (*continued*)

A	C	D	E
86	IFG20)=140,01ANDG20=<160THENC48ELSE0	IFG20)=140,01ANDG20=<160THEND48ELSE0	IFG20)=140,01ANDG20=<160THENE48ELSE0
87	IFG20)=160,01ANDG20=<180THENC49ELSE0	IFG20)=160,01ANDG20=<180THEND49ELSE0	IFG20)=160,01ANDG20=<180THENE49ELSE0
88	IFG20)=180,01ANDG20=<200THENC50ELSE0	IFG20)=180,01ANDG20=<200THEND50ELSE0	IFG20)=180,01ANDG20=<200THENE50ELSE0
89 TOTAL	SUM(C78:C88)	SUM(D78:D88)	SUM(E78:E88)
91 OTS MNH.4	IFG21)0ANDG21<10THENC40ELSE0	IFG21)0ANDG21<10THEND40ELSE0	IFG21)0ANDG21<10THENE40ELSE0
92	IFG21)=10AND621<20THENC41ELSE0	IFG21)=10AND621<20THEND41ELSE0	IFG21)=10AND621<20THENE41ELSE0
93	IFG21)=20,01AND621=<40THENC42ELSE0	IFG21)=20,01AND621=<40THEND42ELSE0	IFG21)=20,01AND621=<40THENE42ELSE0
94	IFG21)=40,01AND621=<60THENC43ELSE0	IFG21)=40,01AND621=<60THEND43ELSE0	IFG21)=40,01AND621=<60THENE43ELSE0
95	IFG21)=60,01AND621=<80THENC44ELSE0	IFG21)=60,01AND621=<80THEND44ELSE0	IFG21)=60,01AND621=<80THENE44ELSE0
96	IFG21)=80,00AND621=<100THENC45ELSE0	IFG21)=80,00AND621=<100THEND45ELSE0	IFG21)=80,00AND621=<100THENE45ELSE0
97	IFG21)=100,01AND621=<120THENC46ELSE0	IFG21)=100,01AND621=<120THEND46ELSE0	IFG21)=100,01AND621=<120THENE46ELSE0
98	IFG21)=120,01AND621=<140THENC47ELSE0	IFG21)=120,01AND621=<140THEND47ELSE0	IFG21)=120,01AND621=<140THENE47ELSE0
99	IFG21)=140,01AND621=<160THENC48ELSE0	IFG21)=140,01AND621=<160THEND48ELSE0	IFG21)=140,01AND621=<160THENE48ELSE0
100	IFG21)=160,01AND621=<180THENC49ELSE0	IFG21)=160,01AND621=<180THEND49ELSE0	IFG21)=160,01AND621=<180THENE49ELSE0
101	IFG21)=180,01AND621=<200THENC50ELSE0	IFG21)=180,01AND621=<200THEND50ELSE0	IFG21)=180,01AND621=<200THENE50ELSE0
102 TOTAL	SUM(C91:C101)	SUM(D91:D101)	(SUM(E91:E101)
104 OTS MNH.5	IFG22)0ANDG22<10THENC40ELSE0	IFG22)0ANDG22<10THEND40ELSE0	IFG22)0ANDG22<10THENE40ELSE0
105	IFG22)=10AND622<20THENC41ELSE0	IFG22)=10AND622<20THEND41ELSE0	IFG22)=10AND622<20THENE41ELSE0
106	IFG22)=20,01AND622=<40THENC42ELSE0	IFG22)=20,01AND622=<40THEND42ELSE0	IFG22)=20,01AND622=<40THENE42ELSE0
107	IFG22)=40,01AND622=<60THENC43ELSE0	IFG22)=40,01AND622=<60THEND43ELSE0	IFG22)=40,01AND622=<60THENE43ELSE0
108	IFG22)=60,01AND622=<80THENC44ELSE0	IFG22)=60,01AND622=<80THEND44ELSE0	IFG22)=60,01AND622=<80THENE44ELSE0
109	IFG22)=80,00AND622=<100THENC45ELSE0	IFG22)=80,00AND622=<100THEND45ELSE0	IFG22)=80,00AND622=<100THENE45ELSE0
110	IFG22)=100,01AND622=<120THENC46ELSE0	IFG22)=100,01AND622=<120THEND46ELSE0	IFG22)=100,01AND622=<120THENE46ELSE0
111	IFG22)=120,01AND622=<140THENC47ELSE0	IFG22)=120,01AND622=<140THEND47ELSE0	IFG22)=120,01AND622=<140THENE47ELSE0
112	IFG22)=140,01AND622=<160THENC48ELSE0	IFG22)=140,01AND622=<160THEND48ELSE0	IFG22)=140,01AND622=<160THENE48ELSE0
113	IFG22)=160,01AND622=<180THENC49ELSE0	IFG22)=160,01AND622=<180THEND49ELSE0	IFG22)=160,01AND622=<180THENE49ELSE0
114	IFG22)=180,01AND622=<200THENC50ELSE0	IFG22)=180,01AND622=<200THEND50ELSE0	IFG22)=180,01AND622=<200THENE50ELSE0
115 TOTAL	SUM(C104:C114)	SUM(D104:D114)	SUM(E104:E114)
117 OTS MNH.6	IFG23)0ANDG23<10THENC40ELSE0	IFG23)0ANDG23<10THEND40ELSE0	IFG23)0ANDG23<10THENE40ELSE0
118	IFG23)=10ANDG23<20THENC41ELSE0	IFG23)=10ANDG23<20THEND41ELSE0	IFG23)=10ANDG23<20THENE41ELSE0
119	IFG23)=20,01AND623=<40THENC42ELSE0	IFG23)=20,01AND623=<40THEND42ELSE0	IFG23)=20,01AND623=<40THENE42ELSE0
120	IFG23)=40,01AND623=<60THENC43ELSE0	IFG23)=40,01AND623=<60THEND43ELSE0	IFG23)=40,01AND623=<60THENE43ELSE0
121	IFG23)=60,01AND623=<80THENC44ELSE0	IFG23)=60,01AND623=<80THEND44ELSE0	IFG23)=60,01AND623=<80THENE44ELSE0

Proforma 11.1 *(continued)*

	F	G	H

```
       F                                    G                                    H

86   IFG20)=140,01ANDG20=<160THENF48ELSE0  IFG20)=140,01ANDG20=<160THENG48ELSE0  IFG20)=140,01ANDG20=<160THENH48ELSE0
87   IFG20)=160,01ANDG20=<180THENF49ELSE0  IFG20)=160,01ANDG20=<180THENG49ELSE0  IFG20)=160,01ANDG20=<180THENH49ELSE0
88   IFG20)=180,01ANDG20=<200THENF50ELSE0  IFG20)=180,01ANDG20=<200THENG50ELSE0  IFG20)=180,01ANDG20=<200THENH50ELSE0
89       SUM(F78;F88)                           SUM(G78;G88)                         SUM(H78;H88)

91   IFG21)0ANDG21<10THENF40ELSE0          IFG21)0ANDG21<10THENG40ELSE0          IFG21)0ANDG21<10THENH40ELSE0
92   IFG21)=10ANDG21<20THENF41ELSE0        IFG21)=10ANDG21<20THENG41ELSE0        IFG21)=10ANDG21<20THENH41ELSE0
93   IFG21)=20,01ANDG21=<40THENF42ELSE0    IFG21)=20,01ANDG21=<40THENG42ELSE0    IFG21)=20,01ANDG21=<40THENH42ELSE0
94   IFG21)=40,01ANDG21=<60THENF43ELSE0    IFG21)=40,01ANDG21=<60THENG43ELSE0    IFG21)=40,01ANDG21=<60THENH43ELSE0
95   IFG21)=60,01ANDG21=<80THENF44ELSE0    IFG21)=60,01ANDG21=<80THENG44ELSE0    IFG21)=60,01ANDG21=<80THENH44ELSE0
96   IFG21)=80,00ANDG21=<100THENF45ELSE0   IFG21)=80,00ANDG21=<100THENG45ELSE0   IFG21)=80,01ANDG21=<100THENH45ELSE0
97   IFG21)=100,01ANDG21=<120THENF46ELSE0  IFG21)=100,01ANDG21=<120THENG46ELSE0  IFG21)=100,01ANDG21=<120THENH46ELSE0
98   IFG21)=120,01ANDG21=<140THENF47ELSE0  IFG21)=120,01ANDG21=<140THENG47ELSE0  IFG21)=120,01ANDG21=<140THENH47ELSE0
99   IFG21)=140,01ANDG21=<160THENF48ELSE0  IFG21)=140,01ANDG21=<160THENG48ELSE0  IFG21)=140,01ANDG21=<160THENH48ELSE0
100  IFG21)=160,01ANDG21=<180THENF49ELSE0  IFG21)=160,01ANDG21=<180THENG49ELSE0  IFG21)=160,01ANDG21=<180THENH49ELSE0
101  IFG21)=180,01ANDG21=<200THENF50ELSE0  IFG21)=180,01ANDG21=<200THENG50ELSE0  IFG21)=180,01ANDG21=<200THENH50ELSE0
102      SUM(F91;F101)                          SUM(G91;G101)                        SUM(H91;H101)

104  IFG22)0ANDG22<10THENF40ELSE0          IFG22)0ANDG22<10THENG40ELSE0          IFG22)0ANDG22<10THENH40ELSE0
105  IFG22)=10ANDG22<20THENF41ELSE0        IFG22)=10ANDG22<20THENG41ELSE0        IFG22)=10ANDG22<20THENH41ELSE0
106  IFG22)=20,01ANDG22=<40THENF42ELSE0    IFG22)=20,01ANDG22=<40THENG42ELSE0    IFG22)=20,01ANDG22=<40THENH42ELSE0
107  IFG22)=40,01ANDG22=<60THENF43ELSE0    IFG22)=40,01ANDG22=<60THENG43ELSE0    IFG22)=40,01ANDG22=<60THENH43ELSE0
108  IFG22)=60,01ANDG22=<80THENF44ELSE0    IFG22)=60,01ANDG22=<80THENG44ELSE0    IFG22)=60,01ANDG22=<80THENH44ELSE0
109  IFG22)=80,00ANDG22=<100THENF45ELSE0   IFG22)=80,00ANDG22=<100THENG45ELSE0   IFG22)=80,01ANDG22=<100THENH45ELSE0
110  IFG22)=100,01ANDG22=<120THENF46ELSE0  IFG22)=100,01ANDG22=<120THENG46ELSE0  IFG22)=100,01ANDG22=<120THENH46ELSE0
111  IFG22)=120,01ANDG22=<140THENF47ELSE0  IFG22)=120,01ANDG22=<140THENG47ELSE0  IFG22)=120,01ANDG22=<140THENH47ELSE0
112  IFG22)=140,01ANDG22=<160THENF48ELSE0  IFG22)=140,01ANDG22=<160THENG48ELSE0  IFG22)=140,01ANDG22=<160THENH48ELSE0
113  IFG22)=160,01ANDG22=<180THENF49ELSE0  IFG22)=160,01ANDG22=<180THENG49ELSE0  IFG22)=160,01ANDG22=<180THENH49ELSE0
114  IFG22)=180,01ANDG22=<200THENF50ELSE0  IFG22)=180,01ANDG22=<200THENG50ELSE0  IFG22)=180,01ANDG22=<200THENH50ELSE0
115  SUM(F104;F114)                            SUM(G104;G114)                       SUM(H104;H114)

117  IFG23)0ANDG23<10THENF40ELSE0          IFG23)0ANDG23<10THENG40ELSE0          IFG23)0ANDG23<10THENH40ELSE0
118  IFG23)=10ANDG23<20THENF41ELSE0        IFG23)=10ANDG23<20THENG41ELSE0        IFG23)=10ANDG23<20THENH41ELSE0
119  IFG23)=20,01ANDG23=<40THENF42ELSE0    IFG23)=20,01ANDG23=<40THENG42ELSE0    IFG23)=20,01ANDG23=<40THENH42ELSE0
120  IFG23)=40,01ANDG23=<60THENF43ELSE0    IFG23)=40,01ANDG23=<60THENG43ELSE0    IFG23)=40,01ANDG23=<60THENH43ELSE0
121  IFG23)=60,01ANDG23=<80THENF44ELSE0    IFG23)=60,01ANDG23=<80THENG44ELSE0    IFG23)=60,01ANDG23=<80THENH44ELSE0
```

Proforma 11.1 (*continued*)

A	C	D	E
122	IFG23>=80,00ANDG23=<100THENC45ELSE0	IFG23>=80,00ANDG23=<100THEND45ELSE0	IFG23>=80,00ANDG23=<100THENE45ELSE0
123	IFG23>=100,01ANDG23=<140THENC46ELSE0	IFG23>=100,01ANDG23=<120THEND46ELSE0	IFG23>=100,01ANDG23=<120THENE46ELSE0
124	IFG23>=120,01ANDG23=<140THENC47ELSE0	IFG23>=120,01ANDG23=<140THEND47ELSE0	IFG23>=120,01ANDG23=<140THENE47ELSE0
125	IFG23>=140,01ANDG23=<160THENC48ELSE0	IFG23>=140,01ANDG23=<160THEND48ELSE0	IFG23>=140,01ANDG23=<160THENE48ELSE0
126	IFG23>=160,01ANDG23=<180THENC49ELSE0	IFG23>=160,01ANDG23=<180THEND49ELSE0	IFG23>=160,01ANDG23=<180THENE49ELSE0
127	IFG23>=180,01ANDG23=<200THENC50ELSE0	IFG23>=180,01ANDG23=<200THEND50ELSE0	IFG23>=180,01ANDG23=<200THENE50ELSE0
128 TOTAL	SUM(C117;C127)	SUM(D117;D127)	SUM(E117;E127)
130 OTS MNH.7	IFG24>0ANDG24<10THENC40ELSE0	IFG24>0ANDG24<10THEND40ELSE0	IFG24>0ANDG24<10THENE40ELSE0
131	IFG24>=10ANDG24<20THENC41ELSE0	IFG24>=10ANDG24<20THEND41ELSE0	IFG24>=10ANDG24<20THENE41ELSE0
132	IFG24>=20,01ANDG24=<40THENC42ELSE0	IFG24>=20,01ANDG24=<40THEND42ELSE0	IFG24>=20,01ANDG24=<40THENE42ELSE0
133	IFG24>=40,01ANDG24=<60THENC43ELSE0	IFG24>=40,01ANDG24=<60THEND43ELSE0	IFG24>=40,01ANDG24=<60THENE43ELSE0
134	IFG24>=60,01ANDG24=<80THENC44ELSE0	IFG24>=60,01ANDG24=<80THEND44ELSE0	IFG24>=60,01ANDG24=<80THENE44ELSE0
135	IFG24>=80,00ANDG24=<100THENC45ELSE0	IFG24>=80,00ANDG24=<100THEND45ELSE0	IFG24>=80,00ANDG24=<100THENE45ELSE0
136	IFG24>=100,01ANDG24=<120THENC46ELSE0	IFG24>=100,01ANDG24=<120THEND46ELSE0	IFG24>=100,01ANDG24=<120THENE46ELSE0
137	IFG24>=120,01ANDG24=<140THENC47ELSE0	IFG24>=120,01ANDG24=<140THEND47ELSE0	IFG24>=120,01ANDG24=<140THENE47ELSE0
138	IFG24>=140,01ANDG24=<160THENC48ELSE0	IFG24>=140,01ANDG24=<160THEND48ELSE0	IFG24>=140,01ANDG24=<160THENE48ELSE0
139	IFG24>=160,01ANDG24=<180THENC49ELSE0	IFG24>=160,01ANDG24=<180THEND49ELSE0	IFG24>=160,01ANDG24=<180THENE49ELSE0
140	IFG24>=180,01ANDG24=<200THENC50ELSE0	IFG24>=180,01ANDG24=<200THEND50ELSE0	IFG24>=180,01ANDG24=<200THENE50ELSE0
141 TOTAL	SUM(C130;C140)	SUM(D130;D140)	SUM(E130;E140)
143 OTS MNH.8	IFG25>0ANDG25<10THENC40ELSE0	IFG25>0ANDG25<10THEND40ELSE0	IFG25>0ANDG25<10THENE40ELSE0
144	IFG25>=10ANDG25<20THENC41ELSE0	IFG25>=10ANDG25<20THEND41ELSE0	IFG25>=10ANDG25<20THENE41ELSE0
145	IFG25>=20,01ANDG25=<40THENC42ELSE0	IFG25>=20,01ANDG25=<40THEND42ELSE0	IFG25>=20,01ANDG25=<40THENE42ELSE0
146	IFG25>=40,01ANDG25=<60THENC43ELSE0	IFG25>=40,01ANDG25=<60THEND43ELSE0	IFG25>=40,01ANDG25=<60THENE43ELSE0
147	IFG25>=60,01ANDG25=<80THENC44ELSE0	IFG25>=60,01ANDG25=<80THEND44ELSE0	IFG25>=60,01ANDG25=<80THENE44ELSE0
148	IFG25>=80,00ANDG25=<100THENC45ELSE0	IFG25>=80,00ANDG25=<100THEND45ELSE0	IFG25>=80,00ANDG25=<100THENE45ELSE0
149	IFG25>=100,01ANDG25=<120THENC46ELSE0	IFG25>=100,01ANDG25=<120THEND46ELSE0	IFG25>=100,01ANDG25=<120THENE46ELSE0
150	IFG25>=120,01ANDG25=<140THENC47ELSE0	IFG25>=120,01ANDG25=<140THEND47ELSE0	IFG25>=120,01ANDG25=<140THENE47ELSE0
151	IFG25>=140,01ANDG25=<160THENC48ELSE0	IFG25>=140,01ANDG25=<160THEND48ELSE0	IFG25>=140,01ANDG25=<160THENE48ELSE0
152	IFG25>=160,01ANDG25=<180THENC49ELSE0	IFG25>=160,01ANDG25=<180THEND49ELSE0	IFG25>=160,01ANDG25=<180THENE49ELSE0
153	IFG25>=180,01ANDG25=<200THENC50ELSE0	IFG25>=180,01ANDG25=<200THEND50ELSE0	IFG25>=180,01ANDG25=<200THENE50ELSE0
154 TOTAL	SUM(C143;C153)	SUM(D143;D153)	SUM(E143;E153)

Proforma 11.1 *(continued)*

	F	G	H
122	IFG23)=80,00ANDG23=<100THENF45ELSE0	IFG23)=80,00ANDG23=<100THENG45ELSE0	IFG23)=80,01ANDG23=<100THENH45ELSE0
123	IFG23)=100,01ANDG23=<120THENF46ELSE0	IFG23)=100,01ANDG23=<120THENG46ELSE0	IFG23)=100,01ANDG23=<120THENH46ELSE0
124	IFG23)=120,01ANDG23=<140THENF47ELSE0	IFG23)=120,01ANDG23=<140THENG47ELSE0	IFG23)=120,01ANDG23=<140THENH47ELSE0
125	IFG23)=140,01ANDG23=<160THENF48ELSE0	IFG23)=140,01ANDG23=<160THENG48ELSE0	IFG23)=140,01ANDG23=<160THENH48ELSE0
126	IFG23)=160,01ANDG23=<180THENF49ELSE0	IFG23)=160,01ANDG23=<180THENG49ELSE0	IFG23)=160,01ANDG23=<180THENH49ELSE0
127	IFG23)=180,01ANDG23=<200THENF50ELSE0	IFG23)=180,01ANDG23=<200THENG50ELSE0	IFG23)=180,01ANDG23=<200THENH50ELSE0
128	SUM(F117;F127)	SUM(G117;G127)	SUM(H117;H127)
130	IFG24>0ANDG24<10THENF40ELSE0	IFG24>0ANDG24<10THENG40ELSE0	IFG24>0ANDG24<10THENH40ELSE0
131	IFG24)=10AND624<20THENF41ELSE0	IFG24)=10AND624<20THENG41ELSE0	IFG24)=10AND624<20THENH41ELSE0
132	IFG24)=20,01ANDG24=<40THENF42ELSE0	IFG24)=20,01ANDG24=<40THENG42ELSE0	IFG24)=20,01ANDG24=<40THENH42ELSE0
133	IFG24)=40,01ANDG24=<60THENF43ELSE0	IFG24)=40,01ANDG24=<60THENG43ELSE0	IFG24)=40,01ANDG24=<60THENH43ELSE0
134	IFG24)=60,01ANDG24=<80THENF44ELSE0	IFG24)=60,01ANDG24=<80THENG44ELSE0	IFG24)=60,01ANDG24=<80THENH44ELSE0
135	IFG24)=80,00ANDG24=<100THENF45ELSE0	IFG24)=80,00ANDG24=<100THENG45ELSE0	IFG24)=80,01ANDG24=<100THENH45ELSE0
136	IFG24)=100,01ANDG24=<120THENF46ELSE0	IFG24)=100,01ANDG24=<120THENG46ELSE0	IFG24)=100,01ANDG24=<120THENH46ELSE0
137	IFG24)=120,01ANDG24=<140THENF47ELSE0	IFG24)=120,01ANDG24=<140THENG47ELSE0	IFG24)=120,01ANDG24=<140THENH47ELSE0
138	IFG24)=140,01ANDG24=<160THENF48ELSE0	IFG24)=140,01ANDG24=<160THENG48ELSE0	IFG24)=140,01ANDG24=<160THENH48ELSE0
139	IFG24)=160,01ANDG24=<180THENF49ELSE0	IFG24)=160,01ANDG24=<180THENG49ELSE0	IFG24)=160,01ANDG24=<180THENH49ELSE0
140	IFG24)=180,01ANDG24=<200THENF50ELSE0	IFG24)=180,01ANDG24=<200THENG50ELSE0	IFG24)=180,01ANDG24=<200THENH50ELSE0
141	SUM(F130;F140)	SUM(G130;G140)	SUM(H130;H140)
143	IFG25>0ANDG25<10THENF40ELSE0	IFG25>0ANDG25<10THENG40ELSE0	IFG25>0ANDG25<10THENH40ELSE0
144	IFG25)=10ANDG25<20THENF41ELSE0	IFG25)=10ANDG25<20THENG41ELSE0	IFG25)=10ANDG25<20THENH41ELSE0
145	IFG25)=20,01ANDG25=<40THENF42ELSE0	IFG25)=20,01ANDG25=<40THENG42ELSE0	IFG25)=20,01ANDG25=<40THENH42ELSE0
146	IFG25)=40,01ANDG25=<60THENF43ELSE0	IFG25)=40,01ANDG25=<60THENG43ELSE0	IFG25)=40,01ANDG25=<60THENH43ELSE0
147	IFG25)=60,01ANDG25=<80THENF44ELSE0	IFG25)=60,01ANDG25=<80THENG44ELSE0	IFG25)=60,01ANDG25=<80THENH44ELSE0
148	IFG25)=80,00ANDG25=<100THENF45ELSE0	IFG25)=80,00ANDG25=<100THENG45ELSE0	IFG25)=80,01ANDG25=<100THENH45ELSE0
149	IFG25)=100,01ANDG25=<120THENF46ELSE0	IFG25)=100,01ANDG25=<120THENG46ELSE0	IFG25)=100,01ANDG25=<120THENH46ELSE0
150	IFG25)=120,01ANDG25=<140THENF47ELSE0	IFG25)=120,01ANDG25=<140THENG47ELSE0	IFG25)=120,01ANDG25=<140THENH47ELSE0
151	IFG25)=140,01ANDG25=<160THENF48ELSE0	IFG25)=140,01ANDG25=<160THENG48ELSE0	IFG25)=140,01ANDG25=<160THENH48ELSE0
152	IFG25)=160,01ANDG25=<180THENF49ELSE0	IFG25)=160,01ANDG25=<180THENG49ELSE0	IFG25)=160,01ANDG25=<180THENH49ELSE0
153	IFG25)=180,01ANDG25=<200THENF50ELSE0	IFG25)=180,01ANDG25=<200THENG50ELSE0	IFG25)=180,01ANDG25=<200THENH50ELSE0
154	SUM(F143;F153)	SUM(G143;G153)	SUM(H143;H153)

Proforma 11.1 (*continued*)

	A	C	D	E
156	OTS MNH,9	IFG26>0ANDG26<10THENC40ELSE0	IFG26>0ANDG26<10THEND40ELSE0	IFG26>0ANDG26<10THENE40ELSE0
157		IFG26>=10ANDG26<20THENC41ELSE0	IFG26>=10ANDG26<20THEND41ELSE0	IFG26>=10ANDG26<20THENE41ELSE0
158		IFG26>=20,01ANDG26=<40THENC42ELSE0	IFG26>=20,01ANDG26=<40THEND42ELSE0	IFG26>=20,01ANDG26=<40THENE42ELSE0
159		IFG26>=40,01ANDG26=<60THENC43ELSE0	IFG26>=40,01ANDG26=<60THEND43ELSE0	IFG26>=40,01ANDG26=<60THENE43ELSE0
160		IFG26>=60,01ANDG26=<80THENC44ELSE0	IFG26>=60,01ANDG26=<80THEND44ELSE0	IFG26>=60,01ANDG26=<80THENE44ELSE0
161		IFG26>=80,00ANDG26=<100THENC45ELSE0	IFG26>=80,00ANDG26=<100THEND45ELSE0	IFG26>=80,00ANDG26=<100THENE45ELSE0
162		IFG26>=100,01ANDG26=<120THENC46ELSE0	IFG26>=100,01ANDG26=<120THEND46ELSE0	IFG26>=100,01ANDG26=<120THENE46ELSE0
163		IFG26>=120,01ANDG26=<140THENC47ELSE0	IFG26>=120,01ANDG26=<140THEND47ELSE0	IFG26>=120,01ANDG26=<140THENE47ELSE0
164		IFG26>=140,01ANDG26=<160THENC48ELSE0	IFG26>=140,01ANDG26=<160THEND48ELSE0	IFG26>=140,01ANDG26=<160THENE48ELSE0
165		IFG26>=160,01ANDG26=<180THENC49ELSE0	IFG26>=160,01ANDG26=<180THEND49ELSE0	IFG26>=160,01ANDG26=<180THENE49ELSE0
166		IFG26>=180,01ANDG26=<200THENC50ELSE0	IFG26>=180,01ANDG26=<200THEND50ELSE0	IFG26>=180,01ANDG26=<200THENE50ELSE0
167	TOTAL	SUM(C156:C166)	SUM(D156:D166)	SUM(E156:E166)
169	OTS MNH,10	IFG27>0ANDG27<10THENC40ELSE0	IFG27>0ANDG27<10THEND40ELSE0	IFG27>0ANDG27<10THENE40ELSE0
170		IFG27>=10ANDG27<20THENC41ELSE0	IFG27>=10ANDG27<20THEND41ELSE0	IFG27>=10ANDG27<20THENE41ELSE0
171		IFG27>=20,01ANDG27=<40THENC42ELSE0	IFG27>=20,01ANDG27=<40THEND42ELSE0	IFG27>=20,01ANDG27=<40THENE42ELSE0
172		IFG27>=40,01ANDG27=<60THENC43ELSE0	IFG27>=40,01ANDG27=<60THEND43ELSE0	IFG27>=40,01ANDG27=<60THENE43ELSE0
173		IFG27>=60,01ANDG27=<80THENC44ELSE0	IFG27>=60,01ANDG27=<80THEND44ELSE0	IFG27>=60,01ANDG27=<80THENE44ELSE0
174		IFG27>=80,00ANDG27=<100THENC45ELSE0	IFG27>=80,00ANDG27=<100THEND45ELSE0	IFG27>=80,00ANDG27=<100THENE45ELSE0
175		IFG27>=100,01ANDG27=<120THENC46ELSE0	IFG27>=100,01ANDG27=<120THEND46ELSE0	IFG27>=100,01ANDG27=<120THENE46ELSE0
176		IFG27>=120,01ANDG27=<140THENC47ELSE0	IFG27>=120,01ANDG27=<140THEND47ELSE0	IFG27>=120,01ANDG27=<140THENE47ELSE0
177		IFG27>=140,01ANDG27=<160THENC48ELSE0	IFG27>=140,01ANDG27=<160THEND48ELSE0	IFG27>=140,01ANDG27=<160THENE48ELSE0
178		IFG27>=160,01ANDG27=<180THENC49ELSE0	IFG27>=160,01ANDG27=<180THEND49ELSE0	IFG27>=160,01ANDG26=<180THENE49ELSE0
179		IFG27>=180,01ANDG27=<200THENC50ELSE0	IFG27>=180,01ANDG27=<200THEND50ELSE0	IFG27>=180,01ANDG27=<200THENE50ELSE0
180	TOTAL	SUM(C169:C179)	SUM(D169:D179)	SUM(E169:E179)
182	OTS MNH,11	IFG28>0ANDG28<10THENC40ELSE0	IFG28>0ANDG28<10THEND40ELSE0	IFG28>0ANDG28<10THENE40ELSE0
183		IFG28>=10ANDG28<20THENC41ELSE0	IFG28>=10ANDG28<20THEND41ELSE0	IFG28>=10ANDG28<20THENE41ELSE0
184		IFG28>=20,01ANDG28=<40THENC42ELSE0	IFG28>=20,01ANDG28=<40THEND42ELSE0	IFG28>=20,01ANDG28=<40THENE42ELSE0
185		IFG28>=40,01ANDG28=<60THENC43ELSE0	IFG28>=40,01ANDG28=<60THEND43ELSE0	IFG28>=40,01ANDG28=<60THENE43ELSE0
186		IFG28>=60,01ANDG28=<80THENC44ELSE0	IFG28>=60,01ANDG28=<80THEND44ELSE0	IFG28>=60,01ANDG28=<80THENE44ELSE0
187		IFG28>=80,00ANDG28=<100THENC45ELSE0	IFG28>=80,00ANDG28=<100THEND45ELSE0	IFG28>=80,00ANDG28=<100THENE45ELSE0
188		IFG28>=100,01ANDG28=<120THENC46ELSE0	IFG28>=100,01ANDG28=<120THEND46ELSE0	IFG28>=100,01ANDG28=<120THENE46ELSE0
189		IFG28>=120,01ANDG28=<140THENC47ELSE0	IFG28>=120,01ANDG28=<140THEND47ELSE0	IFG28>=120,01ANDG28=<140THENE47ELSE0
190		IFG28>=140,01ANDG28=<160THENC48ELSE0	IFG28>=140,01ANDG28=<160THEND48ELSE0	IFG28>=140,01ANDG28=<160THENE48ELSE0

Proforma 11.1   *(continued)*

```
        F                                    G                                    H                              ☐☐☐
                                                                                                                 ☐
156  IFG26>0ANDG26<10THENF40ELSE0      IFG26>0ANDG26<10THENG40ELSE0       IFG26>0ANDG26<10THENH40ELSE0          ☐☐
157  IFG26>=10ANDG26<20THENF41ELSE0    IFG26>=10ANDG26<20THENG41ELSE0     IFG26>=10ANDG26<20THENH41ELSE0        ☐☐
158  IFG26>=20,01ANDG26=<40THENF42ELSE0  IFG26>=20,01ANDG26=<40THENG42ELSE0  IFG26>=20,01ANDG26=<40THENH42ELSE0 ☐☐
159  IFG26>=40,01ANDG26=<60THENF43ELSE0  IFG26>=40,01ANDG26=<60THENG43ELSE0  IFG26>=40,01ANDG26=<60THENH43ELSE0 ☐■
160  IFG26>=60,01ANDG26=<80THENF44ELSE0  IFG26>=60,01ANDG26=<80THENG44ELSE0  IFG26>=60,01ANDG26=<80THENH44ELSE0 ☐☐
161  IFG26>=80,00ANDG26=<100THENF45ELSE0  IFG26>=80,00ANDG26=<100THENG45ELSE0  IFG26>=80,01ANDG26=<100THENH45ELSE0
162  IFG26>=100,01ANDG26=<120THENF46ELSE0  IFG26>=100,01ANDG26=<120THENG46ELSE0  IFG26>=100,01ANDG26=<120THENH46ELSE0
163  IFG26>=120,01ANDG26=<140THENF47ELSE0  IFG26>=120,01ANDG26=<140THENG47ELSE0  IFG26>=120,01ANDG26=<140THENH47ELSE0
164  IFG26>=140,01ANDG26=<160THENF48ELSE0  IFG26>=140,01ANDG26=<160THENG48ELSE0  IFG26>=140,01ANDG26=<160THENH48ELSE0
165  IFG26>=160,01ANDG26=<180THENF49ELSE0  IFG26>=160,01ANDG26=<180THENG49ELSE0  IFG26>=160,01ANDG26=<180THENH49ELSE0
166  IFG26>=180,01ANDG26=<200THENF50ELSE0  IFG26>=180,01ANDG26=<200THENG50ELSE0  IFG26>=180,01ANDG26=<200THENH50ELSE0
167     SUM(F156;F166)                    SUM(G156;G166)                    SUM(H156;H166)

169  IFG27>0ANDG27<10THENF40ELSE0      IFG27>0ANDG27<10THENG40ELSE0       IFG27>0ANDG27<10THENH40ELSE0
170  IFG27>=10ANDG27<20THENF41ELSE0    IFG27>=10ANDG27<20THENG41ELSE0     IFG27>=10ANDG27<20THENH41ELSE0
171  IFG27>=20,01ANDG27=<40THENF42ELSE0  IFG27>=20,01ANDG27=<40THENG42ELSE0  IFG27>=20,01ANDG27=<40THENH42ELSE0
172  IFG27>=40,01ANDG27=<60THENF43ELSE0  IFG27>=40,01ANDG27=<60THENG43ELSE0  IFG27>=40,01ANDG27=<60THENH43ELSE0
173  IFG27>=60,01ANDG27=<80THENF44ELSE0  IFG27>=60,01ANDG27=<80THENG44ELSE0  IFG27>=60,01ANDG27=<80THENH44ELSE0
174  IFG27>=80,00ANDG27=<100THENF45ELSE0  IFG27>=80,00ANDG27=<100THENG45ELSE0  IFG27>=80,01ANDG27=<100THENH45ELSE0
175  IFG27>=100,01ANDG27=<120THENF46ELSE0  IFG27>=100,01ANDG27=<120THENG46ELSE0  IFG27>=100,01ANDG27=<120THENH46ELSE0
176  IFG27>=120,01ANDG27=<140THENF47ELSE0  IFG27>=120,01ANDG27=<140THENG47ELSE0  IFG27>=120,01ANDG27=<140THENH47ELSE0
177  IFG27>=140,01ANDG27=<160THENF48ELSE0  IFG27>=140,01ANDG27=<160THENG48ELSE0  IFG27>=140,01ANDG27=<160THENH48ELSE0
178  IFG27>=160,01ANDG27=<180THENF49ELSE0  IFG27>=160,01ANDG27=<180THENG49ELSE0  IFG27>=160,01ANDG27=<180THENH49ELSE0
179  IFG27>=180,01ANDG26=<200THENF50ELSE0  IFG26>=180,01ANDG26=<200THENG50ELSE0  IFG27>=180,01ANDG27=<200THENH50ELSE0
180     SUM(F169;F179)                    SUM(G169;G179)                    SUM(H169;H179)

182  IFG28>0ANDG28<10THENF40ELSE0      IFG28>0ANDG28<10THENG40ELSE0       IFG28>0ANDG28<10THENH40ELSE0
183  IFG28>=10ANDG28<20THENF41ELSE0    IFG28>=10ANDG28<20THENG41ELSE0     IFG28>=10ANDG28<20THENH41ELSE0
184  IFG28>=20,01ANDG28=<40THENF42ELSE0  IFG28>=20,01ANDG28=<40THENG42ELSE0  IFG28>=20,01ANDG28=<40THENH42ELSE0
185  IFG28>=40,01ANDG28=<60THENF43ELSE0  IFG28>=40,01ANDG28=<60THENG43ELSE0  IFG28>=40,01ANDG28=<60THENH43ELSE0
186  IFG28>=60,01ANDG28=<80THENF44ELSE0  IFG28>=60,01ANDG28=<80THENG44ELSE0  IFG28>=60,01ANDG28=<80THENH44ELSE0
187  IFG28>=80,00ANDG28=<100THENF45ELSE0  IFG28>=80,00ANDG28=<100THENG45ELSE0  IFG28>=80,01ANDG28=<100THENH45ELSE0
188  IFG28>=100,01ANDG28=<120THENF46ELSE0  IFG28>=100,01ANDG28=<120THENG46ELSE0  IFG28>=100,01ANDG28=<120THENH46ELSE0
189  IFG28>=120,01ANDG28=<140THENF47ELSE0  IFG28>=120,01ANDG28=<140THENG47ELSE0  IFG28>=120,01ANDG28=<140THENH47ELSE0
190  IFG28>=140,01ANDG28=<160THENF48ELSE0  IFG28>=140,01ANDG28=<160THENG48ELSE0  IFG28>=140,01ANDG28=<160THENH48ELSE0
```

Proforma 11.1 *(continued)*

	A	C	D	E
191		IFG28)=160,01ANDG28=<180THENC49ELSE0	IFG28)=160,01ANDG28=<180THEND49ELSE0	IFG28)=160,01ANDG28=<180THENE49ELSE0
192		IFG28)=180,01ANDG28=<200THENC50ELSE0	IFG28)=180,01ANDG28=<200THEND50ELSE0	IFG28)=180,01ANDG28=<200THENE50ELSE0
193	TOTAL	SUM(C182;C192)	SUM(D182;D192)	SUM(E182;E192)
195	OTS MNH,12	IFG29>0ANDG29<10THENC40ELSE0	IFG29>0ANDG29<10THEND40ELSE0	IFG29>0ANDG29<10THENE40ELSE0
196		IFG29)=10ANDG29<20THENC41ELSE0	IFG29)=10ANDG29<20THEND41ELSE0	IFG29)=10ANDG29<20THENE41ELSE0
197		IFG29)=20,01ANDG29=<40THENC42ELSE0	IFG29)=20,01ANDG29=<40THEND42ELSE0	IFG29)=20,01ANDG29=<40THENE42ELSE0
198		IFG29)=40,01ANDG29=<60THENC43ELSE0	IFG29)=40,01ANDG29=<60THEND43ELSE0	IFG29)=40,01ANDG29=<60THENE43ELSE0
199		IFG29)=60,01ANDG29=<80THENC44ELSE0	IFG29)=60,01ANDG29=<80THEND44ELSE0	IFG29)=60,01ANDG29=<80THENE44ELSE0
200		IFG29)=80,00ANDG29=<100THENC45ELSE0	IFG29)=80,00ANDG29=<100THEND45ELSE0	IFG29)=80,00ANDG29=<100THENE45ELSE0
201		IFG29)=100,01ANDG29=<120THENC46ELSE0	IFG29)=100,01ANDG29=<120THEND46ELSE0	IFG29)=100,01ANDG29=<120THENE46ELSE0
202		IFG29)=120,01ANDG29=<140THENC47ELSE0	IFG29)=120,01ANDG29=<140THEND47ELSE0	IFG29)=120,01ANDG29=<140THENE47ELSE0
203		IFG29)=140,01ANDG29=<160THENC48ELSE0	IFG29)=140,01ANDG29=<160THEND48ELSE0	IFG29)=140,01ANDG29=<160THENE48ELSE0
204		IFG29)=160,01ANDG29=<180THENC49ELSE0	IFG29)=160,01ANDG29=<180THEND49ELSE0	IFG29)=160,01ANDG29=<180THENE49ELSE0
205		IFG29)=180,01ANDG29=<200THENC50ELSE0	IFG29)=180,01ANDG29=<200THEND50ELSE0	IFG29)=180,01ANDG29=<200THENE50ELSE0
206	TOTAL	SUM(C195;C205)	SUM(D195;D205)	SUM(E195;E205)

Proforma 11.1 *(concluded)*

	F	G	H
191	IFG28)=160,01ANDG28=<180THENF49ELSE0	IFG28)=160,01ANDG28=<180THENG49ELSE0	IFG28)=160,01ANDG28=<180THENH49ELSE0
192	IFG28)=180,01ANDG28=<200THENF50ELSE0	IFG28)=180,01ANDG28=<200THENG50ELSE0	IFG28)=180,01ANDG28=<200THENH50ELSE0
193	SUM(F182;F192)	SUM(G182;G192)	SUM(H182;H192)
195	IFG29>0ANDG29<10THENF40ELSE0	IFG29>0ANDG29<10THENG40ELSE0	IFG29>0ANDG29<10THENH40ELSE0
196	IFG29)=10ANDG29<20THENF41ELSE0	IFG29)=10ANDG29<20THENG41ELSE0	IFG29)=10ANDG29<20THENH41ELSE0
197	IFG29)=20,01ANDG29=<40THENF42ELSE0	IFG29)=20,01ANDG29=<40THENG42ELSE0	IFG29)=20,01ANDG29=<40THENH42ELSE0
198	IFG29)=40,01ANDG29=<60THENF43ELSE0	IFG29)=40,01ANDG29=<60THENG43ELSE0	IFG29)=40,01ANDG29=<60THENH43ELSE0
199	IFG29)=60,01ANDG29=<80THENF44ELSE0	IFG29)=60,01ANDG29=<80THENG44ELSE0	IFG29)=60,01ANDG29=<80THENH44ELSE0
200	IFG29)=80,00ANDG29=<100THENF45ELSE0	IFG29)=80,00ANDG29=<100THENG45ELSE0	IFG29)=80,01ANDG29=<100THENH45ELSE0
201	IFG29)=100,01ANDG29=<120THENF46ELSE0	IFG29)=100,01ANDG29=<120THENG46ELSE0	IFG29)=100,01ANDG29=<120THENH46ELSE0
202	IFG29)=120,01ANDG29=<140THENF47ELSE0	IFG29)=120,01ANDG29=<140THENG47ELSE0	IFG29)=120,01ANDG29=<140THENH47ELSE0
203	IFG29)=140,01ANDG29=<160THENF48ELSE0	IFG29)=140,01ANDG29=<160THENG48ELSE0	IFG29)=140,01ANDG29=<160THENH48ELSE0
204	IFG29)=160,01ANDG29=<180THENF49ELSE0	IFG29)=160,01ANDG29=<180THENG49ELSE0	IFG29)=160,01ANDG29=<180THENH49ELSE0
205	IFG29)=180,01ANDG29=<200THENF50ELSE0	IFG29)=180,01ANDG29=<200THENG50ELSE0	IFG29)=180,01ANDG29=<200THENH50ELSE0
206	SUM(F195;F205)	SUM(G195;G205)	SUM(H195;H205)

Example 11.1   Marketing investment model

■□
□

	A	B	C	D	E	F	G	H
4		MARKETING INVESTMENT						
6	BUDGET$	230000						
8	MEDIA							
9	EFFECT%	100						
12	BUDGET	230000						
14	GRP/$0	1						
15	GRP TOT.	230						
17	CAMPAIGN	MONTH	%TOTAL	%SALES	AD.COST	INDEX	EFF.GRP	1+COVER
18	STRUCT	1	30	10	1.2	1.00040	69.0276	58
19		2	15	2	0.9	0.26677	9.20368	51.1
20		3	10	5	0.9	0.66693	15.3395	56.77
21		4	5	3	1	0.36014	4.14166	50.239
22		5	0	10	1	1.20048	0	35.1673
23		6	0	15	1	1.80072	0	24.16171
24		7	20	5	1	0.60024	27.6110	43.8320
25		8	20	10	1	1.20048	55.2221	64.2824
26		9	0	10	1	1.20048	0	44.9977
27		10	0	5	1	0.60024	0	31.4984
28		11	0	15	1	1.80072	0	22.0489
29		12	0	10	1	1.20048	0	15.4342
30	TOTAL		100	100	12		180.546	497.987
33	MONTHLY							
34	DECAY%	30						
36							COVER	
37	FREQUENCY							
38	DIST		1	2	3	4	5	6
39		GRP						
40		10	15	8	4	0	0	0
41		20	30	20	10	0	0	0
42		40	38	26	15	5	3	2
43		60	48	30	20	9	7	5

Example 11.1 *(continued)*

	I	J	K
	I	J	K
4			
6			
8			
9			
12			
14			
15			
17	2+COVER	3+COVER	4+COVER
18	38	25	13
19	32.2	20.3	9.1
20	36.54	21.21	6.37
21	31.178	17.674	4.459
22	21.8246	12.3529	3.1213
23	15.2722	8.64703	2.18491
24	28.8941	16.5529	5.02944
25	41.2258	25.5870	9.82061
26	28.8581	17.9109	6.87422
27	20.2007	12.5377	4.81210
28	14.1405	8.77636	3.36847
29	9.89832	6.14345	2.35793
30	318.237	192.665	70.4982

Note: This example omits the 5 and 6+Cover columns and summarises the OTS data
by month. For the sake of clarity all 12 OTS months are shown but only those
lines with an information content have been selected from the spreadsheet
print out.

Example 11.1 *(concluded)*

A	B	C	D	E	F	G	H
44	80	58	38	25	13	11	7
45	100	69	42	30	18	15	10
46	120	80	49	35	25	20	14
47	140	85	55	40	35	23	17
48	160	87	63	45	38	27	22
49	180	89	67	48	42	32	25
50	200	91	75	52	45	38	32
52 OTS MNH.1		0	0	0	0	0	0
56		58	38	25	13	11	7
63 TOTAL		58	38	25	13	11	7
65 OTS MNH.2		15	8	4	0	0	0
76 TOTAL		15	8	4	0	0	0
78 OTS MNH.3		0	0	0	0	0	0
79		30	20	10	0	0	0
89 TOTAL		30	20	10	0	0	0
91 OTS MNH.4		15	8	4	0	0	0
102 TOTAL		15	8	4	0	0	0
104 OTS MNH.5		0	0	0	0	0	0
117 OTS MNH.6		0	0	0	0	0	0
130 OTS MNH.7		0	0	0	0	0	0
132		38	26	15	5	3	2
141 TOTAL		38	26	15	5	3	2
143 OTS MNH.8		0	0	0	0	0	0
146		48	30	20	9	7	5
154 TOTAL		48	30	20	9	7	5
156 OTS MNH.9		0	0	0	0	0	0
169 OTS MNH.10		0	0	0	0	0	0
182 OTS MNH.11		0	0	0	0	0	0
195 OTS MNH.12		0	0	0	0	0	0

12 Test markets

The concept of using small areas for testing purposes has been part of marketing philosophy for many years, and with the increasing level of investment required for new product launches or alterations in existing strategy, the pre-testing of such changes becomes more and more vital.

The underlying idea of the operation is straightforward. The organisation determines its final form of product, promotion, packaging, distribution, and so on, and sells it in a typical area over a period of time, collects the sales data relating to the test, and analyses it. A comparison will be made with control areas where the test is not being made to ensure that major national changes are not affecting the local markets and that the difference seen is a 'real' one. Once this is complete the organisation will be able to decide whether the exercise has been worthwhile and should or should not be continued.

When each of these theoretical items is considered practically, obvious problems start to emerge. The first will be the selection of area, which should be as representative as possible of the country as a whole. This in the majority of countries is a major stumbling block, as most countries show strong regional differences between north and south, east and west. These can be further compounded by the contrast between urban and rural life, and magnified by language and culture. Compromises at this early stage of the test design become practically inevitable. Problems also arise in the choice of promotional techniques and distribution channels. Though certain promotional methods lend themselves very effectively to extremely localised promotion – the use of coupons and posters are obvious examples – other media may only operate over a wider area, with both radio and television not available on a regional basis in many countries. Similar restrictions generally apply also to press and magazine usage which may also limit the effectiveness of the test market performance.

Evaluating test market data

With the growing strength of certain national retail chains in many countries the acquisition of distribution for the test market is becoming increasingly difficult, as chains may refuse to stock the product on a regional basis. With the loss of such an important element, the validity of the comparison between the test and control areas becomes much more difficult to ascertain.

Provided the majority of these constraints have been overcome the problems of the data collection and the length of time that the test needs to continue remain to be considered, as they are both inter-dependent. The larger the number of observations available the greater the reliability of the results: as the number of data points increases, variation in one direction will tend to be balanced by variation in another. Nevertheless, from a Nielsen survey, a sales data figure is never completely accurate however well defined the sample may be or however large the brand. Further, the error will be proportionately more important for small brands than large, particularly relevant with new brand introductions.

In consequence, the more variable the data, the higher the number of observations which need to be taken and the longer the test run, particularly if the changed level of sales is likely to be small. To be sure that a changed media strategy was increasing sales by 3 per cent a manufacturer with a major share of the tinned soup market had to continue the test in four regions for over a year using Nielsen bi-month data for sales information.

But sales may also fluctuate significantly in the case of a large brand thereby increasing the problems of analysing changes in effectiveness even over a long period. A major carbonated drinks brand, for example, fluctuated in sales over a two-year period from 16 per cent to 21 per cent of the total market. Unless the variation in the data is taken into account it is unlikely even in this case – of a brand with a major market share – that changes in sales of less than 30 per cent could have been determined.

The interrelationship between the variation in the sales data, the percentage change that is taking place and the degree of confidence that the management wishes to place in the results can be summarised in the equation:

$$N = \frac{(x)^2 p^2}{s^2}$$

N = the number of observations required (regions × time)
x = the confidence limits that management wish the operation to achieve
p = the level of variation in the data
s = the sales change that is to be observed.

The larger the perceived change the smaller N need be; the more variable the data the larger.

One of the main problems encountered with test market data therefore is the degree of variation that occurs and whether this can be explained by chance or not. Readers will be aware of the concept of a standard distribution with a bell-shaped curve representing a standard distribution around the mean. The introduction of a new product into the market place will tend to shift the distribution of the data points (Figure 12.1). Obviously the changes in the test market need to be

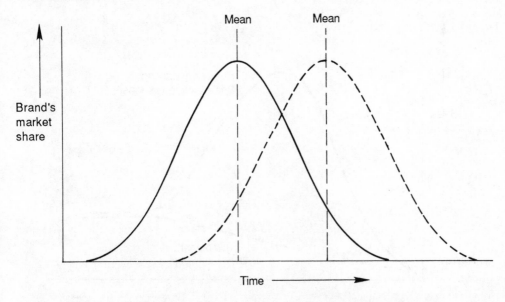

Figure 12.1 Effect of new product introduction on market structure

analysed to ensure that any reported alterations cannot be explained by chance variations in the data. This also extends to the question of whether changes in brand ranking can be explained by chance or not.

Full analysis of the variation in the data will require an understanding of the underlying causal factors or a measure of whether the perceived changes are occurring by chance or not. The first approach is used by the pharmaceutical and foods group Beechams (1). This system called AMTES (Measuring Advertising Effects by Test Areas), develops an econometric model to explain the movements in the market. Factors such as competitors' pricing, distribution levels, advertising weight, and so on, are taken into account for the explanation of the changes that are taking place.

The influence of the market

When the data has been analysed to ascertain the statistical probability that it could have occurred by chance there still exists the problem of long-term stability of the market: whether the changes seen in the short term will truly be reflective of the long-term patterns. The introduction of a new product follows two broad patterns (Figure 12.2). One is a sharp growth in sales followed by a decline – often the classic response to heavy advertising and discounting in the early stages of the brand's development. The other shows a steady slow growth in sales. This is called by some companies a 'slow burner' brand, one that eventually will gain acceptance and a similar brand share to other introductions. Indeed it can be seen that both brand development patterns can eventually settle down at the same level when the market returns to equilibrium.

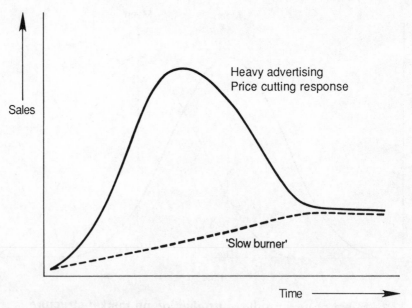

Figure 12.2   Different sales growth rates

These two different growth patterns of the new brand obviously imply that an understanding of the market dynamics and how the consumer attitudes are changing over time are essential to determine when the new equilibrium will be achieved. Though a wide range of data can be collected via a number of specific surveys including brand image, buying intention, whether the advertising has been seen or not, likes/dislikes of the product area, many of them fail to address the central issue of how the market equilibrium will become re-established.

The major components of brand share are the current level of share (penetration) and whether the consumer will buy the product again (repeat buying rate). In the case of new product launches the penetration rate is generally taken to be synonymous with trial. Thus a high penetration and high repeat purchase would mean a large initial brand share stabilising at a high level; high penetration followed by low repeat purchase would show a peak of sales followed by a decline.

On an individual level there is evidence that there is a high degree of brand switching with individuals changing between brands. Typically, it has been found in a number of consumer brand areas that only 50 per cent of the consumers buying the brand in one purchase cycle will be buying it in the next, the product gaining consumers who are switching 'out' of other products. The individual switching will not, however, be a random affair, but will occur within a grouping of brands. For example, an individual might switch between Camay, Lux, and Shield toilet soaps, but would not buy retailer own brands, Imperial Leather or Palmolive. The nature of the consumer's buying patterns could be seen as a series of interlocking Venn diagrams (see Figure 12.3) with the individuals moving from brand to brand within the encompassing circles, and the brand share of the product at any one particular time being made up by consumers purchasing that brand during their

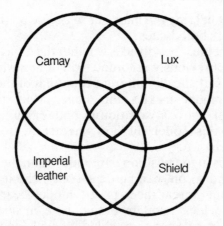

Figure 12.3   Simple schematic diagram of brand portfolio in toilet soap market

'walkabout' amongst the competing brands. Shifts in this brand purchasing pattern will obviously be affected by a number of factors covered in other chapters, such as distribution, price, and promotion, all of which are relevant in the test market phase.

The launch price may have an important effect on the initial penetration, confusing the eventual level of market share. Thus a low initial price will encourage the bargain shoppers to buy the product while it is on special offer, but the brand will inevitably lose the bulk if not all of the sales this generates once the price is elevated. In consequence it can be seen that the simulation of the introduction of new products does not only depend on an understanding of likely penetration rates and repeat sales; it also demands an understanding of the market dynamics and the likely movement of consumers between alternate brands.

The simulation of the likely progress of the brand in the market can provide important information as to when the equilibrium is likely to be established. Thus if the new brand is taking share evenly from others it may be considered to be more likely to maintain a stable position than one which is taking share from distributors' own brands. This could be explained by price effects: the low introductory price encouraging individuals to switch into the product – consumers that would be lost when the price is increased. In contrast the brand that is tending to take share from the more established premium brands should maintain its position when the introductory period is complete.

Three test market models

Three simple models can serve the manager as effective working tools in helping to resolve some of the difficulties discussed earlier.

The two main problems in the analysis of test market data are the variability of the data and the effects of where the market share is being taken from. Any practical work aimed at helping the manager to decide on the effectiveness of the test market must address both issues.

The first question that must be solved is whether the data that is available differs substantially from that previously recorded – analysing whether the data that is seen in the first case is statistically different from that of the second. The normal distribution analysis model tackles this issue. Market shares or sales to supermarket groups will show a variation in both cases, and the use of simple statistical techniques in this model will show whether the two different sets of data could be explained by chance.

Secondly, the changes in the position of brands within the market, brand leader becoming number 2 and so on, can be explored by the use of rank correlation analysis adapted for the spreadsheet in the model bearing that title. It will compare the level of achievement in brand share in one period with that in another. Variation in the two rankings could be explained by chance if the two rankings are reasonably similar – but once the variation is considerable the changes in brand share perceived in the market are caused by the introduction of a new market entrant.

Finally, one needs to consider the changes in the market and the likely new equilibrium that will or will not be established. The test markets model provides a framework within which the effects of various levels of brand switching can be identified, and from that builds up a method of simulating the movement of the brand and from where it is likely to gain market share.

Starting from the current market position, the effect of various levels of trial and repeat purchase are developed in the test markets model. The unit of time used is the purchase cycle, the length of time that the individual leaves between each purchase. This for sugar or pet food tends to be short, for durables such as light bulbs considerably longer. The model uses the projected brand share of the new product introduction to determine via the brand switching level what, in theory, should be the market shares of the other products as the launch progresses. The manager can then evaluate the actual changes in the market place and whether the new introduction is taking equally from all other brands in the market place or predominantly from one sector.

Changes in the brand switching rate and the speed at which the new product is gaining market share will obviously affect the performance of the new product and the effects of such changes can be examined.

Using the three test market models

The *Go To* column in Listings 12.1, 12.2 and 12.3 tells you the cell number and the cursor position. The next column specifies the spreadsheet option (LO = Label Option; VO = Value Option). The *Type In* column gives you instructions within the inverted commas which you must type in or asks you to supply the necessary data. These commas are not part of the instructions supplied here and should not be typed in, but beware that some spreadsheets, the *Lotus 1-2-3* for example, enter the Label Option by using the inverted-comma key. Under the

Type In column the symbols * = multiply and / = divide. R in the *Return* column
instructs you to commit the information to memory by pressing the Return key.
Remember: When you have finished, save your model.

Listing 12.1 Normal distribution analysis model

Go To		Type In	Return	Go To		Type In	Return
A2/	LO	"NORMAL	R	D16	VO	"B16*B16"	R
B2/		DISTRIBUTION"	R	D17	VO	"B17*B17"	R
C2			R	D18	VO	"B18*B18"	R
A3	LO	"ANALYSIS"	R	D19	VO	"B19*B19"	R
B5	LO	"DATA"	R	D20	VO	"B20*B20"	R
B6 to B20	VO	Enter data points for evaluation	R	D21	VO	"SUM(D6:D20)"	R
				D22	VO	"D21+E21"	R
B21	VO	"SUM(B6:B20)"	R	D23	VO	"C23/29"	R
B22	VO	"B21+C21"	R	E6	VO	"C6*C6"	R
B23	VO	"B22/30"	R	E7	VO	"C7*C7"	R
C6 to C20	VO	Enter data points for evaluation	R	E8	VO	"C8*C8"	R
				E9	VO	"C9*C9"	R
				E10	VO	"C10*C10"	R
C21	VO	"SUM(C6:C20)"	R	E11	VO	"C11*C11"	R
C22	VO	"B22*B22"	R	E12	VO	"C12*C12"	R
C23	VO	"D22−E22"	R	E13	VO	"C13*C13"	R
D6	VO	"B6*B6"	R	E14	VO	"C14*C14"	R
D7	VO	"B7*B7"	R	E15	VO	"C15*C15"	R
D8	VO	"B8*B8"	R	E16	VO	"C16*C16"	R
D9	VO	"B9*B9"	R	E17	VO	"C17*C17"	R
D10	VO	"B10*B10"	R	E18	VO	"C18*C18"	R
D11	VO	"B11*B11"	R	E19	VO	"C19*C19"	R
D12	VO	"B12*B12"	R	E20	VO	"C20*C20"	R
D13	VO	"B13*B13"	R	E21	VO	"SUM(E6:E20)"	R
D14	VO	"B14*B14"	R	E22	VO	"C22/30"	R
D15	VO	"B15*B15"	R				

Listing 12.1   *(concluded)*

Go To		Type In	Return	Go To		Type In	Return
E23	VO	"SQ RT D23"	R	B28	VO	"E23/5.47"	R
A25	LO	"Normal"	R	A29	LO	"Var"	R
A26	LO	"Mean"	R	B29	VO	"B27/B28"	R
B26	VO	Enter value for normal mean	R	B30	VO	"IF1.96>=B29THEN10 ELSE0"	R
B27	VO	"B23−B26"	R				

Listing 12.2   Rank correlation model

Go To		Type In	Return	Go To		Type In	Return
A3/	LO	"RANK	R	E8	VO	"(C8−D8)*(C8−D8)"	R
B3		CORRELATION"	R	E9	VO	"(C9−D9)*(C9−D9)"	R
B5	LO	"ITEM"	R	E10	VO	"(C10−D10)*(C10−D10)"	R
C5	LO	"RANK-A"	R				
D5	LO	"RANK-B"	R	E11	VO	"(C11−D11)*(C11−D11)"	R
E5	LO	"(A−B)2" i.e. A−B squared	R	E12	VO	"(C12−D12)*(C12−D12)"	R
B8	LO	"1"	R				
B9	LO	"2"	R	E13	VO	"(C13−D13)*(C13−D13)"	R
B10	LO	"3"	R				
B11	LO	"4"	R	E14	VO	"(C14−D14)*(C14−D14)"	R
B12	LO	"5"	R	E15	VO	"(C15−D15)*(C15−D15)"	R
B13	LO	"6"	R				
B14	LO	"7"	R	E16	VO	"(C16−D16)*(C16−D16)"	R
B15	LO	"8"	R				
B16	LO	"9"	R	E17	VO	"(C17−D17)*(C17−D17)"	R
B17	LO	"10"	R				
C8 to C17	VO	Enter ranking values of Group A	R	E18	VO	"SUM(E8:E17)"	R
				B19	VO	"1−6*E18/990"	R
D8 to D17	VO	Enter ranking values of Group B	R	B20	VO	"IFB19>=0.746THEN10 ELSE0"	R

Proforma 12.1 Normal distribution analysis model

	A	B	C	D	E
2	NORMAL	DISTRIBUTION			
3	ANALYSIS				
5		DATA			
6		94	68	B6*B6	C6*C6
7		95	49	B7*B7	C7*C7
8		48	86	B8*B8	C8*C8
9		58	74	B9*B9	C9*C9
10		75	79	B10*B10	C10*C10
11		69	100	B11*B11	C11*C11
12		55	88	B12*B12	C12*C12
13		51	62	B13*B13	C13*C13
14		89	83	B14*B14	C14*C14
15		91	52	B15*B15	C15*C15
16		89	63	B16*B16	C16*C16
17		93	89	B17*B17	C17*C17
18		69	83	B18*B18	C18*C18
19		81	71	B19*B19	C18*C19
20		81	73	B20*B20	C20*C20
21		SUM(B6:B20)	SUM(C6:C20)	SUM(D6:D20)	SUM(E6:E20)
22		B21+C21	B22*B22	D21+E21	C22/30
23		B22/30	D22-E22	C23/29	SQ.RT.D23
25	Normal				
26	mean	75			
27		B23-B26			
28		E23/5.47			
29	var	B27/B28			
30		IF1.96>=B29THEN10ELSE0			

Proforma 12.2   Rank correlation model

	A	B	C	D	E
3	RANK CORRELATION				
5		ITEM	RANK-A	RANK-B	(A-B)2
8		1	7	4	(C8-D8)*(C8-D8)
9		2	3	5	(C9-D9)*(C9-D9)
10		3	4	3	(C10-D10)*(C10-D10)
11		4	9	1	(C11-D11)*(C11-D11)
12		5	1	8	(C12-D12)*(C12-D12)
13		6	5	7	(C13-D13)*(C13-D13)
14		7	6	6	(C14-D14)*(C14-D14)
15		8	2	2	(C15-D15)*(C15-D15)
16		9	10	9	(C16-D16)*(C16-D16)
17		10	8	10	(C17-D17)*(C17-D17)
18					SUM(E8:E17)
19		1-6*E18/990			
20		IFB19>=0,746THEN10ELSE0			

Listing 12.3   Test markets model

Go To		Type In	Return	Go To		Type In	Return
A2	LO	"TEST MKT"	R	A20	LO	"Cons. avb" for consumer availability	R
A5	LO	"BRAND A"	R	B4	LO	"P. CYCLE 1"	R
A7	LO	"BRAND B"	R	B5	VO	Enter current market share for Brand A at beginning of purchase cycle 1	R
A9	LO	"BRAND C"	R				
A11	LO	"BRAND D"	R				
A13	LO	"BRAND E"	R	B7	VO	Enter current market share for Brand B at beginning of purchase cycle 1	R
A15	LO	"NEW BRAND"	R				
A17/	LO	"Brand	R				
A18		Switch %" i.e. the % of consumers changing the brand they purchase from one purchase cycle to another	R	B9	VO	Enter current market share for Brand C at beginning of purchase cycle 1	R

Listing 12.3   *(concluded)*

Go To		Type In	Return
B11	VO	Enter current market share for Brand D at beginning of purchase cycle 1	R
B13	VO	Enter current market share for Brand E at beginning of purchase cycle 1	R
B15	VO	Enter proposed initial brand share for New Brand at the start of purchase cycle 1	R
B18	VO	Enter % of consumers switching brands during each purchase cycle	R
B20	VO	"SUM(B5:B13)*B18/100"	R
C5	VO	"B5*B18/100+B5/100*C20"	R
C7	VO	"B7*B18/100+B7/100*C20"	R
C9	VO	"B9*B18/100+B9/100*C20"	R
C11	VO	"B11*B18/100+B11/100*C20"	R
C13	VO	"B13*B18/100+B13/100*C20"	R
C15	VO	"B15"	R
C20	VO	"B20−B15"	R
D4	LO	"P.CYCLE 2"	R
D5	VO	"C5"	R
D7	VO	"C7"	R
D9	VO	"C9"	R
D11	VO	"C11"	R
D13	VO	"C13"	R
D15	VO	Enter proposed value of new brand's market	

Go To		Type In	Return
		share at end of second Purchase Cycle	R
D20	VO	"B20−D15"	R
E5	VO	"B5*B18/100+B5/100*D20"	R
E7	VO	"B7*B18/100+B7/100*D20"	R
E9	VO	"B9*B18/100+B9/100*D20"	R
E11	VO	"B11*B18/100+B11/100*D20"	R
E13	VO	"B13*B18/100+B13/100*D20"	R
E15	VO	"D15"	R
F4	LO	"P.CYCLE 3"	R
F5	VO	"E5"	R
F7	VO	"E7"	R
F9	VO	"E9"	R
F11	VO	"E11"	R
F13	VO	"E13"	R
F15	VO	Enter proposed value for new brand's market share at end of third Purchase Cycle	R
F20	VO	"B20−F15"	R
G5	VO	"B5*B18/100+B5/100*F20"	R
G7	VO	"B7*B18/100+B7/100*F20"	R
G9	VO	"B9*B18/100+B9/100*F20"	R
G11	VO	"B11*B18/100+B11/100*F20"	R
G13	VO	"B13*B18/100+B13/100*F20"	R
G15	VO	"F15"	R

Proforma 12.3 Test markets model

	A	B	C	D	E	F	G
2	TEST MKT.						
4		P.CYCLE1		P.CYCLE2		P.CYCLE3	
5	BRAND A	50	B5*B18/100+B5/100*C20		B5*B18/100+B5/100*D20		B5*B18/100+B5/100*F20
7	BRAND B	25	B7*B18/100+B7/100*C20		B7*B18/100+B7/100*D20		B7*B18/100+B7/100*F20
9	BRAND C	10	B9*B18/100+B9/100*C20		B9*B18/100+B9/100*D20		B9*B18/100+B9/100*F20
11	BRAND D	5	B11*B18/100+B11/100*C20		B11*B18/100+B11/100*D20		B11*B18/100+B11/100*F20
13	BRAND E	10	B13*B18/100+B13/100*C20		B13*B18/100+B13/100*D20		B13*B18/100+B13/100*F20
15	NEW BRND	5	B15	7.5	D15	8	F15
17	Brand/						
18	Switch%	50					
20	Cons.Avb	SUM(B5:B13)*B18/100	B20-B15	B20-D15		B20-F15	

248

Example 12.1   Normal distribution analysis model

	A	B	C	D	E
	A	B	C	D	E
2	NORMAL	DISTRIBUTION			
3	ANALYSIS				
5		DATA			
6		94	68	8836	4624
7		95	49	9025	2401
8		48	86	2304	7396
9		58	74	3364	5476
10		75	79	5625	6241
11		69	100	4761	10000
12		55	88	3025	7744
13		51	62	2601	3844
14		89	83	7921	6889
15		91	52	8281	2704
16		89	63	7921	3969
17		93	89	8649	7921
18		69	83	4761	6889
19		81	71	6561	5041
20		81	73	6561	5329
21		1138	1120	90196	86468
22		2258	5098564	176664	169952
23		75.2667	6711.87	231.444	15.19
25	Normal				
26	mean	75			
27		0.26667			
28		2.77697			
29	var	0.09603			
30		10			

Example 12.2   Rank correlation model

	A	B	C	D	E
3	RANK CORRELATION				
5		ITEM	RANK-A	RANK-B	(A-B)2
8		1	7	4	9
9		2	3	5	4
10		3	4	3	1
11		4	9	1	64
12		5	1	8	49
13		6	5	7	4
14		7	6	6	0
15		8	2	2	0
16		9	10	9	1
17		10	8	10	4
18					136
19		0.17576			
20		0			

Example 12.3 Test markets model

	A	B	C	D	E	F	G
2	TEST MKT.						
4		P.CYCLE1		P.CYCLE2		P.CYCLE3	
5	BRAND A	50	47.5	47.5	46.25	46.25	46
7	BRAND B	25	23.75	23.75	23.125	23.125	23
9	BRAND C	10	9.5	9.5	9.25	9.25	9.2
11	BRAND D	5	4.75	4.75	4.625	4.625	4.6
13	BRAND E	10	9.5	9.5	9.25	9.25	9.2
15	NEW BRND	5	5	7.5	7.5	8	8
17	Brand/						
18	Switch%	50					
20.	Cons.Avb	50	45	42.5		42	

251

Test market commentary

Example 12.3 shows the effects of the new product entry and where sales are being achieved from competing brands. In this example, product sales are being taken equally from all brands which may differ from the reality in the market place.

Reference

1 M.J. Stewart, 'Measuring Advertising Effects by Test Areas', *ADMAP*, March 1980.

13 Price evaluation

This area of marketing management is one of the most complex, impinging as it does on various aspects of microeconomic theory, the legal framework of the country, the psychology of the individual – and in competitive bids the psychology of the firm, business theory and practice.

The importance of correct pricing to a firm can hardly be overstated. One study has shown that for the firms studied the only major correlation that could be derived between operating ratios and continuing success was gross profit margin levels (1). One aspect of business policy that is quite often ignored is the effect of even minor changes in profit margin on overall profitability. Thus one can draw the standard chart showing the interaction of fixed and variable overhead against sales revenue (Figure 13.1). Minor changes in the sales revenue curve can have a

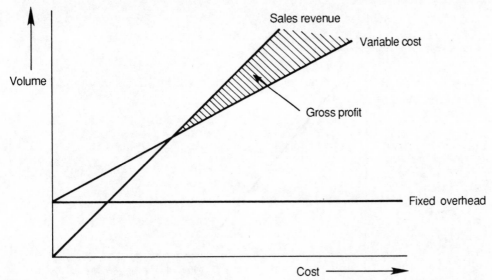

Figure 13.1 Interaction between fixed overheads, variable cost and sales revenue

considerable impact with a 5 per cent increase in gross margin often leading to a doubling of overall profitability (2).

Within companies dealing with rapid turnover of a large volume of items the difference between rags and riches is normally very small. If one draws a similar line to that in Figure 13.1 for a number of producers of fast moving consumer goods, especially those in the bulk food business, it would show that they begin making money from about the second week in December. Retailers are often even more pressed.

The pricing environment

Because of the opportunities and problems that correct or incorrect pricing can bring, it is worth considering the impact that economic theory, behavioural science, the legal framework, and business practice have had on the pricing equation.

First, economic theory broadly paints a picture of the interrelationship between supply and demand, mediated by the common denominator, price. Elementary textbooks on economics discuss initially the price elasticity, that is the rate at which demand drops when price increases in real, or more usefully, in relative terms (3, 4). However, the equation can be restated to yield a relationship between an incremental increase in price, leading to an incremental increase in quantity. This relationship can be used to define in a *homogeneous, objective* market what changes in price could mean in terms of volume increase or decline (Figure 13.2).

The main practical application of this standard economic theory is in the area of price elasticity. Commonly each product area will have a demand curve which is *generally* applicable. Thus changes in the price of butter will have a considerable effect on sales, whereas prestige sports cars are not greatly affected. One says that

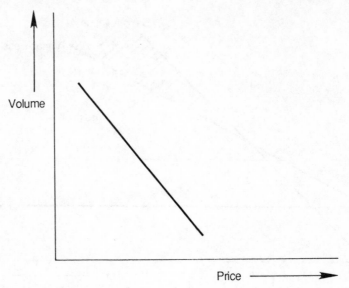

Figure 13.2   Price elasticity curve

butter therefore has a high price elasticity – in Europe it is typically a factor of 10 – whereas the sales of Rolls-Royce cars show a much lower factor. This means that a 1 per cent increase in relative price would in the case of butter imply a 10 per cent drop in sales. Graphically this can be represented as a series of price volume relationships (Figure 13.3). The elasticity seen in the market place will not always be the same as different parts of the curve will show different properties. In practice there will, generally, be a narrow range of price variation and therefore a standard price elasticity can be considered to exist for the majority of markets over the medium term.

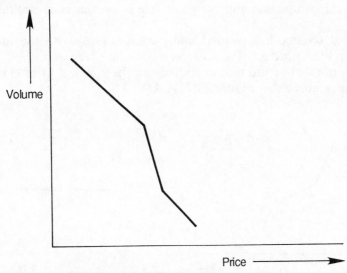

Figure 13.3   Changes in price elasticity curve

The understanding of the general price relationships in the market is important in many areas of marketing activity, such as sales productivity analysis, and the effects of advertising – topics covered elsewhere. However, the realities of pricing effects seen in the market are often far from the smooth changes of demand, and here we need to break ranks with the economists and consider the reality of the business environment. Any pricing decision must take into account a whole spectrum of decision making that moves beyond the traditional area of smooth changes in price leading to smooth changes in demand. Insufficient attention is given to the whole question of price/quality relationships. Take the example of the daily newspaper. Does the price solely influence the purchase of one title in competition with another? No one would believe this to be the case, with many other factors being considered important. Indeed the more useful incremental assessment might be one of profit margin/quantity or page cost/quantity.

Though the contribution of theoretical economics within the pricing environment has not been wholly effective; its use in competitive bidding and within the area of opportunity costing has become widespread.

The legal framework generally offers little guidance for the overall business pricing decisions but is relevant in two ways. One is in countries where pre-set

profit levels or price control operates. The second is more subtle but no less
prevalent, the pricing structure imposed by the threat of anti-monopoly action by
the government. Thus following a report by the Monopolies Commission in the
United Kingdom on the activities of Procter and Gamble and Unilever, both
companies agreed to introduce low-priced detergent powders, Surf and Daz.
Surf has for many years maintained broadly the same formulation as Omo,
another powder which continues to be sold at a higher price. In addition to the
legal framework, the 'illegal' framework or cartel can have fundamental effects
on pricing. There have been numerous reports on both the international
pharmaceutical companies and oil giants claiming that such influences are at
work (5, 6).

Behavioural science has yielded many useful clues as to the interaction of
consumers and the product. They all show that the reaction of the consumer can
be a very complex one, and that in contrast to the classical price elasticity curve
other structures may exist (Figure 13.4, A–D).

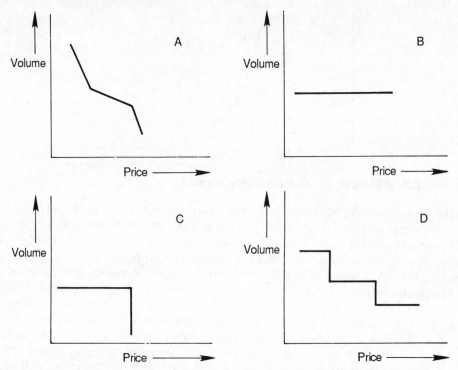

Figure 13.4   Varying market price effects

Thus in A, demand will vary in a step fashion either side of a median reference
point. In B, the demand is practically totally elastic in respect of price. An
example of this can be found in the world of arms sales where demand exists
practically in isolation to price. In C, there is a limited market for a particular
product which will sell up to a specific price, but not beyond. In D, the market

reacts in a series of step functions at particular price points. An example of this is the conversion of consumers from butter to margarine as the price differential widens.

Thus the mechanisms at work do not follow a clear, easily understood pattern which can be rapidly evaluated. In addition to this, the establishment of the firm in a particular market or market segment makes substantial changes in the price element of the marketing mix more difficult. So in addition to the direct economic factors, psychological factors and legal factors, the public relations aspects and competitive nature of pricing should not be ignored.

Approaches to pricing

Firms tend to follow a number of traditional approaches to the pricing problem. These systems are generally in line with the firms' objectives, and can be described as follows:

1 Cost-orientated pricing

This is one of the most common methods particularly in retailing and engineering-led companies. A standard profit margin is assigned to the overall range or one of the particular product group. The advantage of this system is simplicity in that products can be quickly priced in response to rapidly changing external circumstances such as inflation. Moreover, within complex product ranges a standard costing approach requires the minimum of management time. Finally, it copes with the effect of varying demand by ignoring it over most levels of output. The disadvantages are that this approach will rarely if ever yield the position of maximum profit. Secondly, the system leads to serious inflexibility where there are considerable economies of scale, and factory overheads can be allocated in a variety of areas.

2 Recovery orientated pricing

Organisations having high fixed overheads to recover – high plant investment, large advertising support – often set target prices to recover these overheads at a certain volume, the equation being fixed cost plus variable cost plus margin equalling price. The obvious problem in this area is the effect of price on the likely sales achieved. Companies can, using this system, enter a spiral from which there is little escape. Under-recovery of overhead can lead to the establishment of higher target prices, causing a further under-recovery of overhead and the subsequent adoption of still higher target prices and so ad infinitum – or what is more common, the arrival of creditors en masse.

3 Marketplace pricing

In its most common form this derives from the conventional wisdom that if other major firms in the market are following a certain pricing path this should be considered as the tablet of stone. Within cartels the benefits of such a system are self-evident, but the pitfalls for other companies are significant. Consolidation of a standard price position by a group of companies can, and does, allow a new entrant to become firmly established relatively quickly. A recent example of this has been the phenomenal penetration by the Japanese car manufacturers into the American car market.

4   Fashionability pricing

With a unique product a number of organisations will price at levels which cannot be sustained over the long term once competitors appear. Electronic games are a good case in point – high initial pricing will enable high returns in the initial 'fashionable' phase followed by price reductions during the following year. Toys and fashion fabrics contain many good examples of this type of pricing policy.

5   Introductory pricing

This is based on the concept that the use of low initial pricing will enable the company to rapidly build up brand share in order to dominate the market. Many Japanese concerns have followed this corporate objective in such markets as watches, cameras, cars, televisions, audio equipment and increasingly, photocopiers.

6   Segmental pricing

The market is divided into a series of sectors each with differing value perceptions. Package holiday companies charge more for holidays at peak periods not because there is generally a shortage of such holidays at such periods but because the consumer has grown accustomed to such a system. Customisation of cars shows a similar trend at work, with the addition of small amounts of trim and different seat coverings allowing the change in designation from L to GL or GL to GLS or GLS to SR and so on. All these alterations to the product require little additional investment and in consequence are considerably more profitable to the parent company.

Business theory lastly considers that there will be a variety of pricing phases tied to the product life cycle, during the growth, maturation and senility phases (see Chapter 1 on product viability). During the phase of market development, there should be a concentration on trade discounting and sampling, followed by continued promotional discounting at the consumer level. Once the market becomes mature, the emphasis should switch more to defensive pricing to prevent further entrants into the marketplace. Finally, during the period of decline, the brand should be priced at a level to yield the maximum profitability to the organisation even if this implies a loss of market share.

Once these differing approaches to pricing have been identified, it becomes clear that the pricing problem is far more complex than the simple price elasticity proposal, though analyses on this basis do have their value.

Two pricing models

Due to the complexities of the pricing problem there are two models. One provides the classical evaluation of pricing elasticity and profit potential within a macro-economic method and the other evaluates price within a decision framework system.

The pricing model

The pricing model is designed to determine the development of demand for the particular product type; to calculate the likely share of the product within the market; and to measure the contribution of each unit sold.

This model produces what could be termed the 'pure' price effects. That is the price effects operating within an ideal market where the factors dealt with in the confines of the second model do not operate. It attempts to produce a framework upon which the secondary evaluation can be completed.

The model calculates the current market average price weighted by respective volumes of the brands in the market, based on the input of current price, market share, and total market sales. The model will then take the current inflation rate operating in the market and calculate the likely market price in the forthcoming time periods. The manager is then asked to enter his views as to whether the price forecast is a reasonable one, entering either the same or a different price level. The model will then use the price elasticity factor to calculate the likely changes in market share and volume as a consequence of these changes.

This model can be easily linked with the marginal profitability model in Chapter 5 to provide the profitability analysis of the revised volumes. It enables the manager to carry out sensitivity analyses at varying price levels and to study the effects of a growing or declining market on the total brand sales and market share.

The pricing strategy model

The pricing model assumes that the response to differing price levels will be smooth depending on the underlying nature of the market conditions. It ignores the other features of the market which have already been discussed, namely the effects of time costs, search efforts, learning costs, design compromise costs, risk costs, quality factors, and place costs. These rather feature in the pricing strategy model.

1   Time costs

This postulates that there is a pay-off between the product/service and the amount of time that it consumes, and the price that it costs. Thus there has been a dramatic growth in the take-away food market due to the combination of minimal time taken and costs of food. There is, however, a limit which can be reached in such exercises. There have been many failures in food products due to such constraints; the launch of duo-can (vegetable and meat in one can divided by a central wall) is a case in point. Here the value of the combined product was more than offset by the increased cost, to the extent that the product was not perceived as competitive by the consumer.

2   Search efforts

Inextricably combined with price is the availability of the product in question. Here we meet the 'better mousetrap syndrome'. There is a limit to the amount of time that the consumer can be expected to spend in searching for any particular item. This will obviously vary from industry to industry and from product to product. Thus in a famine, considerable effort will be exerted in the search for basic foodstuffs; in the Western world however the majority of individuals will be lazy in their quest for a specific brand of baked beans. Naturally, both advertising, as a means of information spread, and physical distribution to the maximum possible extent can overcome problems in this area.

3   Risk costs

The buyer is aware that each purchase contains an element of uncertainty; that is, the product will not meet their expectations. An unknown product will carry a higher risk than products which have previously given satisfaction. For each market there will be a discount rate operating which offsets the risk factor by a lower price. For gasoline, this will be small (brand X will be bought in preference to Shell if the differential is one or two cents) but for a product such as perfume it would probably be insurmountable.

4   Repeat purchase factors

Within the industrial environment the continuity of supply is often crucial as well as being of major importance in the area of consumer durables.Thus the purchase of a vacuum cleaner may often be dependent on whether a continuing supply of disposal bags and drive bands are available.

5   Quality factor

No particular product will ever totally meet the purchasers' requirements even if it is custom built. The further one moves away from individual products the greater the difficulty of balancing a whole range of conflicting customer demands. Thus one may not like the colour of one particular packet of frozen peas; another will be disliked because of the toughness of the plastic, and so on.

6   Learning costs

The introduction of any product into the market place entails the consumer taking time to understand the nature of the concept and how it could be of value to him- or herself. These costs will be low when it is an untechnical product introduced into a non-technical sector, for example a new brand of jam, but it will be high in the case of highly technical products in a new sector. Thus the growth of thermal printing technology and the development of lasers have both been slow due to factors of this nature. This is no less true for authors of textbooks on new aspects of marketing policy!

7 Perceptual difference

There is a large body of evidence that shows that the individual is unable to differentiate between items which are closely but not exactly similarly priced. This again will vary from industry to industry, but in general terms it would appear that price differences of around 10 per cent are the limits of awareness. Thus a product priced at $3.25 may easily achieve the same sales as one at $3.55.

8 Price point

Consumer markets contain a number of examples of products which have sold well at say $2.99, but have failed at $3.09, even though they still remain a bargain in any other quantifiable approach. The more expensive the product, the less likely that this will occur, and it will also be diminished by any period of rapid price inflation. It will therefore be most marked in low priced, frequently purchased items in periods of economic stability.

9 Historic pricing

There are many examples of historic pricing or 'price lining' in operation in consumer and industrial goods. Thus the consumer will expect candy bars to sell at a particular price be it $0.50 or $0.10 and any manufacturer not providing it at that point will face severe problems. The author was aware of the trauma that rising prices created for the Mars bar when the product finally went through the 10 pence barrier in the UK. The other aspect of historic pricing is that the consumers often become segmented with respect to price; expectations are apparent at each price point and the consumer will not trade up or down on price within that band. A washing machine may be chosen from a particular price bracket because the buyer is accustomed to it and will not consider another type of machine even if a new entry provides significantly improved value for money on an objective basis.

10 Prestige factor

There are a number of studies which do substantiate the commonly held view that there is, in many product sectors, a close correlation between quality and price. This is particularly important in well established prestige markets where dramatic changes in price can have deleterious effects on the products' performance. Atkinsons held for many years a prestigious position within the United Kingdom perfumery market; indeed the famous doll's house at Windsor Castle has examples of their products as the main perfumery lines. After their acquisition by Unilever a lower cost range of products was introduced to sell in discount stores with the resultant effect that the brand is now practically unknown in the English market.

11   Halo effect

When consumers are purchasing a range of products from the same source the effect of one item can spill over onto other items, the acceptance that because some S is P all S is P. Many retail chains have managed to build up a tremendous consumer franchise on this basis, examples of which include Migros in Switzerland and Marks and Spencer in England. There is evidence that this is a common phenomenon in other fields. Respondents asked to guess the height of an individual seen in a piece of film will add two or three extra inches when the person is identified as a leader of industry compared with being described as a dustman.

12   Over-pricing factors

There are instances when a mid-priced product (priced say at $0.35) will sell less than one priced at $0.39. The underlying evaluation method at work appears to consider the $0.35 overpriced: that it should be priced at $0.30 or $0.29 whereas the other item is a bargain reduced as it is from $0.40.

13   Price reference factors

These refer to situations where the consumer may have an underlying comparison which is made to determine the pricing of a particular item. For example, the price of baked beans certainly seems to have close links with tinned spaghetti: when the price of baked beans goes up the sales of spaghetti tend to increase. It would appear in this particular instance that the consumer is comparing the prices across two differing convenience foods and purchasing the most cost-effective.

14   Morality factors

This can be found most commonly in the gift market. For children's parties, for example, expenditure on gifts is regarded to be acceptable within a certain price bracket. Manufacturers failing to provide products without a sufficiently high price tag will miss out on this market, especially valuable as the profit margins are potentially much higher than might be expected for 'normal' business. A second area is in the area of 'add-ons'. Thus a pair of trousers may be purchased with a belt included in the price only if the consumer considers the price differential between the trousers without belt and with as being 'reasonable'.

The pricing strategy model provides a decision framework for evaluating these factors. Each of those mentioned has a value assigned to it according to the particular problems associated with the industry or that particular product.

Probabilities are then assigned as to how likely the event will be and the overall value of that particular pricing decision based on the macro-economic model can be re-assessed.

Using the two pricing models

The *Go To* column in Listings 13.1 and 13.2 tells you the cell number and the cursor position. The next column specifies the spreadsheet option (LO = Label Option; VO = Value Option). The *Type In* column gives you instructions within the inverted commas which you must type in or asks you to supply the necessary data. These commas are not part of the instructions supplied here and should not be typed in but beware that some spreadsheets, the *Lotus 1-2-3* for example, enter the Label Option by pressing the inverted-comma key. Under the *Type In* column the symbols * = multiply and / = divide. R in the *Return* column reminds you to commit the information to memory by pressing the Return Key.
Remember: When you have finished, save your model.

Listing 13.1 Pricing model

Go To		Type In	Return	Go To		Type In	Return
A2/	LO	"PRICING	R	A8	LO	"BRAND B"	R
B2		MODEL"	R	A9	LO	"BRAND C"	R
B5/	LO	"CURRENT	R	A10	LO	"BRAND D"	R
C5		MARKET"	R	A11	LO	"BRAND E"	R
G5	LO	"MKT. FCST." for Market Forecast	R	A12	LO	"BRAND F"	R
				A13	LO	"BRAND G"	R
B6	LO	"% SHARE"	R	A14	LO	"BRAND H"	R
C6	LO	"PRICE"	R	A15	LO	"BRAND I"	R
D6	LO	"VOLUME"	R	A16	LO	"BRAND J"	R
F6	LO	"PR. PROJ." for Price Projection in line with inflation	R	A17	LO	"OTHERS"	R
				A21	LO	"TOT. VOL"	R
G6	LO	"PR. FCST." for Price Forecast	R	A22	LO	"INFL.%" for % rate of inflation	R
J6	LO	"REV. VOL" for Revised Volume	R	A23	LO	"ELAST." for price elasticity	R
K6	LO	"REV. SHR" for Revised Share	R	B7 to B17	VO	Insert market share values for Brands A to Others	R
A7	LO	"BRAND A"	R				

Listing 13.1 *(continued)*

Go To		Type In	Return	Go To		Type In	Return
B18	VO	"SUM(B7:B17)"	R	E16	VO	"C16*D16"	R
B21	VO	Enter total unit sales in market	R	E17	VO	"C17*D17"	R
				E18	VO	"SUM(E7:E17)"	R
B22	VO	Enter % inflation rate	R	F7	VO	"C7*(1+B22/100)"	R
B23	VO	Enter price elasticity coefficient for respective market	R	F8	VO	"C8*(1+B22/100)"	R
				F9	VO	"C9*(1+B22/100)"	R
C7 to C17	VO	Enter price for Brands A to Others	R	F10	VO	"C10*(1+B22/100)"	R
				F11	VO	"C11*(1+B22/100)"	R
D7	VO	"B7/100*B21"	R	F12	VO	"C12*(1+B22/100)"	R
D8	VO	"B8/100*B21"	R	F13	VO	"C13*(1+B22/100)"	R
D9	VO	"B9/100*B21"	R	F14	VO	"C14*(1+B22/100)"	R
D10	VO	"B10/100*B21"	R	F15	VO	"C15*(1+B22/100)"	R
D11	VO	"B11/100*B21"	R	F16	VO	"C16*(1+B22/100)"	R
D12	VO	"B12/100*B21"	R	F17	VO	"C17*(1+B22/100)"	R
D13	VO	"B13/100*B21"	R	F21	LO	"REV. VOL." for Revised Volume	R
D14	VO	"B14/100*B21"	R	F22	LO	"REV. PR" for Revised Price	R
D15	VO	"B15/100*B21"	R				
D16	VO	"B16/100*B21"	R	G7 to G17	VO	Enter company forecast of likely prices for Brands A to Others	R
D17	VO	"B17/100*B21"	R				
D21	LO	"MKT. AV." for Market Average Price	R	G21	VO	Enter company forecast for likely total volumes	R
D22	VO	"E18/B21"	R				
E7	VO	"C7*D7"	R	G22	VO	"D22*(1+B23/100)"	R
E8	VO	"C8*D8"	R	H7	VO	"G7/G22/(F7/G22)"	R
E9	VO	"C9*D9"	R	H8	VO	"G8/G22/(F8/G22)"	R
E10	VO	"C10*D10"	R	H9	VO	"G9/G22/(F9/G22)"	R
E11	VO	"C11*D11"	R	H10	VO	"G10/G22/(F10/G22)"	R
E12	VO	"C12*D12"	R	H11	VO	"G11/G22/(F11/G22)"	R
E13	VO	"C13*D13"	R	H12	VO	"G12/G22/(F12/G22)"	R
E14	VO	"C14*D14"	R	H13	VO	"G13/G22/(F13/G22)"	R
E15	VO	"C15*D15"	R	H14	VO	"G14/G22/(F14/G22)"	R

Listing 13.1   *(concluded)*

Go To		Type In	Return	Go To		Type In	Return
H15	VO	"G15/G22/(F15/G22)"	R	K9	VO	"J9/J18∗100"	R
H16	VO	"G16/G22/(F16/G22)"	R	K10	VO	"J10/J18∗100"	R
H17	VO	"G17/G22/(F17/G22)"	R	K11	VO	"J11/J18∗100"	R
I7	VO	"1/H7∗B23−1"	R	K12	VO	"J12/J18∗100"	R
I8	VO	"1/H8∗B23−1"	R	K13	VO	"J13/J18∗100"	R
I9	VO	"1/H9∗B23−1"	R	K14	VO	"J14/J18∗100"	R
I10	VO	"1/H10∗B23−1"	R	K15	VO	"J15/J18∗100"	R
I11	VO	"1/H11∗B23−1"	R	K16	VO	"J16/J18∗100"	R
I12	VO	"1/H12∗B23−1"	R	K17	VO	"J17/J18∗100"	R
I13	VO	"1/H13∗B23−1"	R	K22	LO	"EST. PR." for Estimated average market price per unit	R
I14	VO	"1/H14∗B23−1"	R				
I15	VO	"1/H15∗B23−1"	R	K23	LO	"% DIFF" for % Difference	R
I16	VO	"1/H16∗B23−1"	R				
I17	VO	"1/H17∗B23−1"	R	L7	VO	"G7∗J7"	R
J7	VO	"B7/100∗G21∗I7"	R	L8	VO	"G8∗J8"	R
J8	VO	"B8/100∗G21∗I8"	R	L9	VO	"G9∗J9"	R
J9	VO	"B9/100∗G21∗I9"	R	L10	VO	"G10∗J10"	R
J10	VO	"B10/100∗G21∗I10"	R	L11	VO	"G11∗J11"	R
J11	VO	"B11/100∗G21∗I11"	R	L12	VO	"G12∗J12"	R
J12	VO	"B12/100∗G21∗I12"	R	L13	VO	"G13∗J13"	R
J13	VO	"B13/100∗G21∗I13"	R	L14	VO	"G14∗J14"	R
J14	VO	"B14/100∗G21∗I14"	R	L15	VO	"G15∗J15"	R
J15	VO	"B15/100∗G21∗I15"	R	L16	VO	"G16∗J16"	R
J16	VO	"B16/100∗G21∗I16"	R	L17	VO	"G17∗J17"	R
J17	VO	"B17/100∗G21∗I17"	R	L18	VO	"SUM(L7:L17)"	R
J18	VO	"SUM(J7:J17)"	R	L22	VO	"L18/J18"	R
K7	VO	"J7/J18∗100"	R	L23	VO	"L22/G22∗100−100"	R
K8	VO	"J8/J18∗100"	R				

Proforma 13.1 Pricing model

■□

	A	B	C	D	E	F	G
2	PRICING MODEL						
5		CURRENT	MARKET				MKT, FCST
6		% SHARE	PRICE	VOLUME		PR, PROJ,	PR, FCST,
7	BRANDA	20	34	B7/100*B21	C7*D7	C7*(1+B22/100)	37
8	BRANDB	12	34	B8/100*B21	C8*D8	C8*(1+B22/100)	36
9	BRANDC	5	27	B9/100*B21	C9*D9	C9*(1+B22/100)	28
10	BRANDD	7	29	B10/100*B21	C10*D10	C10*(1+B22/100)	31
11	BRANDE	8	31	B11/100*B21	C11*D11	C11*(1+B22/100)	33
12	BRANDF	3	32	B12/100*B21	C12*D12	C12*(1+B22/100)	32
13	BRANDG	3	38	B13/100*B21	C13*D13	C13*(1+B22/100)	39
14	BRANDH	4	37	B14/100*B21	C14*D14	C14*(1+B22/100)	38
15	BRANDI	5	38	B15/100*B21	C15*D15	C15*(1+B22/100)	40
16	BRANDJ	6	29	B16/100*B21	C16*D16	C16*(1+B22/100)	31
17	OTHERS	27	26	B17/100*B21	C17*D17	C17*(1+B22/100)	28
18		SUM(B7:B17)			SUM(E7:E17)		
21	TOT, VOL	5,E8		MKT, AV,		REV, VOL	5,5E8
22	INFL %	5		E18/B21		REV, PR	D22*(1+B23/100)
23	ELAST,	2					

Proforma 13.1   *(concluded)*

◻️■

H	I	J	K	L
2				
5				
6		REV.VOL.	REV. SHR	
7 G7/G22/(F7/G22)	1/H7*B23-1	B7/100*G21*I7	J7/J18*100	G7*J7
8 G8/G22/(F8/G22)	1/H8*B23-1	B8/100*G21*I8	J8/J18*100	G8*J8
9 G9/G22/(F9/G22)	1/H9*B23-1	B9/100*G21*I9	J9/J18*100	G9*J9
10G10/G22/(F10/G22)	1/H10*B23-1	B10/100*G21*I10	J10/J18*100	G10*J10
11G11/G22/(F11/G22)	1/H11*B23-1	B11/100*G21*I11	J11/J18*100	G11*J11
12G12/G22/(F12/G22)	1/H12*B23-1	B12/100*G21*I12	J12/J18*100	G12*J12
13G13/G22/(F13/G22)	1/H13*B23-1	B13/100*G21*I13	J13/J18*100	G13*J13
14G14/G22/(F14/G22)	1/H14*B23-1	B14/100*G21*I14	J14/J18*100	G14*J14
15G15/G22/(F15/G22)	1/H15*B23-1	B15/100*G21*I15	J15/J18*100	G15*J15
16G16/G22/(F16/G22)	1/H16*B23-1	B16/100*G21*I16	J16/J18*100	G16*J16
17G17/G22/(G17/G22)	1/H17*B23-1	B17/100*G21*I17	J17/J18*100	G17*J17
18		SUM(J7:J17)		SUM(L7:L17
21				
22			EST.PR.	L18/J18
23			% DIFF	L22/G22*100-100

Listing 13.2 Pricing strategy model

Go To		Type In	Return	Go To		Type In	Return
D4/	LO	"Pricing	R	A32/	LO	"Over	R
E4		Strategy"	R	B32		Pricing"	R
E6/	LO	"PROBABILITY	R	A34/	LO	"Reference	R
F6/		OF	R	B34		Price"	R
G6		OCCURRENCE"	R	A36/	LO	"Morality	R
A8	LO	"CATEGORY"	R	B36		Pricing"	R
C8	LO	"Value"	R	C10	VO	Insert values for Time cost	R
D8	LO	"V.GOOD"	R				
E8	LO	"GOOD"	R	C12	VO	Insert values for Search Cost	R
F8	LO	"AVERAGE"	R				
G8	LO	"POOR"	R	C14	VO	Insert Risk value	R
H8	LO	"V.POOR"	R	C16	VO	Insert Repeat Purchase value	R
A10/	LO	"Time	R				
B10		Cost"	R	C18	VO	Insert Quality Factor value	R
A12/	LO	"Search	R				
B12		Cost"	R	C20	VO	Insert Learning Cost value	R
A14	LO	"Risk"	R				
A16/	LO	"Repeat	R	C22	VO	Insert Perceptual value	R
B16		Purchase"	R	C24	VO	Insert Price Point value	R
A18/	LO	"Quality	R	C26	VO	Insert Historic Pricing value	R
B18		Factor"	R				
A20/	LO	"Learning	R	C28	VO	Insert Prestige Pricing value	R
B20		Cost"	R				
A22	LO	"Perceptual"	R	C30	VO	Insert value for Halo Effect	R
A24/	LO	"Price	R				
B24		Point"	R	C32	VO	Insert Over Pricing value	R
A26/	LO	"Historic	R				
B26		Pricing"	R	C34	VO	Insert Reference Price value	R
A28/	LO	"Prestige	R				
B28		Pricing"	R	C36	VO	Insert Morality Pricing value	R
A30/	LO	"Halo	R				
B30		Effect"	R				

Note: Together the values assigned from C10 to C36 must add up to 100.

| C37 | VO | "IFSUM(C10:C36)=100 THEN100ELSE0" | R |

Listing 13.2 *(continued)*

Go To		Type In	Return	Go To		Type In	Return
D10 to H10	VO	Insert probability values of occurrence for Time Cost assigned to Very Good, Good, Average, Poor, Very Poor. They must together add up to one	R	H15	VO	"C14*H14*10"	R
				I15	VO	"SUM(D15:H15)/I14"	R
				I16	VO	"IFSUM(D16:H16)=1 THEN1ELSE0"	R
I10	VO	"IFSUM(D10:H10)=1 THEN1ELSE0"	R	D16 to H16	VO	Insert Repeat Purchase occurrence probabilities as per D10–H10	R
D11	VO	"C10*D10*2"	R	D17	VO	"C16*D16*2"	R
E11	VO	"C10*E10*4"	R	E17	VO	"C16*E16*4"	R
F11	VO	"C10*F10*6"	R	F17	VO	"C16*F16*6"	R
G11	VO	"C10*G10*8"	R	G17	VO	"C16*G16*8"	R
H11	VO	"C10*H10*10"	R	H17	VO	"C16*H16*10"	R
I11	VO	"SUM(D11:H11)/I10"	R	I17	VO	"SUM(D17:H17)/I16"	R
D12 to H12	VO	Insert probability values of occurrence for Search Cost as per D10–H10	R	I18	VO	"IFSUM(D18:H18)=1 THEN1ELSE0"	R
				D18 to H18	VO	Insert Quality Factor occurrence probabilities as per D10–H10	R
I12	VO	"IFSUM(D12:H12)=1 THEN1ELSE0"	R	D19	VO	"C18*D18*2"	R
D13	VO	"C12*D12*2"	R	E19	VO	"C18*E18*4"	R
E13	VO	"C12*E12*4"	R	F19	VO	"C18*F18*6"	R
F13	VO	"C12*F12*6"	R	G19	VO	"C18*G18*8"	R
G13	VO	"C12*G12*8"	R	H19	VO	"C18*H18*10"	R
H13	VO	"C12*H12*10"	R	I19	VO	"SUM(D19:H19)/I18"	R
I13	VO	"SUM(D13:H13)/I12"	R	I20	VO	"IFSUM(D20:H20)=1 THEN1ELSE0"	R
D14 to H14	VO	Insert Risk occurrence probabilities as per D10–H10	R	D20 to H20	VO	Insert Learning Cost occurrence probabilities as per D10–H10	R
I14	VO	"IFSUM(D14:H14)=1 THEN1ELSE0"	R	D21	VO	"C20*D20*2"	R
D15	VO	"C14*D14*2"	R	E21	VO	"C20*E20*4"	R
E15	VO	"C14*E14*4"	R	F21	VO	"C20*F20*6"	R
F15	VO	"C14*F14*6"	R	G21	VO	"C20*G20*8"	R
G15	VO	"C14*G14*8"	R	H21	VO	"C20*H20*10"	R

Listing 13.2 *(continued)*

Go To		Type In	Return	Go To		Type In	Return
I21	VO	"SUM(D21:H21)/I20"	R	I28	VO	"IFSUM(D28:H28)=1 THEN1ELSE0"	R
I22	VO	"IFSUM(D22:H22)=1 THEN1ELSE0"	R	D28 to H28	VO	Insert occurrence probabilities for Prestige Pricing as per D10–H10	R
D22 to H22	VO	Insert Perceptual occurrence probabilities as per D10–H10	R	D29	VO	"C28*D28*2"	R
D23	VO	"C22*D22*2"	R	E29	VO	"C28*E28*4"	R
E23	VO	"C22*E22*4"	R	F29	VO	"C28*F28*6"	R
F23	VO	"C22*F22*6"	R	G29	VO	"C28*G28*8"	R
G23	VO	"C22*G22*8"	R	H29	VO	"C28*H28*10"	R
H23	VO	"C22*H22*10"	R	I29	VO	"SUM(D29:H29)/I28"	R
I23	VO	"SUM(D23:H23)/I22"	R	I30	VO	"IFSUM(D30:H30)=1 THEN1ELSE0"	R
I24	VO	"IFSUM(D24:H24)=1 THEN1ELSE0"	R	D30 to H30	VO	Insert occurrence probabilities for Halo Effect as per D10–H10	R
D24 to H24	VO	Insert occurrence probabilities for Price Point as per D10–H10	R	D31	VO	"C30*D30*2"	R
D25	VO	"C24*D24*2"	R	E31	VO	"C30*E30*4"	R
E25	VO	"C24*E24*4"	R	F31	VO	"C30*F30*6"	R
F25	VO	"C24*F24*6"	R	G31	VO	"C30*G30*8"	R
G25	VO	"C24*G24*8"	R	H31	VO	"C30*H30*10"	R
H25	VO	"C24*H24*10"	R	I31	VO	"SUM(D31:H31)/I30"	R
I25	VO	"SUM(D25:H25)/I24"	R	I32	VO	"IFSUM(D32:H32)=1 THEN1ELSE0"	R
I26	VO	"IFSUM(D26:H26)=1 THEN1ELSE0"	R	D32 to H32	VO	Insert occurrence probabilities for Over Pricing as per D10–H10	R
D26 to H26	VO	Insert occurrence probabilities for Historic Pricing as per D10–H10	R	D33	VO	"C32*D32*2"	R
D27	VO	"C26*D26*2"	R	E33	VO	"C32*E32*4"	R
E27	VO	"C26*E26*4"	R	F33	VO	"C32*F32*6"	R
F27	VO	"C26*F26*6"	R	G33	VO	"C32*G32*8"	R
G27	VO	"C26*G26*8"	R	H33	VO	"C32*H32*10"	R
H27	VO	"C26*H26*10"	R	I33	VO	"SUM(D33:H33)/I32"	R
I27	VO	"SUM(D27:H27)/I26"	R				

Listing 13.2   *(concluded)*

Go To		Type In	Return	Go To		Type In	Return
I34	VO	"IFSUM(D34:H34)=1 THEN1ELSE0"	R	to H36		probabilities for Morality Pricing as per D10−H10	R
D34 to H34	VO	Insert occurrence probabilities for Reference Price as per D10−H10	R	D37	VO	"C36*D36*2"	R
				E37	VO	"C36*E36*4"	R
				F37	VO	"C36*F36*6"	R
D35	VO	"C34*D34*2"	R	G37	VO	"C36*G36*8"	R
E35	VO	"C34*E34*4"	R				
F35	VO	"C34*F34*6"	R	H37	VO	"C36*H36*10"	R
G35	VO	"C34*G34*8"	R	I37	VO	"SUM(D37:H37)/I36"	R
H35	VO	"C34*H34*10"	R	I38	VO	"SUM(I13:I37)−14"	R
I35	VO	"SUM(D35:H35)/I34"	R	A39/	LO	"PRICE	R
I36	VO	"IFSUM(D36:H36)=1 THEN1ELSE0"	R	B39/		ACHIEVEMENT"	R
				C39			R
D36	VO	Insert occurrence		C40	VO	"I38/C37"	R

Pricing commentary

The two charts show examples of the various pricing factors at work. The market share forecast (Example 13.1) identifies likely effects on future volume on a brand by brand basis. Because of the relatively small changes in relative prices of the brands the market share figures do not change significantly, though it can be seen that Brands E & F are showing small market gains.

In the pricing decision model (Examples 13.2.1 and 13.2.2) the manager has identified the fact that price points are particularly important for the particular brand under consideration. Entering the probability of occurrence under each heading indicates that there is a good chance of missing the price point problems that exist with the brand and that the pricing decision will be likely to meet the brand manager's requirements.

References

1 Centre for Interfirm Comparison, *Management Policies, Practices and Business Performance*, Colchester, England, 1978.
2 R. Winkler, *Pricing for Results*, Heinemann, 1983.
3 J. Pen, *Modern Economics*, Pelican, 1965.
4 R. Turvey, *Demand and Supply*, George Allen and Unwin, 1971.
5 W. Breckon, *The Drug Makers*, Eyre Methuen, 1972.
6 A. Sampson, *The Seven Sisters*, Hodder and Stoughton, 1978.

Proforma 13.2 Pricing strategy model

A/B	C	D	E	F	G	H	I
4		Pricing	Strategy				
6			Probability of Occurrence				
8 CATEGORY	Value	V. Good	Good	Average	Poor	V. Poor	
10 Time Cost	5	0.3	0.3	0.3	0.1	0	IFSUM(D10;H10)=1THEN1ELSE0
11		C10*D10*2	C10*E10*4	C10*F10*6	C10*G10*8	C10*H10*10	SUM(D11:H11)/10
12 Search Cost	4	0.2	0.5	0.2	0.1	0	IFSUM(D12;H12)=1THEN1ELSE0
13		C12*D12*2	C12*E12*4	C12*F12*6	C12*G12*8	C12*H12*10	SUM(D13;H13)/I12
14 Risk	2	0.2	0.3	0.2	0.3	0	IFSUM(D14;H14)=1THEN1ELSE0
15		C14*2*D14	C14*E14*4	C14*F14*6	C14*G14*8	C14*H14*10	SUM(D15;H15)/I14
16 Repeat Purchase	4	0.6	0.1	0.3	0	0	IFSUM(D16;H16)=1THEN1ELSE0
17		C16*2*D16	C16*E16*4	C16*F16*6	C16*G16*8	C16*H16*10	SUM(D17;H17)/I16
18 Quality Factor	10	0	0.2	0.2	0.5	0.1	IFSUM(D18;H18)=1THEN1ELSE0
19		C18*2*D18	C18*E18*4	C18*F18*6	C18*G18*8	C18*H18*10	SUM(D19;H19)/I18
20 Learning Cost	4	0.3	0	0	0	0.7	IFSUM(D20;H20)=1THEN1ELSE0
21		C20*D20	C20*E20*4	C20*F20*6	C20*G20*8	C20*H20*10	SUM(D21;HF21)/I20
22 Perceptual	5	0	0.2	0.3	0.2	0.3	IFSUM(D22;H22)=1THEN1ELSE0
23		C22*2*D22	C22*E22*4	C22*F22*6	C22*G22*8	C22*H22*10	SUM(D23;H23)/I22

A/B	C	D	E	F	G	H	I
24 Price Point	12	0	0	0.3	0.7	0	IFSUM(O24;H24)=1THEN1ELSE0
25		C24*D24*2	C24*E24*4	C24*F24*6	C24*G24*8	C24*H24*10	SUM(O25;H25)/I24
26 Historic Pricing	2	0	0	0.5	0.3	0.2	IFSUM(O26;H26)=1THEN1ELSE0
27		C26*D26*2	C26*E26*4	C26*F26*6	C26*G26*8	C26*H26*10	SUM(O27;H27)/I26
28 Prestige Pricing	2	0	0.2	0.8	0	0	IFSUM(O28;H28)=1THEN1ELSE0
29		C28*2*D28	C28*E28*4	C28*F28*6	C28*G28*8	C28*H28*10	SUM(O29;H29)/I28
30 Halo Effect	7	0.2	0.2	0.2	0.2	0.2	IFSUM(O30;H30)=1THEN1ELSE0
31		C30*2*D30	C30*E30*4	C30*F30*6	C30*G30*8	C30*H30*10	SUM(O31;H31)/I30
32 Over Pricing	3	0	0.6	0.4	0	0	IFSUM(O32;I32)=1THEN1ELSE0
33		C32*2*D32	C32*E32*4	C32*F32*6	C32*G32*8	C32*H32*10	SUM(O33;H33)/I32
34 Reference Price	25	0	0	0.5	0.5	0	IFSUM(O34;H34)=1THEN1ELSE0
35		C34*2*D34	C34*E34*4	C34*F34*6	C34*G34*8	C34*H34*10	SUM(O35;H35)/I34
36 Morality Pricing	15	0.6	0	0.4	0	0	IFSUM(O36;H36)=1THEN1ELSE0
37	(%)	C36*2*D36	C36*E36*4	C36*F36*6	C36*G36*8	C36*H36*10	SUM(O37;H37)/I36
38							SUM(I13;I37)-14
39 PRICE ACHIEVEMENT							
40		I38/C37					

(%) C37 Formula: IF SUM(C10:C36)>100THENOELSESUM(C10:C36)

273

Example 13.1   Pricing model

■□

	A	B	C	D	E	F	G
2	PRICING MODEL						
5		CURRENT	MARKET				MKT. FCST
6		% SHARE	PRICE	VOLUME		PR. PROJ.	PR. FCST.
7	BRANDA	20	34	1.E8	3.4E9	35.7	37
8	BRANDB	12	34	6.E7	2.04E9	35.7	36
9	BRANDC	5	27	2.5E7	6.75E8	28.35	28
10	BRANDD	7	29	3.5E7	1.015E9	30.45	31
11	BRANDE	8	31	4.E7	1.24E9	32.55	33
12	BRANDF	3	32	1.5E7	4.8E8	33.6	32
13	BRANDG	3	38	1.5E7	5.7E8	39.9	39
14	BRANDH	4	37	2.E7	7.4E8	38.85	38
15	BRANDI	5	38	2.5E7	9.5E8	39.9	40
16	BRANDJ	6	29	3.E7	8.7E8	30.45	31
17	OTHERS	27	26	1.35E8	3.51E9	27.3	28
18		100			1.55E10		
21	TOT. VOL	5.E8		MKT. AV.		REV. VOL	5.5E8
22	INFL %	5		30.98		REV. PR	31.5996
23	ELAST.	2					

Example 13.1 *(concluded)*

	H	I	J	K	L	□ ■
2						
5						
6			REV. VOL.	REV. SHR		
7	1.03641	0.92973	1.023E8	19.1534	3.784E9	
8	1.00840	0.98333	6.49E7	12.1546	2.336E9	
9	0.98765	1.025	2.819E7	5.27901	7.893E8	
10	1.01806	0.96452	3.713E7	6.95451	1.151E9	
11	1.01382	0.97273	4.280E7	8.01567	1.412E9	
12	0.95238	1.1	1.815E7	3.39917	5.808E8	
13	0.97744	1.04615	1.726E7	3.23278	6.732E8	
14	0.97812	1.04474	2.298E7	4.30453	8.734E8	
15	1.00251	0.995	2.736E7	5.12451	1.095E9	
16	1.01806	0.96452	3.183E7	5.96101	9.867E8	
17	1.02564	0.95000	1.41E8	26.4208	3.95E9	
18			5.340E8		1.76E10	
21						
22				EST PR	33.0214	
23				% DIFF	4.49939	

Example 13.2.1 Pricing strategy model

A/B	C	D	E	F	G	H	I
4			Pricing	Strategy			
6				Probability of Occurrence			
8 CATEGORY	Value	V. Good	Good	Average	Poor	V. Poor	
10 Time Cost	5	0.3	0.3	0.3	0.1	0	1
11		3	6	9	4	0	22
12 Search Cost	4	0.2	0.5	0.2	0.1	0	1
13		1.6	8	4.8	3.2	0	17.6
14 Risk	2	0.2	0.3	0.2	0.3	0	1
15		0.8	2.4	2.4	4.8	0	10.4
16 Repeat Purchase	4	0.6	0.1	0.3	0	0	1
17		4.8	1.6	7.2	0	0	13.6
18 Quality Factor	10	0	0.2	0.2	0.5	0.1	1
19		0	8	12	40	10	70
20 Learning Cost	4	0.3	0	0	0	0.7	1
21		2.4	0	0	0	28	30.4
22 Perceptual	5	0	0.2	0.3	0.2	0.3	1

A/B	C	D	E	F	G	H	I
23		0	4	9	8	15	36
24 Price Point	12	0	0	0.3	0.7	0	1
25		0	0	21.6	67.2	0	88.8
26 Historic Pricing	2	0	0	0.5	0.3	0.2	1
27		0	0	6	4.8	4	14.8
28 Prestige Pricing	2	0	0.2	0.8	0	0	1
29		0	1.6	9.6	0	0	11.2
30 Halo Effect	7	0.2	0.2	0.2	0.2	0.2	1
31		2.8	5.6	8.4	11.2	14	42
32 Over Pricing	3	0	0.6	0.4	0	0	1
33		0	7.2	7.2	0	0	14.4
34 Reference Price	25	0	0	0.5	0.5	0	1
35		0	0	75	100	0	175
36 Morality Pricing	15	0.6	0	0.4	0	0	1
37	100	18	0	36	0	0	54
38							575.2
39 PRICE ACHIEVEMENT							
40		5.752					

Example 13.2.2 Pricing strategy model

A/B	C	D	E	F	G	H	I
		Pricing	Strategy				
			Probability of Occurrence				
CATEGORY	Value	V. Good	Good	Average	Poor	V. Poor	
Time Cost	5	0.3	0.3	0.3	0.1	0	1
		3	6	9	4	0	22
Search Cost	0	0.2	0.5	0.2	0.1	0	1
		0	0	0	0	0	0
Risk	0	0.2	0.3	0.2	0.3	0	1
		0	0	0	0	0	0
Repeat Purchase	3	0.6	0.1	0.3	0	0	1
		3.6	1.2	5.4	0	0	10.2
Quality Factor	5	0	0.2	0.2	0.5	0.1	1
		0	4	6	20	5	35
Learning Cost	0	0.3	0	0	0	0.7	1
		0	0	0	0	0	0
Perceptual	5	0	0.2	0.3	0.2	0.3	1
		0	4	9	8	15	36

A/B	C	D	E	F	G	H	I
24 Price Point	50	0.7	0.3	0	0	0	1
25		70	60	0	0	0	130
26 Historic Pricing	10	0.5	0.5	0	0	0	1
27		10	20	0	0	0	30
28 Prestige Pricing	2	0	0.2	0.8	0	0	1
29		0	1.6	9.6	0	0	11.2
30 Halo Effect	5	0.2	0.2	0.2	0.2	0.2	1
31		2	4	6	8	10	30
32 Over Pricing	0	0	0.6	0.4	0	0	1
33		0	0	0	0	0	0
34 Reference Price	15	0.8	0.1	0.1	0	0	1
35		24	6	9	0	0	39
36 Morality Pricing	0	0.6	0	0.4	0	0	1
37	100	0	0	0	0	0	0
38							319.4
39 PRICE ACHIEVEMENT							
40		3.194					

□■

14 Distribution

The role of distribution in gaining competitive advantage is often ignored by many companies: advertising and packaging are far more visible and therefore tend to receive considerably more attention.

However, distribution costs make up a far more significant proportion of the final price than might be expected. A recent survey in the United States showed that the costs related to distribution made up a significant percentage of the final product price in many industries:

Industry	*percentage*
Food and food factors	29.6
Machinery	9.8
Chemicals	23.1
Paper	16.7
Primary metal	26.1
Wood products	16.1

Of the industries studied it was found that the average cost of distribution related factors was 19 per cent, broken down as follows:

Administration	2.4
Transport	6.7
Warehousing	3.8
Costs of stock (inventory)	3.7
Order processing	1.2
Cost of incoming materials	1.7

A number of issues will affect the level of distribution costs and need also to be considered by the firm as to how they should be used to gain competitive advantage within an industry:

1   The level of distribution required to meet strategic requirements (the required service level of distribution).
2   The way the company reaches the consumer (channel decisions).
3   Where the company produces its product (production and supply alternatives).
4   How the company stores its product (warehousing options).
5   The way in which the company moves its product (transport).
6   The level of stock that the company needs to maintain (inventory).
7   The way in which orders are received and despatched (communication).

The level of service

All industries will demand that investment in distribution systems meet the required level of supply; some companies will perceive an opportunity to gain competitive advantage by offering an improved level of distribution.

These companies will in consequence need to invest more heavily in the distribution network than the industry traditionally requires; delivery on a daily basis might mean that the investment in vehicles and drivers would be 40 per cent higher than one operating a twice-weekly service.

High levels of service will not just involve a higher level of investment, they will often reduce the level of out-of-stock goods at the end user. They will also allow a far higher level of market coverage – a firm could achieve a 90 per cent market coverage compared with a 60 per cent coverage at a lower level of service. Past a certain point the costs of supplying the market will increase exponentially, and the firm will have to decide what level of cost is acceptable to achieve the necessary level of distribution. Efficient distribution will also allow the firm to offer improved delivery discounts.

Channel decisions

Organisations will also need to consider as part of the service provided the way in which goods reach the final consumer. In broad terms, two possible approaches exist; sending goods straight to the consumer or end user (direct distribution) or using an intermediary (indirect). A typical intermediary would be a wholesaler, or a franchisee.

In order to determine whether direct or indirect distribution is most appropriate, firms will need to evaluate the needs of the market on certain criteria:

Factor	High	Low
Geographical concentration	Direct	Indirect
Number of buyers	Indirect	Direct
Complexity of product	Direct	Indirect
Unit price	Direct	Indirect

Standardisation	Indirect	Direct
Servicing requirements	Direct	Indirect
Price negotiation	Direct	Indirect
Frequency of purchase	Indirect	Direct
Financial strength	Direct	Indirect
Payment problems	Indirect	Direct

For example, a chocolate bar is low in price, purchased frequently by large numbers of consumers, is standard and requires no servicing or installation. The manufacturer of the chocolate bar needs to ensure that the widest possible distribution is achieved and will use wholesalers and other intermediaries to achieve it. Contrast the supplier of turbines for power stations. The product is not standard, requires a large amount of attention to installation and servicing. Distribution will be direct from manufacturer to end-user.

Channel conflict

In all industries there will be competition or conflict within the channels of distribution. This can either occur between firms at the same level of the distribution chain, retailer to retailer for example, between retailer and department store or wholesaler and between suppliers and end-users.

Production and supply alternatives

There will be a number of interrelating factors that affect the choice of where the company manufactures.

1 Economies of scale As has been mentioned elsewhere, the greater the volume produced, the lower the unit cost of the production. It may be in the interests of the company to concentrate production in one site.

2 Vulnerability Concentrating all production in one site may make the entire company vulnerable to political and economic upheaval.

3 Flexibility Large production plants cannot easily or cost-effectively cope with small volume production which may be demanded by a change in the market.

Each of the production points that the company chooses will have an effect on the distribution costs: the more widely spread the manufacturing sites the lower the distribution costs on average.

Warehousing

The location of the warehouse, the way in which both incoming and outgoing product is handled, and the way in which product is stored will all have an impact on the distribution costs.

1 Warehouse numbers

One of the more important decisions that the growing company has to take is whether to increase the number of warehouses that it uses to service its customers.

Many of the costs will increase (such as the cost of stock which will need to be substantially higher in five separate warehouses compared with one central operation) but some will decrease. Transport costs, for example, will decline when comparing the use of regional depots to deliver from, rather than a central national depot. Other costs may initially grow and then decline or vice versa. The best option for the expanding company would therefore be where the combined costs would be minimal. This is outlined in the following example:

Factor	Warehouse numbers						
	1	2	3	4	5	6	7
Warehouse costs	10	15	20	25	30	35	40
Transport costs	60	45	35	28	25	22	20
Costs of stock	20	30	35	50	60	70	80
Obsolescent stock	5	7	9	11	13	15	17
Customer service cost	12	8	7	8	9	10	11
Supply alternatives	18	14	10	9	7	5	8
Add. costs from single sourcing	0	2	3	5	9	10	12
Communication cost	2	3	4	5	5	5	5
Totals	127	124	123	141	154	172	191

2 Warehouse organisation

The way in which the warehouse is organised can make a substantial difference to the efficiency and costing of the operation.

(a) Traffic flow Warehouses that can separate the unloading and loading processes are generally more efficient than others where the two areas are combined; reductions in labour cost of 15 per cent have been reported by firms.

(b) Mechanisation The introduction of fork-lift trucks and containerisation has done much to reduce the levels of labour and to increase the speed at which goods can be transferred with the consequent effect on cost.

(c) Automation Large-scale investment in product handling equipment can lead to substantial reductions in the labour force and speed of assembly.

(d) Packaging Well designed packaging which can be efficiently stacked and moved can substantially increase the speed of warehouse operation. Many products are now stacked on wooden platforms or pallets; a well organised batch

of cases on a pallet will hold together like an interlocking wall, allowing the pallet to be stacked high up on warehouse racking systems.

Transport issues

The manufacturer has a number of options available to achieve the target distribution levels: rail; road; air; water (both inland and sea).

Each will offer a level of speed and security coupled with a level of cost which will, when combined, decide the most appropriate transport system for the organisation. In addition, the firm will need to consider the inventory cost for each transport option as part of the overall equation. For example, to supply the Middle East overland with consumer goods will take around 14 days; by sea around 5 weeks. The additional cost of financing the 3 weeks' stock required for delivery by sea would be a potential saving if the company changed from sea to road which might offset the higher transport costs.

Rail   The advantage of rail transport is the ability to move large quantities with fair speed and at low cost. However the system is inflexible, often requires special containers, and is vulnerable to disruption. In consequence many firms no longer use rail for transport unless they are immediately adjacent to a railway line.

Road   Road has become the preferred method of transport for a wide range of consumer and industrial goods. It offers the advantages of fair flexibility, with good security, and is much less vulnerable to disruption. There are higher costs to be considered and substantial legislation that governs the length of time that drivers can work, the maximum weight of vehicles and many other constraints.

For the firm many of these problems can be solved by contracting transport rather than owning a fleet of transport vehicles. This further improves the flexibility offered by the use of road transport; but for a large firm will often be the more expensive option. The point at which it becomes more cost-effective for a firm to own and operate their own vehicles will vary according to the nature of the industry in which it operates and the level of service that it is trying to supply. In the late 1960s the point at which for the average firm it was economic to employ their own drivers was around 8 vehicles; it has since risen to 12 as independent transport operators have become more cost-competitive.

Air   Air transport provides an extremely rapid and secure means of transporting product, thereby minimising inventory and packaging problems. Though it is the most expensive option available there has been a steady growth in its use and it now accounts for around 5 per cent of total freight movements.

Water   Inland water transport in the United Kingdom is very limited accounting for far less than 1 per cent of total freight movements. In Europe the advantages of river transport – those of low cost and flexibility – have continued to ensure a healthy level of investment in barge transport, particularly on the Rhine in Germany.

Inventory control

The level of stocks that the organisation needs to maintain will be a result partly of the level of service that it is trying to offer and the fluctuations in demand within the market. The firm will need to establish three levels of stock; 'buffer stock', reorder levels at which a new production run will be required, and maximum stock levels (Figure 14.1).

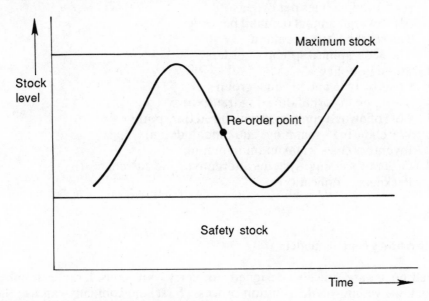

Figure 14.1   Fluctuations in stock level

The firm can easily calculate the optimum number of orders per year, the optimum level of stock required for each order and the optimum level of stock cover that should be ordered.

Communication factors

The speed at which orders are processed will affect the level of inventory and transport costs. The introduction of computers has greatly increased the efficiency of many distribution systems. In Germany the issue of computers to certain salesforces has reduced the time from receipt of the order to despatch by up to 3 days – an example of how effective technology can be in improving the distribution process.

Analysing distribution

Reassessing the distribution system can provide large savings for any company;

Dupont, the major American chemical concern, managed to save over $350 million dollars by a careful re-appraisal of its distribution system.

The firm will need to evaluate:

1   Present distribution
    (a)   frequency of orders
    (b)   size of orders
    (c)   product lines per order
    (d)   overall annual demand per order
2   The seasonality of demand
3   The geographical spread of orders
4   Strategic policy
5   Costs by type and product group
6   Variation in cost of differing transport systems
7   Cost of owned compared with hired transport
8   Warehousing – manning, equipment, design
9   Inventory costs – maximum/minimum
10 Order processing: systems alternatives and current costs
11 Packaging implications

The inventory control model

Spreadsheets are ideally designed to carry out considerable numbers of evaluations within the distribution process. First, the company can use them to evaluate the most sensible choice of distribution channel by an evaluation process similar to those in the packaging, product viability and other chapters.

Secondly, the analysis of warehouse numbers required within the network is ideally suited to spreadsheet manipulation. The calculation of stock levels and re-order quantities is slightly less straightforward. By using a set spreadsheet model the manager can however quickly calculate:

1   The economic order quantity.
2   The optimum number of units per order.
3   The optimum number of days' supply per order.

The data required is:

1   The total number of units sold or used in the year.
2   The total value of the units sold during the year.
3   The average per unit price of the stock.
4   The percentage cost of maintaining the level of required inventory as a percentage of the overall cost of the volume of stock sold in the year. For example, the total sales in the year would be 10000, the normal inventory level 1250; percentage cost equals 12.5 per cent.

Using the inventory control model

The *Go To* column in Listing 14.1 tells you the cell number and the cursor position. The next column specifies the spreadsheet option (LO = Label Option; VO = Value Option). The *Type In* column gives you instructions within the inverted commas which you must type in or asks you to supply the necessary data. These commas are not part of the instructions supplied here and should not be typed in. Beware that some spreadsheets, the *Lotus 1-2-3* for example, enter the Label Option by using the inverted-comma key. Under the *Type In* column the symbols * = multiply and / = divide. R in the *Return* column instructs you to commit the information to memory by pressing the Return key.
Remember: When you have finished, save your model.

Listing 14.1 Inventory control model

Go To		Type In	Return	Go To		Type In	Return
A2/	LO	"Inventory	R	A19/	LO	"Opt.	R
B2		control"	R	B19	LO	stock"	R
A4/B4	LO	"Input data"	R	C6	VO	Enter total value of product sold in year($)	R
A6/B6	LO	"Total value/item"	R				
A8/B8	LO	"Cost of order"	R	C8	VO	Enter administrative cost of each order ($)	R
A10/	LO	"Storage	R	C10	VO	Enter % cost of storage	R
B10	LO	cost"	R				
A12/	LO	"Unit	R	C12	VO	Enter unit price of item	R
B12	LO	price"	R	C14	VO	Enter total units sold in year	R
A14/	LO	"Total units	R				
B14	LO	/yr"	R	C17	VO	"SQ.RT.(C6*C10/100/(C8*2))"	R
A17/	LO	"Opt.	R				
B17	LO	orders"	R	C18	VO	"SQ.RT.(C14*2*C8/(C12*C10/100))"	R
A18/	LO	"Units/	R				
B18	LO	order"	R	C19	VO	"SQ.RT.(266450*C8/(C14*C12*C10/100))"	R

Proforma 14.1   Inventory control model

A/B		C
2	Inventory Control	
4	Input data	
6	Total value/item	10000
8	Cost of order	25
10	Storage cost (%)	12.5
12	Unit price	1
14	Total units/yr	10000
17	Opt. orders	SQ.RT(C6*C10/100/(C8*2))
18	Units/order	SQ.RT(C14*2*C8/(C12*C10/100))
19	Opt. stock	SQ.RT266450*C8/(C14*C12*C10/100)

Example 14.1   Inventory control model

A/B		C
2	Inventory Control	
4	Input data	
6	Total value/item	10000
8	Cost of order	25
10	Storage cost (%)	12.5
12	Unit price	1
14	Total units/yr	10000
17	Opt. orders	5
18	Units/order	2000
19	Opt. stock	73

Inventory control commentary

The model (Example 14.1) shows the effects of a particular sales volume and value on the re-order process.

Additional reading

1 Fitzroy, A. *Analytical Methods for Marketing Management*. Prentice-Hall, 1982.

2 Hayslett, H.T. *Statistics Made Simple*. WH Allen, 1967.

3 Hughes, G. *Marketing Management*. Addison-Wesley, 1982.

4 Laric, M.V., Stiff, R. *Lotus 1-2-3 for Marketing and Sales*. Prentice-Hall, 1984.

5 Rodger, L.W. *Statistics for Marketing*. McGraw-Hill, 1984.